the daily lives of high school boys

2

yasunobu yamauchi

CONTENTS

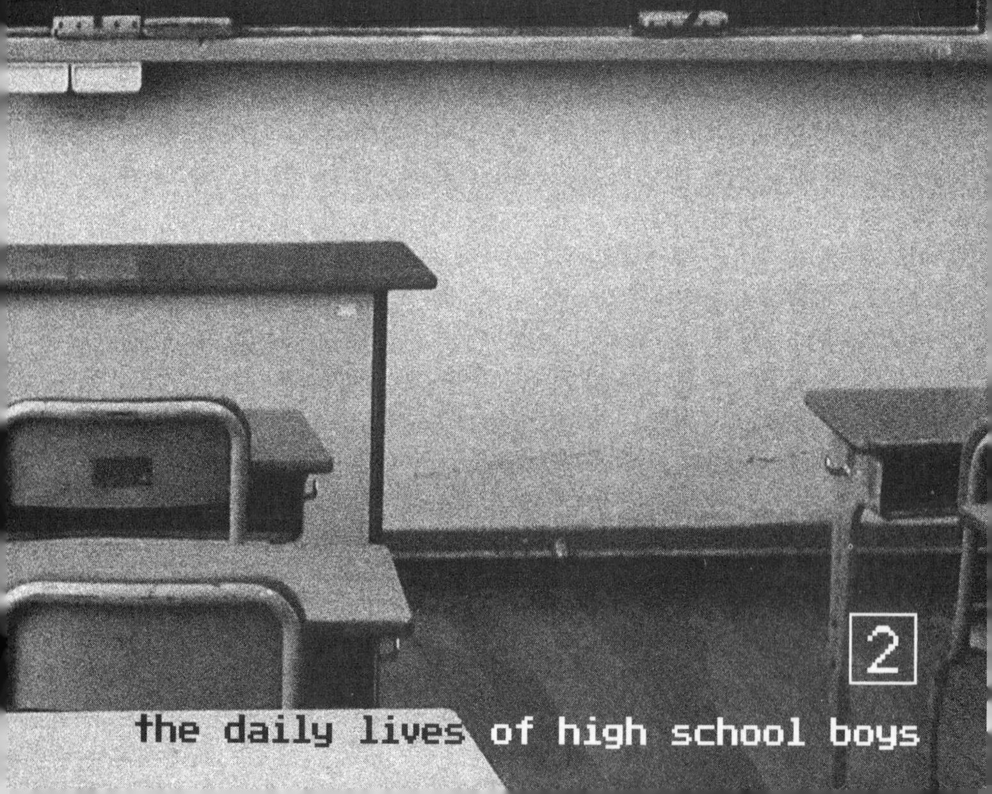

2

the daily lives of high school boys

chapter 16:
high school boys and boyhood

*Evening cicadas chirping

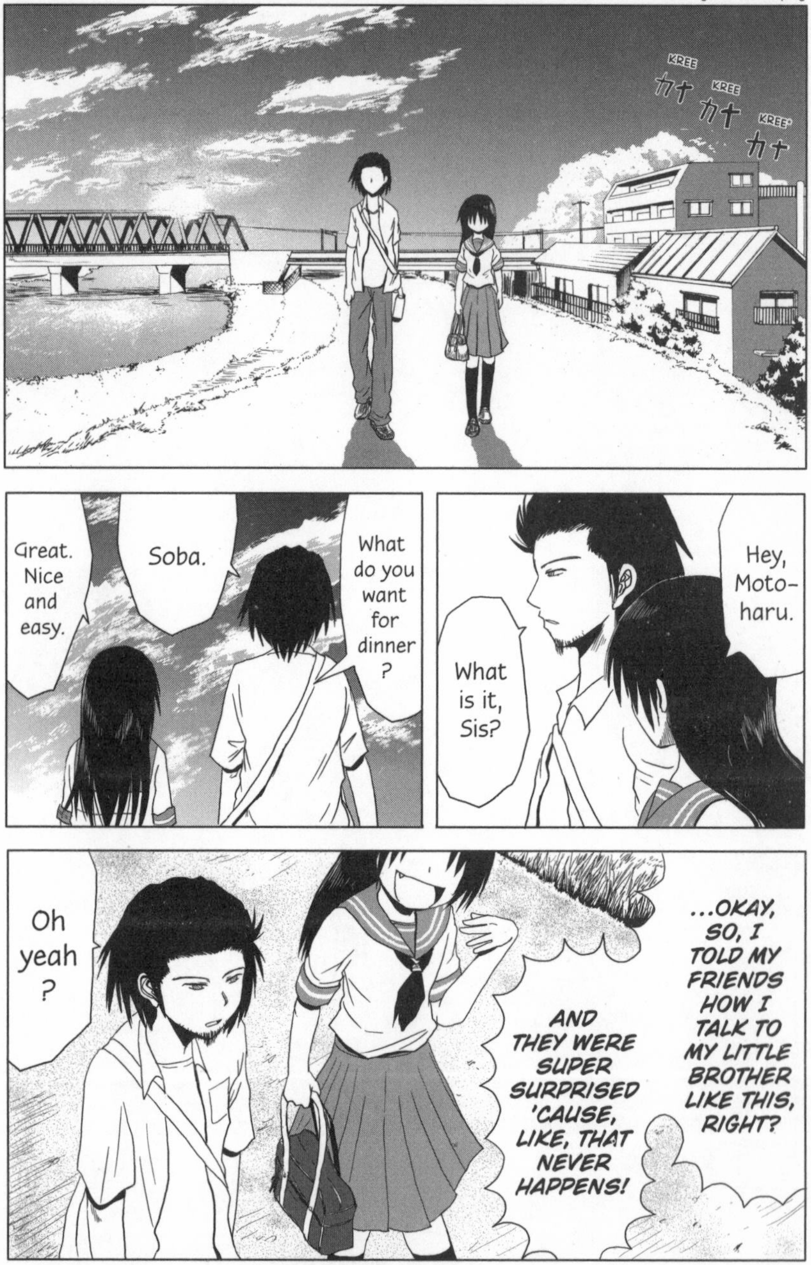
KREE
カナ
KREE
カナ
KREE*
カナ
Hey, Moto-haru.
What is it, Sis?
What do you want for dinner?
Soba.
Great. Nice and easy.
...OKAY, SO, I TOLD MY FRIENDS HOW I TALK TO MY LITTLE BROTHER LIKE THIS, RIGHT?
AND THEY WERE SUPER SURPRISED 'CAUSE, LIKE, THAT NEVER HAPPENS!
Oh yeah?

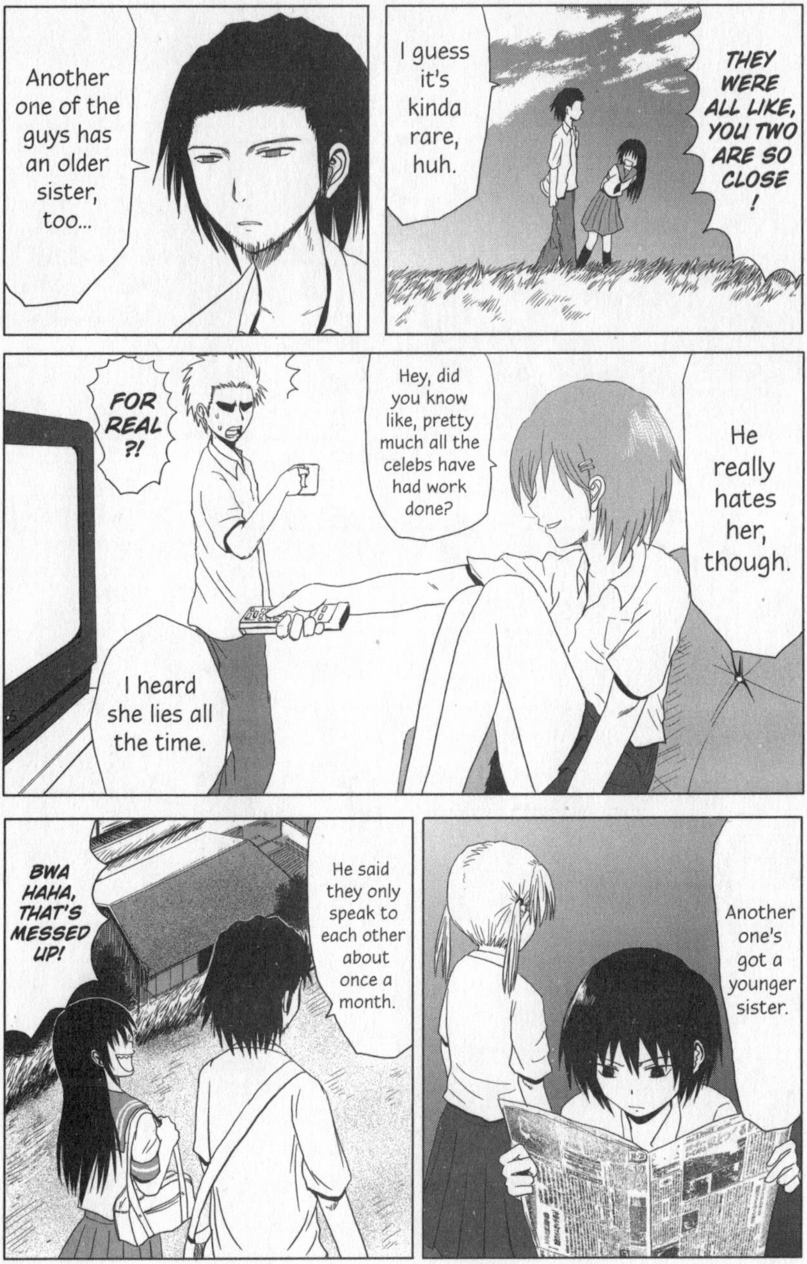

I guess it's kinda rare, huh.
THEY WERE ALL LIKE, YOU TWO ARE SO CLOSE!
Another one of the guys has an older sister, too...
He really hates her, though.
Hey, did you know like, pretty much all the celebs have had work done?
FOR REAL?!
I heard she lies all the time.
Another one's got a younger sister.
He said they only speak to each other about once a month.
BWA HAHA, THAT'S MESSED UP!

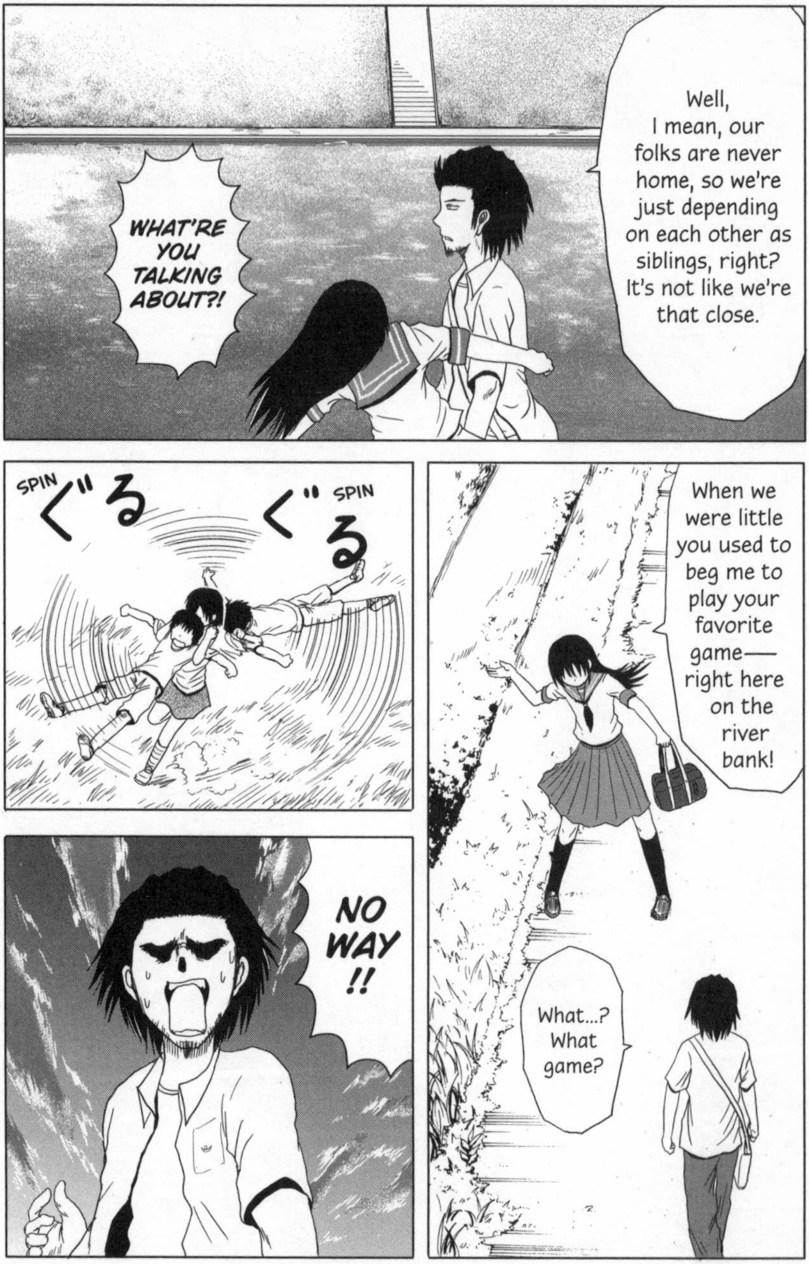
Well, I mean, our folks are never home, so we're just depending on each other as siblings, right? It's not like we're that close.
WHAT'RE YOU TALKING ABOUT?!
When we were little you used to beg me to play your favorite game— right here on the river bank!
What...? What game?
SPIN ぐる
ぐる SPIN
NO WAY !!

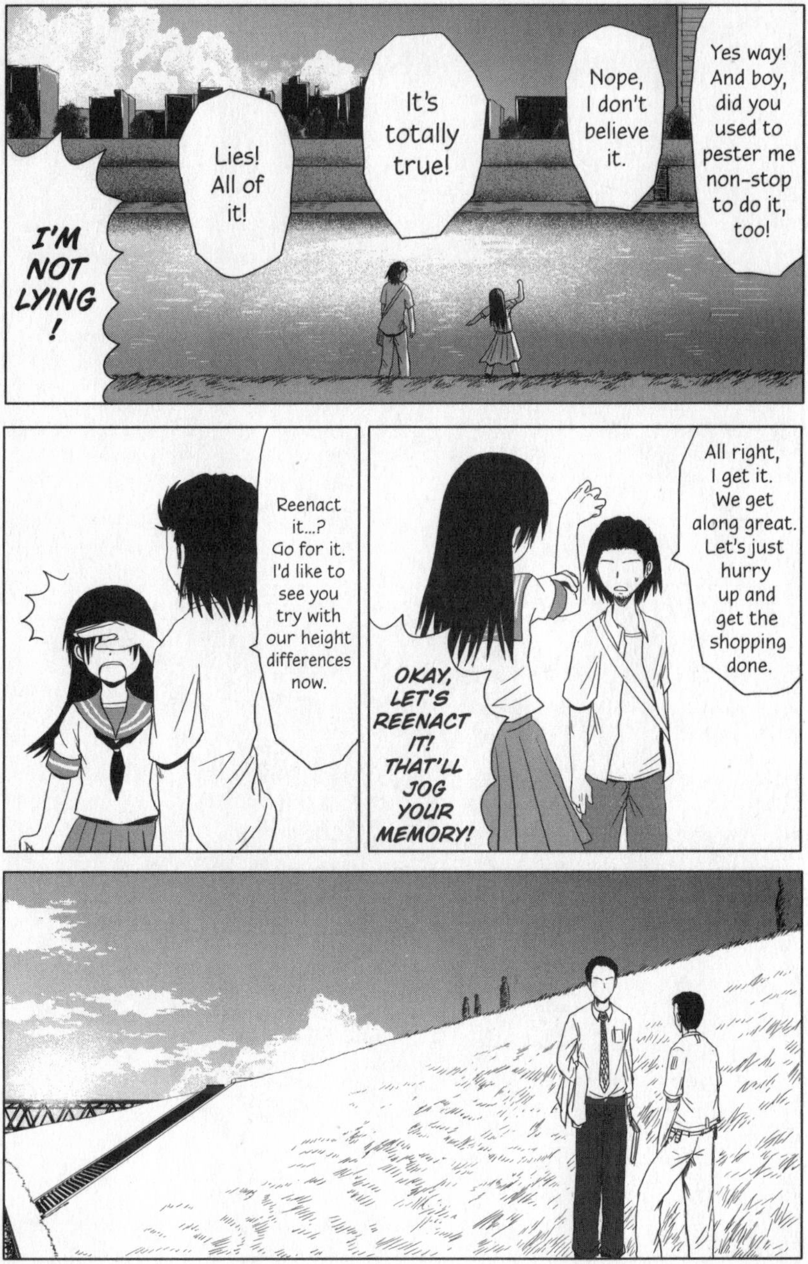
Yes way! And boy, did you used to pester me non-stop to do it, too!
Nope, I don't believe it.
It's totally true!
Lies! All of it!
I'M NOT LYING!
All right, I get it. We get along great. Let's just hurry up and get the shopping done.
OKAY, LET'S REENACT IT! THAT'LL JOG YOUR MEMORY!
Reenact it...? Go for it. I'd like to see you try with our height differences now.

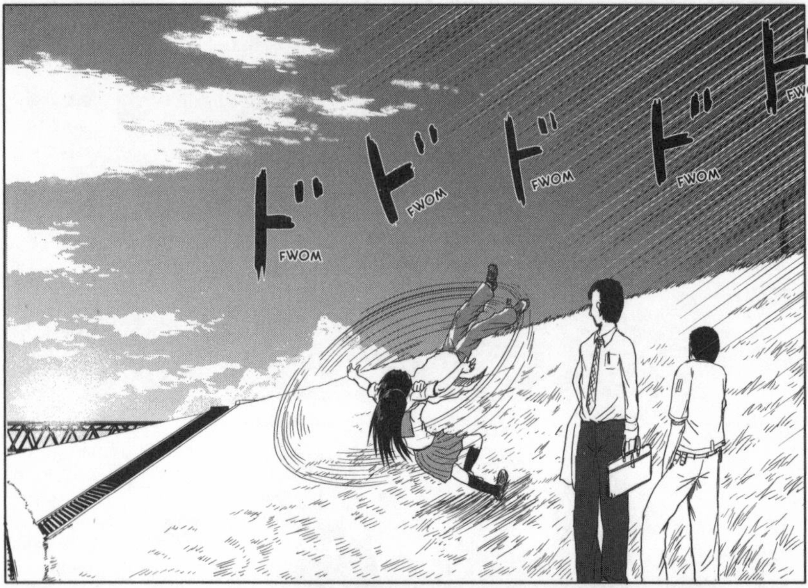
ド FWOM
ド FWOM
ド FWOM
ド FWOM
ド FWOM

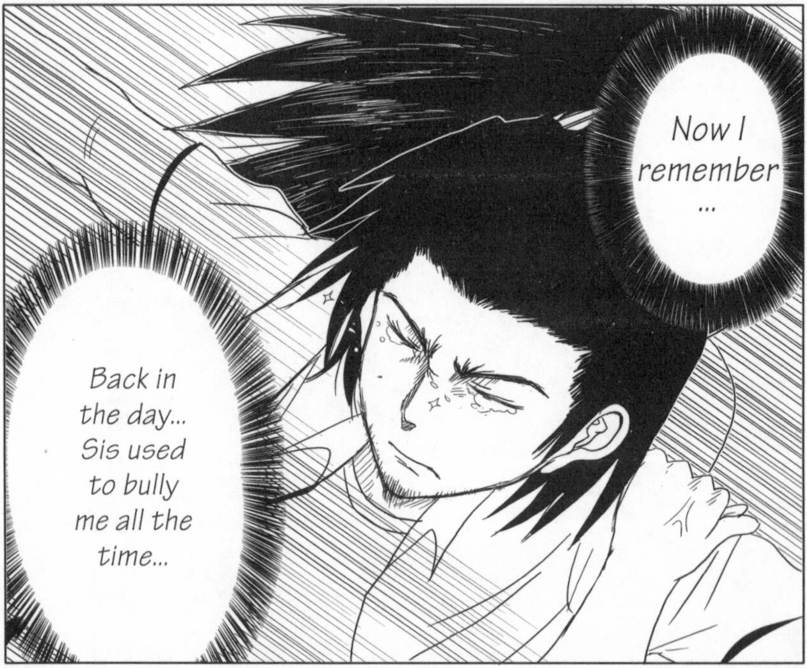
Now I remember ...
Back in the day... Sis used to bully me all the time...

chapter 17:
high school boys and ghost stories, pt. 2

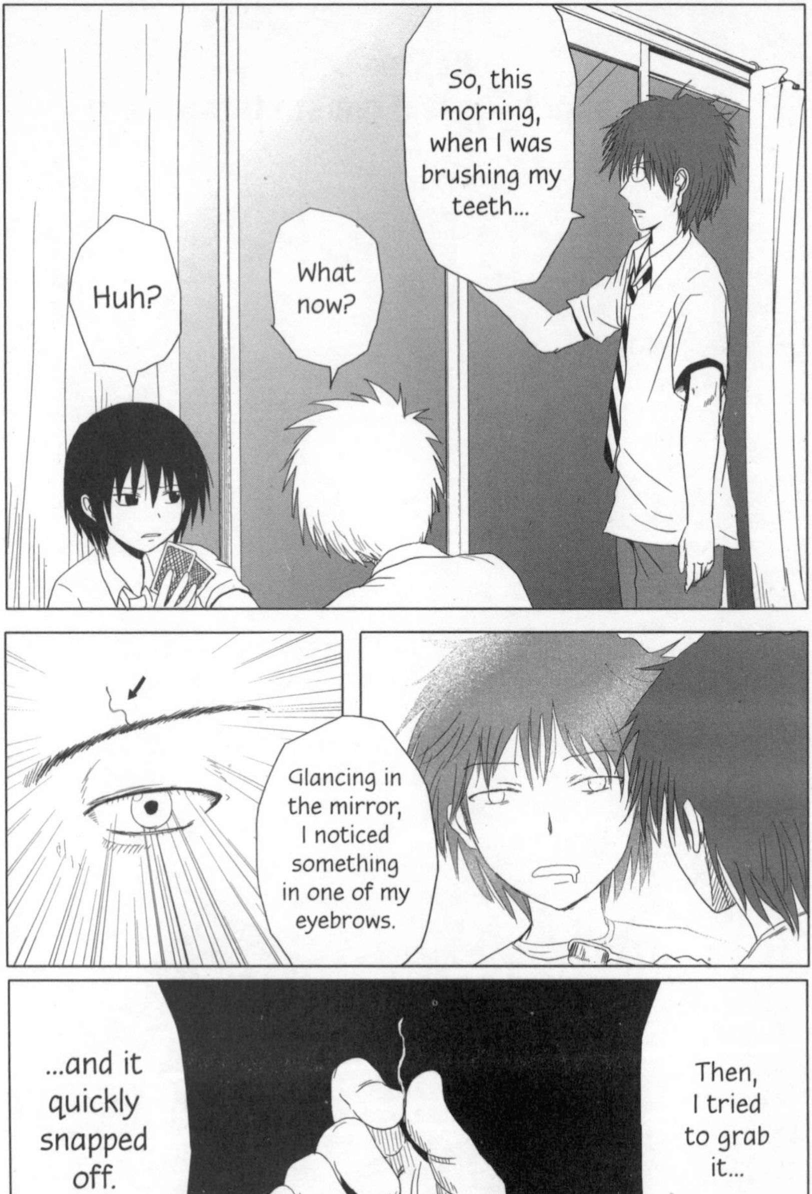
So, this morning, when I was brushing my teeth...
What now?
Huh?
Glancing in the mirror, I noticed something in one of my eyebrows.
Then, I tried to grab it...
...and it quickly snapped off.

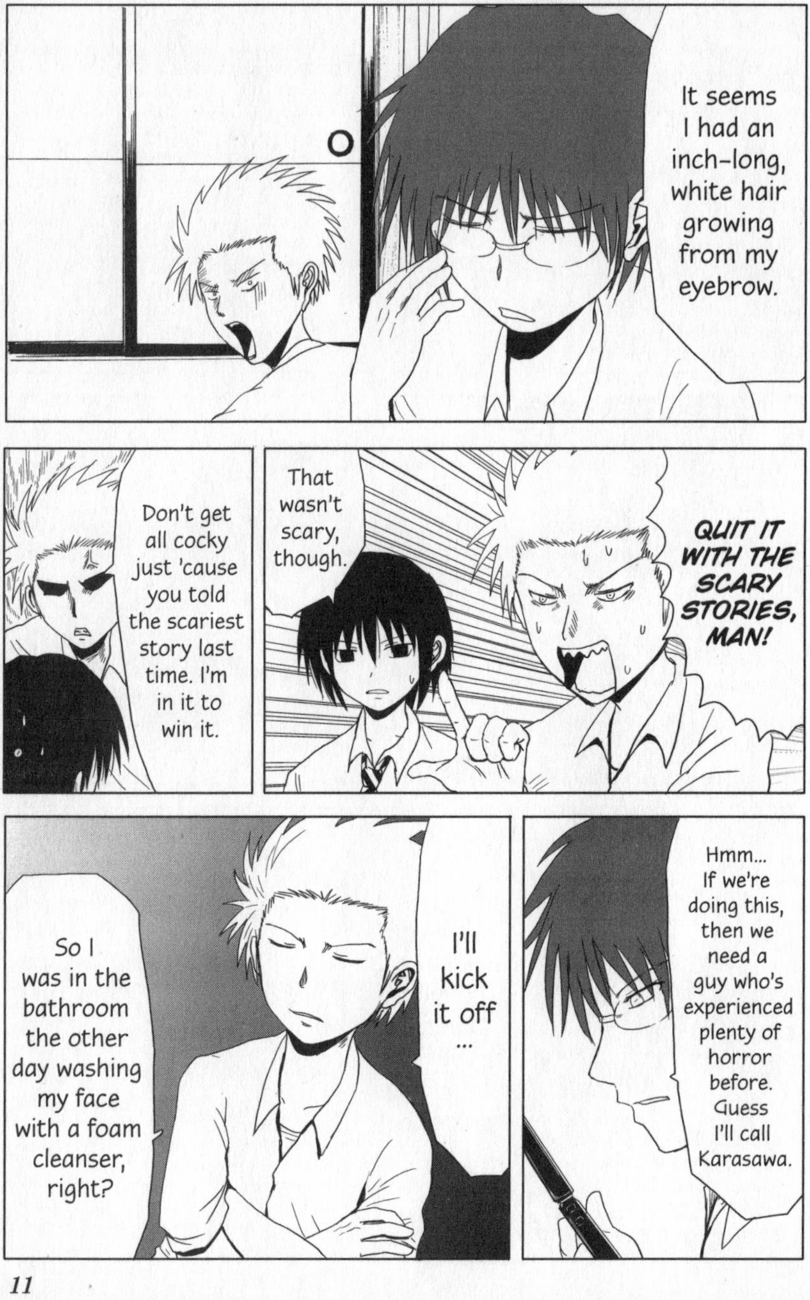
It seems I had an inch-long, white hair growing from my eyebrow.
QUIT IT WITH THE SCARY STORIES, MAN!
That wasn't scary, though.
Don't get all cocky just 'cause you told the scariest story last time. I'm in it to win it.
Hmm... If we're doing this, then we need a guy who's experienced plenty of horror before. Guess I'll call Karasawa.
I'll kick it off ...
So I was in the bathroom the other day washing my face with a foam cleanser, right?

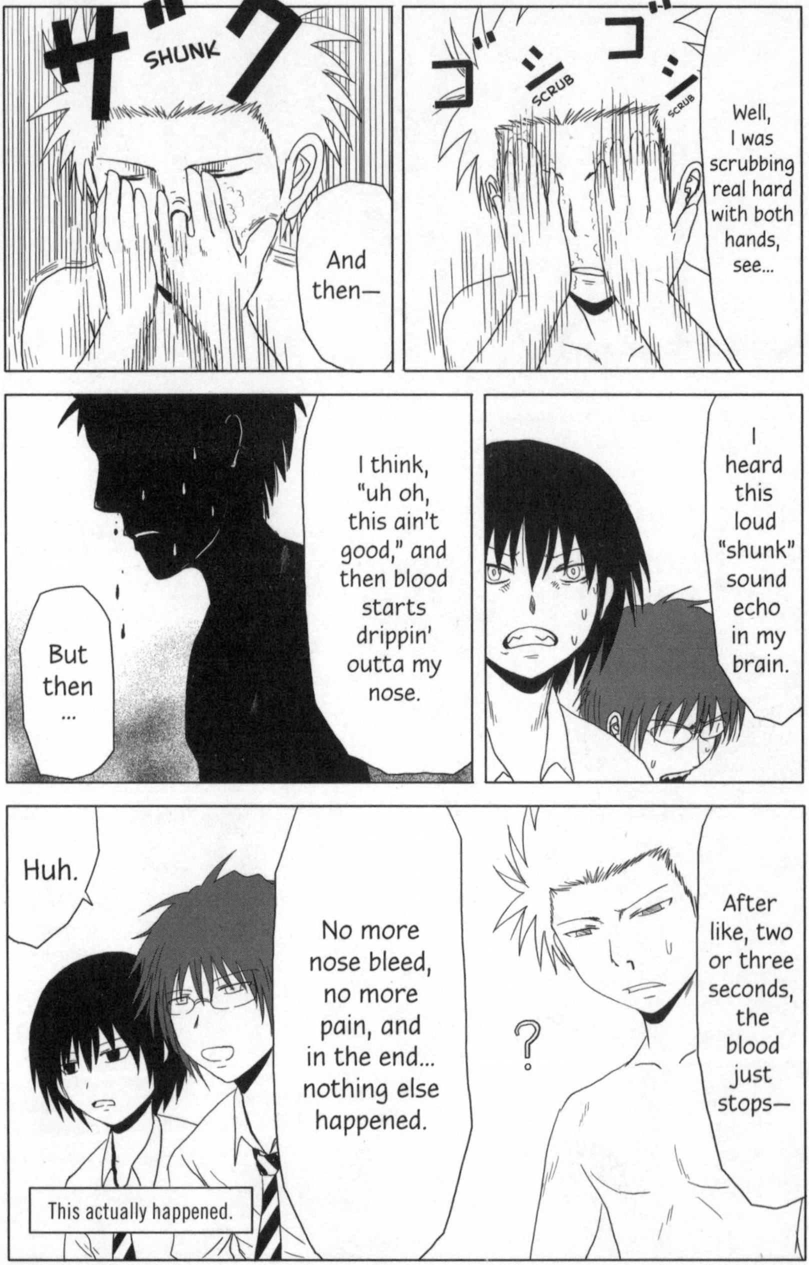

ゴシ ゴシ
SCRUB SCRUB
Well, I was scrubbing real hard with both hands, see...
ザク
SHUNK
And then—
I heard this loud "shunk" sound echo in my brain.
I think, "uh oh, this ain't good," and then blood starts drippin' outta my nose.
But then ...
After like, two or three seconds, the blood just stops—
No more nose bleed, no more pain, and in the end... nothing else happened.
Huh.
?
This actually happened.

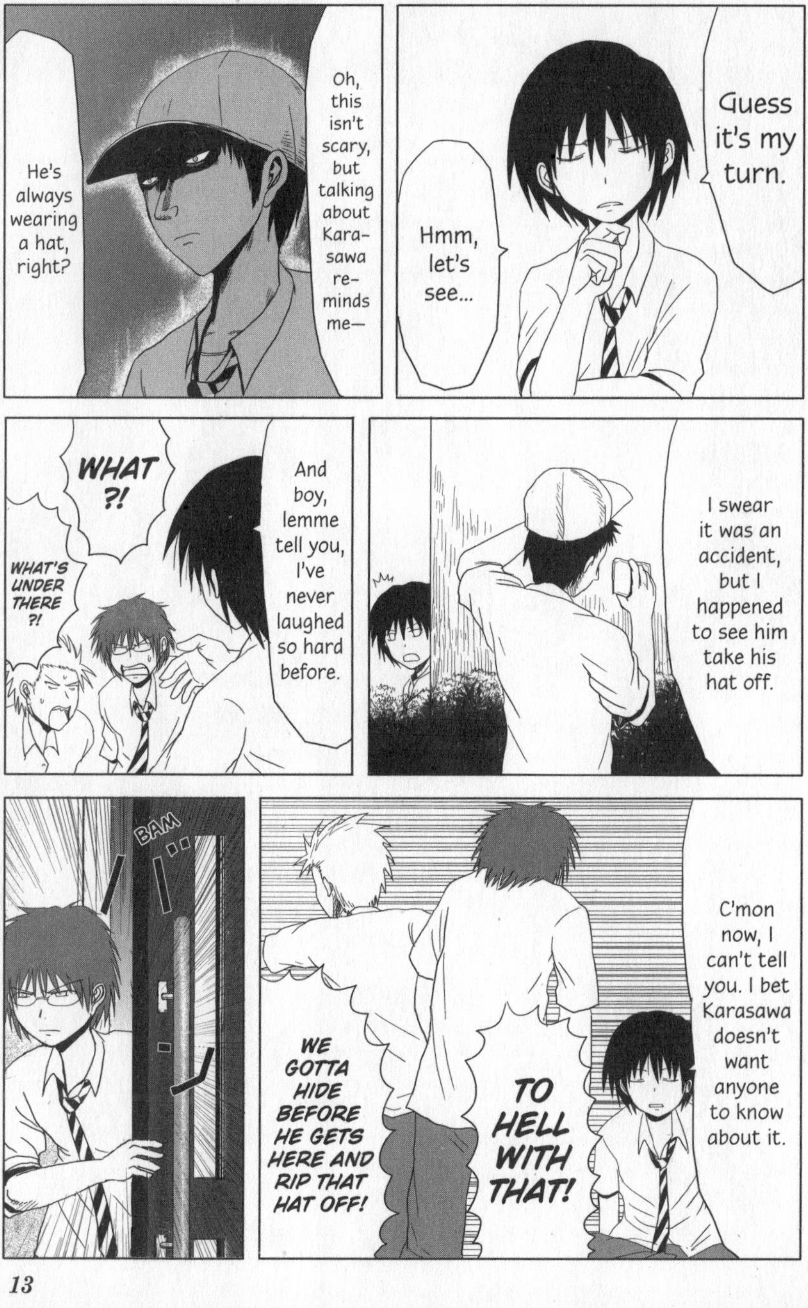
Guess it's my turn.
Hmm, let's see...
Oh, this isn't scary, but talking about Kara-sawa re-minds me—
He's always wearing a hat, right?
I swear it was an accident, but I happened to see him take his hat off.
And boy, lemme tell you, I've never laughed so hard before.
WHAT ?!
WHAT'S UNDER THERE ?!
C'mon now, I can't tell you. I bet Karasawa doesn't want anyone to know about it.
TO HELL WITH THAT!
WE GOTTA HIDE BEFORE HE GETS HERE AND RIP THAT HAT OFF!
BAM

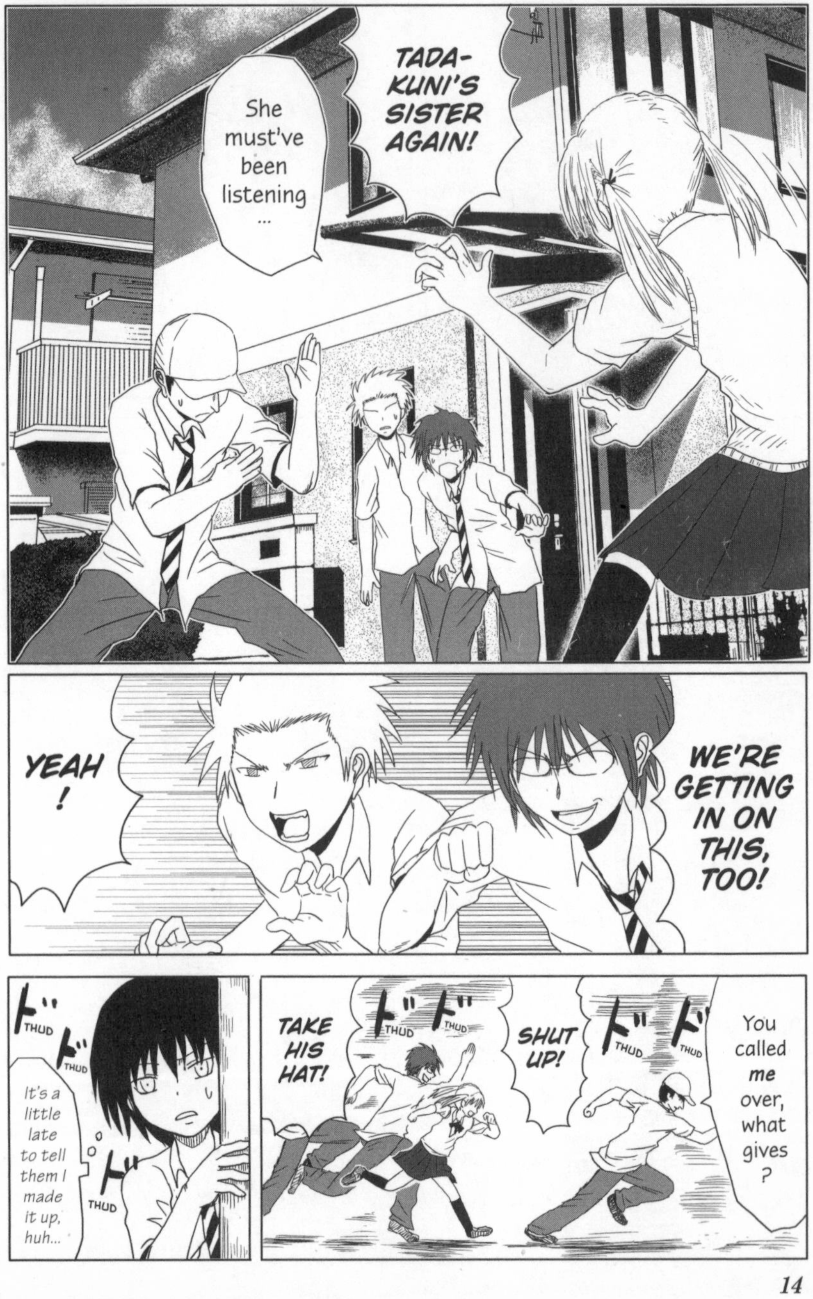
TADA-KUNI'S SISTER AGAIN!
She must've been listening ...
WE'RE GETTING IN ON THIS, TOO!
YEAH !
You called *me* over, what gives ?
ドド THUD THUD
SHUT UP!
ドド THUD THUD
TAKE HIS HAT!
ド THUD
ド THUD
It's a little late to tell them I made it up, huh...
ド THUD

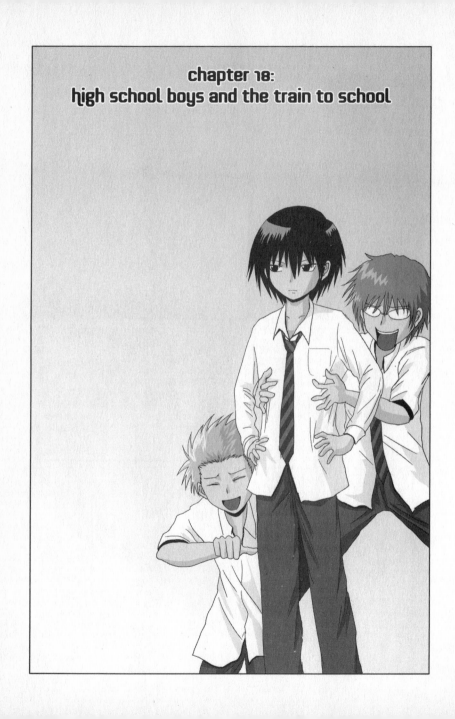

chapter 18: high school boys and the train to school

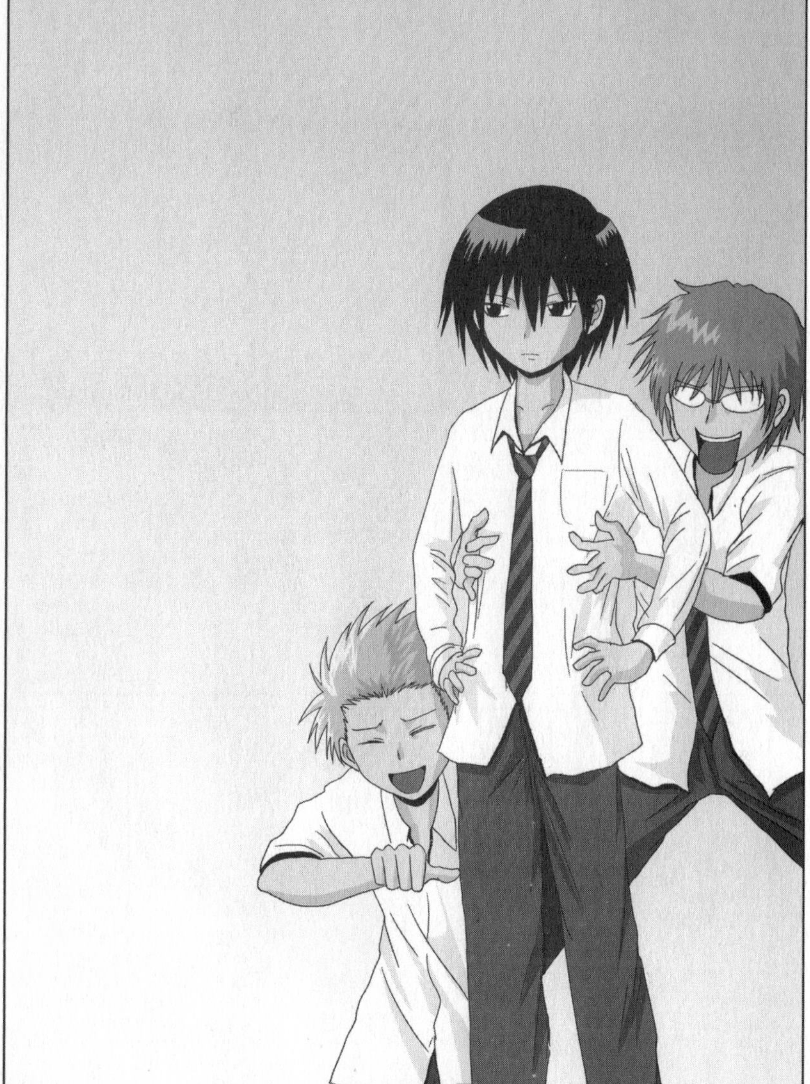

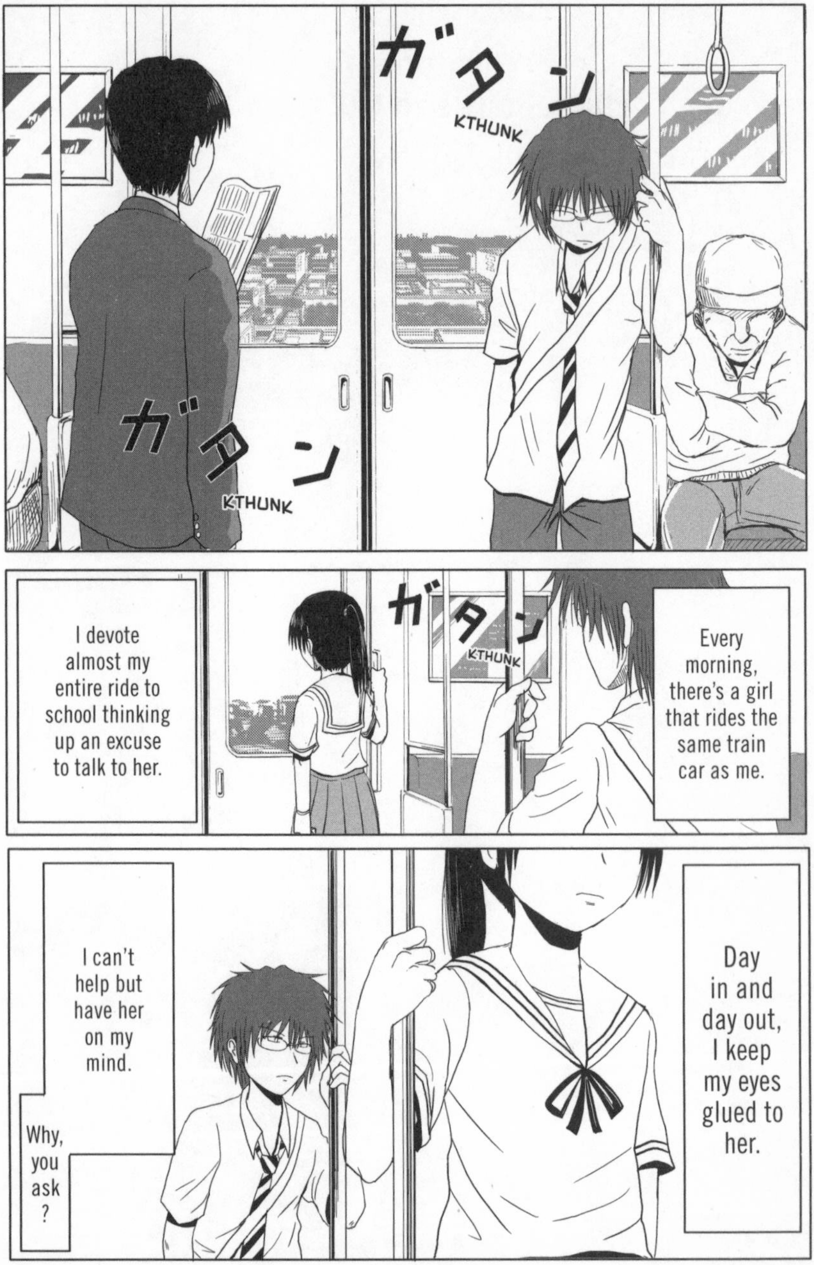
ガタン
KTHUNK
ガタン
KTHUNK
Every morning, there's a girl that rides the same train car as me.
ガタン
KTHUNK
I devote almost my entire ride to school thinking up an excuse to talk to her.
Day in and day out, I keep my eyes glued to her.
I can't help but have her on my mind.
Why, you ask?

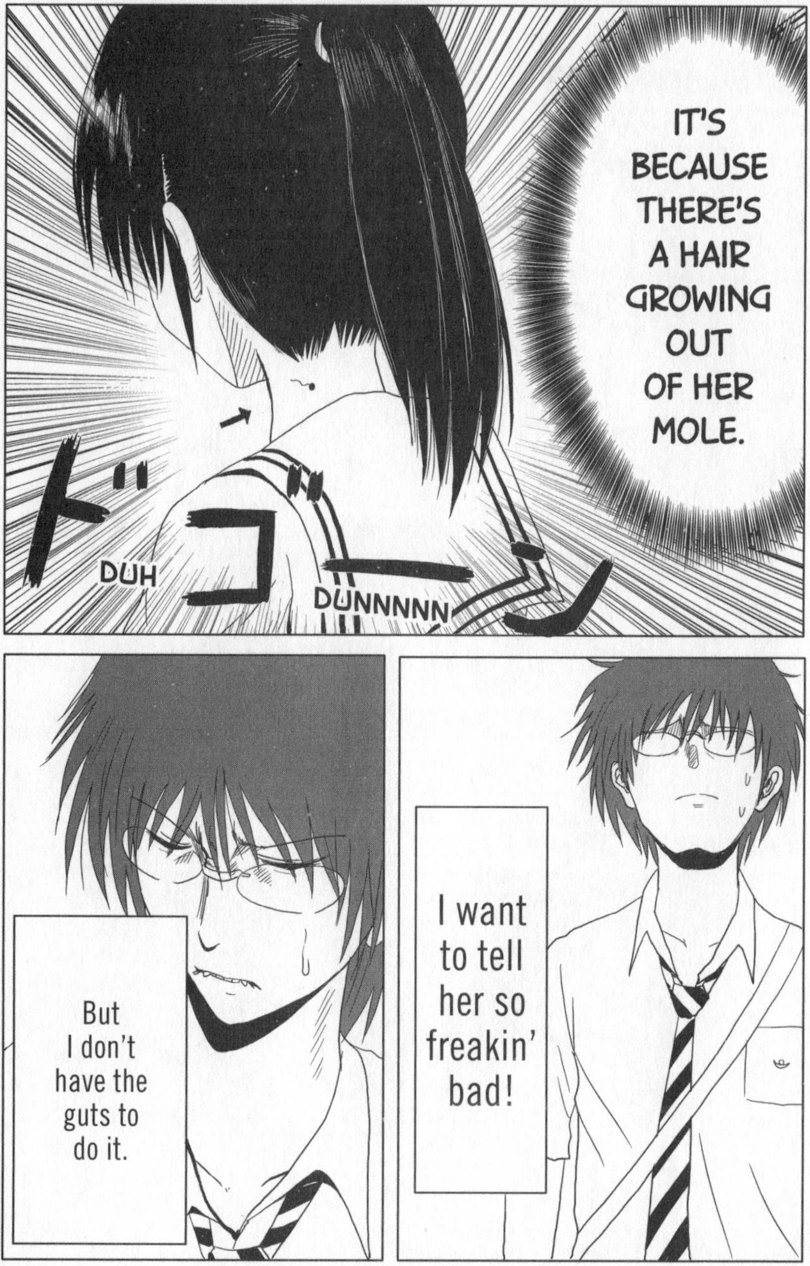
IT'S BECAUSE THERE'S A HAIR GROWING OUT OF HER MOLE.
ドコーン
DUH
DUNNNNN
I want to tell her so freakin' bad!
But I don't have the guts to do it.

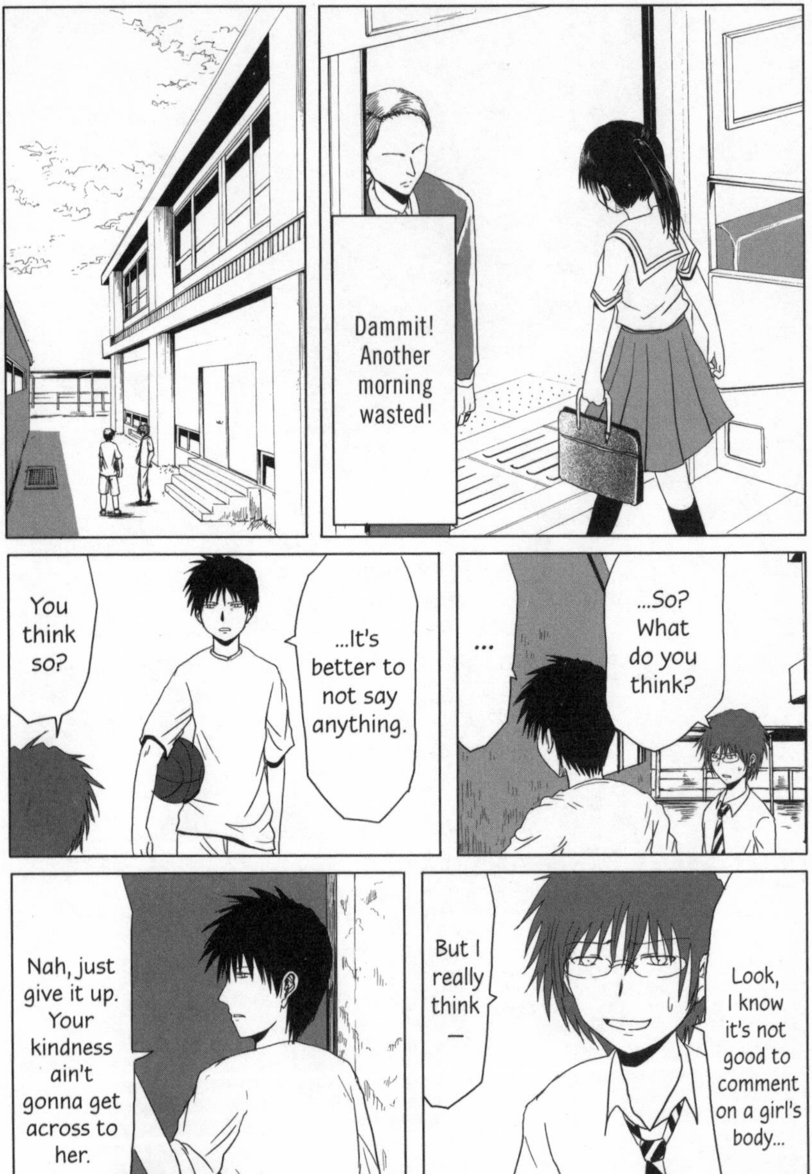
Dammit! Another morning wasted!
...So? What do you think?
...
...It's better to not say anything.
You think so?
Look, I know it's not good to comment on a girl's body...
But I really think—
Nah, just give it up. Your kindness ain't gonna get across to her.

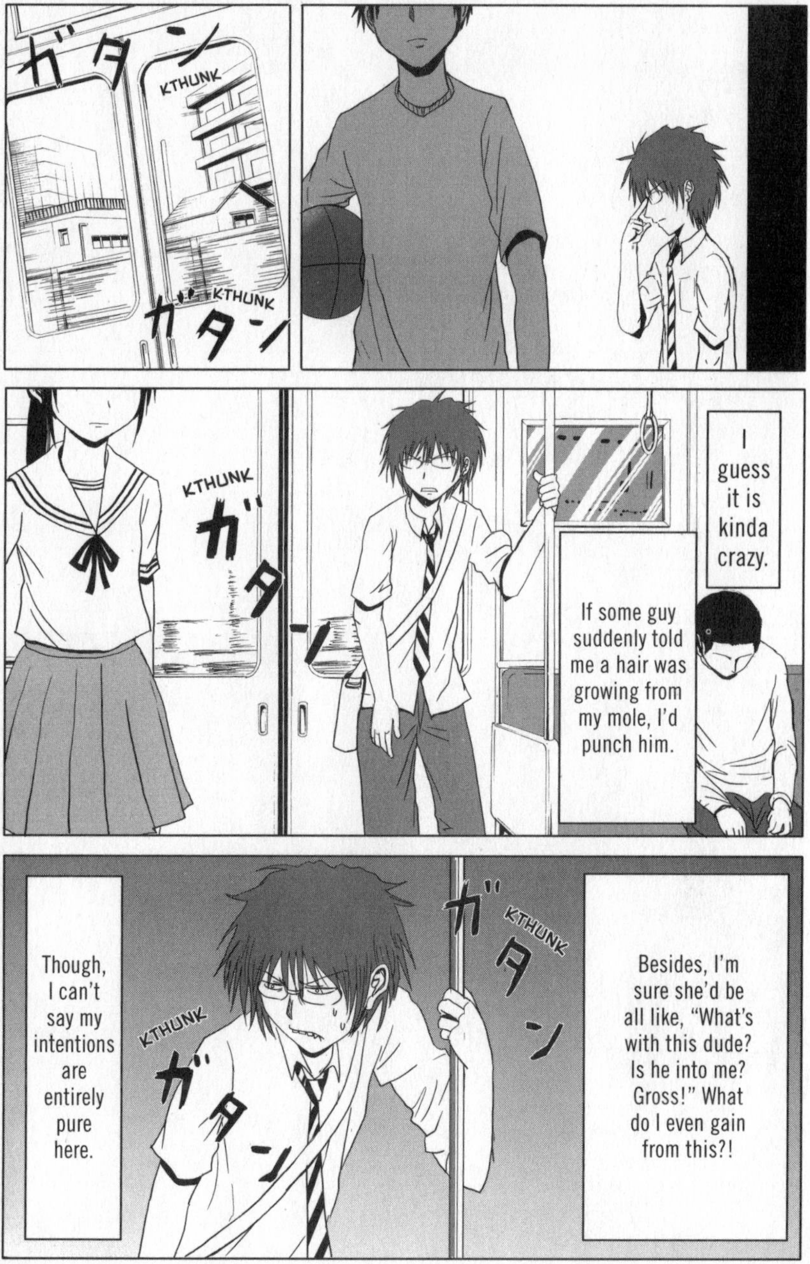
ガタン
KTHUNK
KTHUNK
ガタン
I guess it is kinda crazy.
If some guy suddenly told me a hair was growing from my mole, I'd punch him.
KTHUNK
ガタン
Besides, I'm sure she'd be all like, "What's with this dude? Is he into me? Gross!" What do I even gain from this?!
KTHUNK
ガタン
KTHUNK
ガタン
Though, I can't say my intentions are entirely pure here.

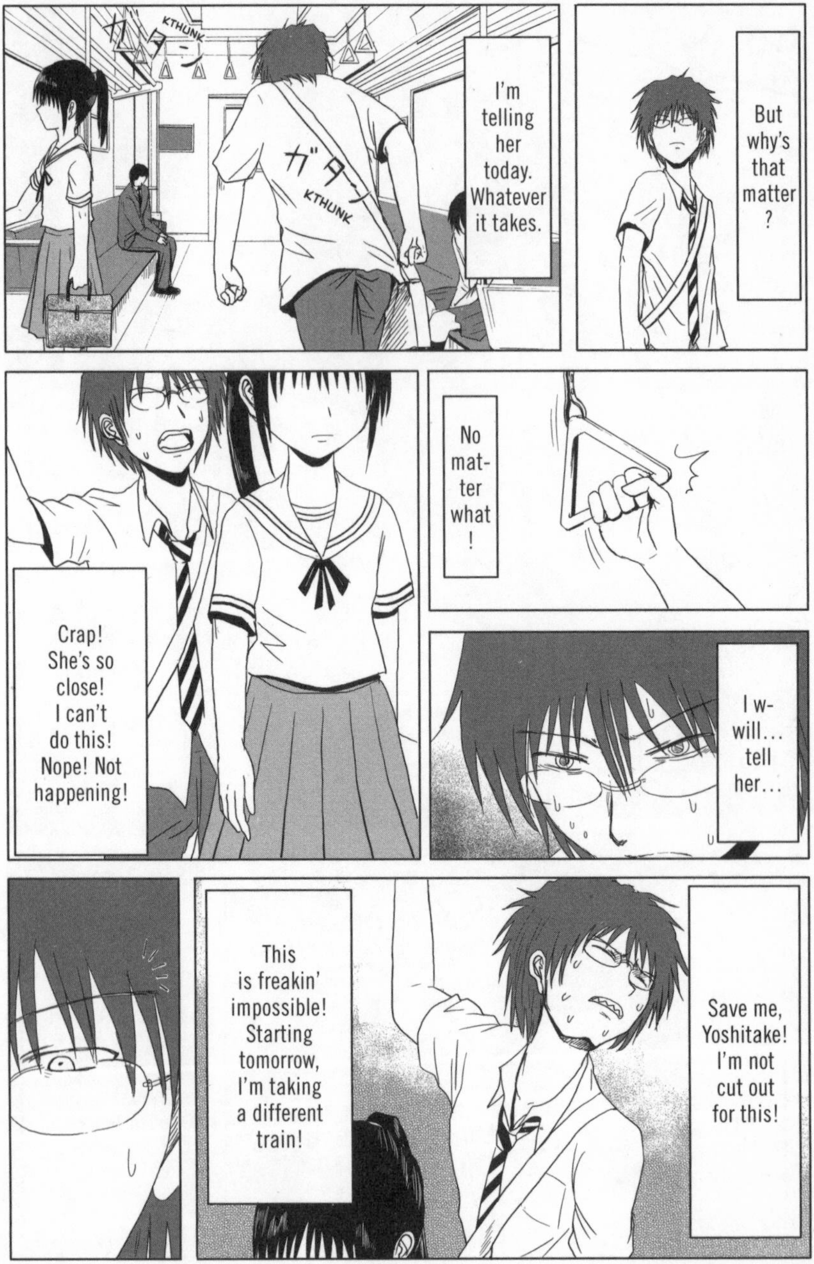

But why's that matter?
I'm telling her today. Whatever it takes.
KTHUNK
KTHUNK
No mat-ter what!
I w-will… tell her…
Crap! She's so close! I can't do this! Nope! Not happening!
Save me, Yoshitake! I'm not cut out for this!
This is freakin' impossible! Starting tomorrow, I'm taking a different train!

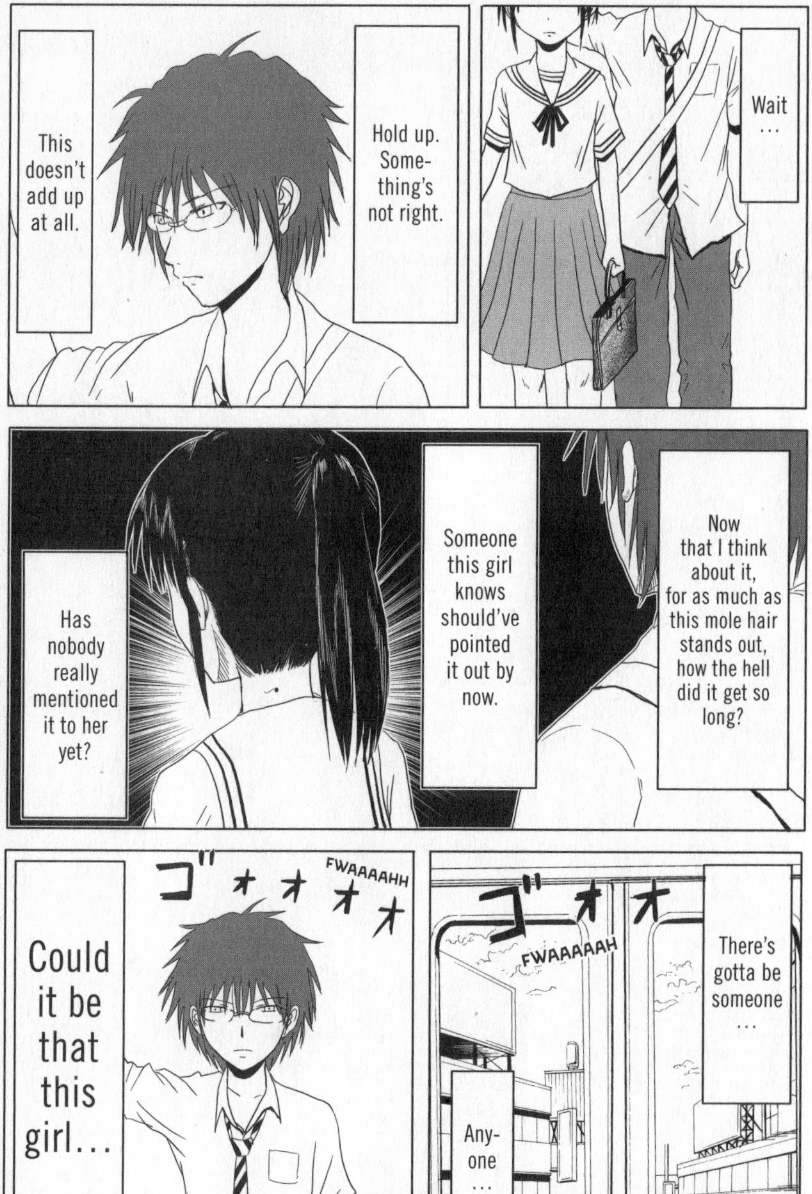

Wait…
Hold up. Something's not right.
This doesn't add up at all.
Now that I think about it, for as much as this mole hair stands out, how the hell did it get so long?
Someone this girl knows should've pointed it out by now.
Has nobody really mentioned it to her yet?
There's gotta be someone…
ゴォオ
FWAAAAAH
Anyone…
FWAAAAAHH
ゴォオオ
Could it be that this girl…

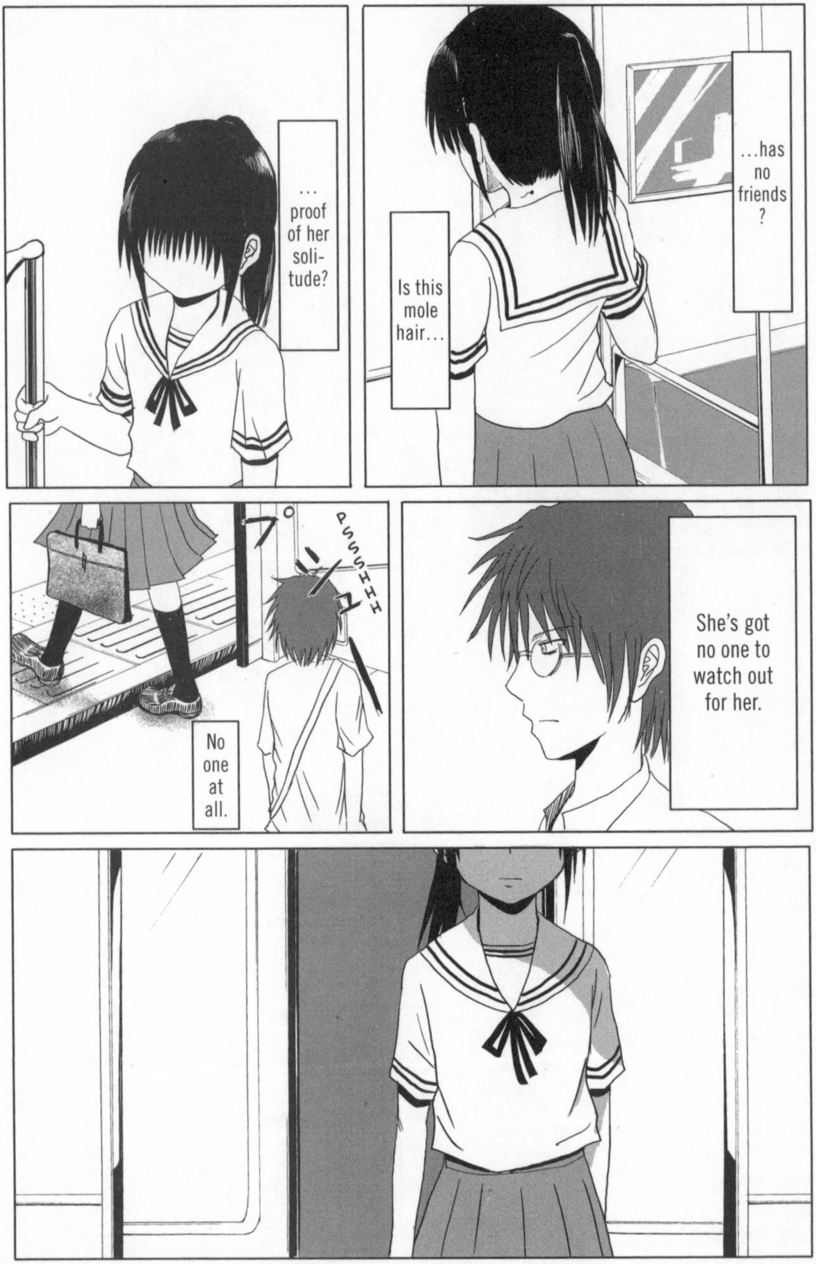

…has no friends?
Is this mole hair…
…proof of her solitude?
She's got no one to watch out for her.
PSSSHHH
No one at all.

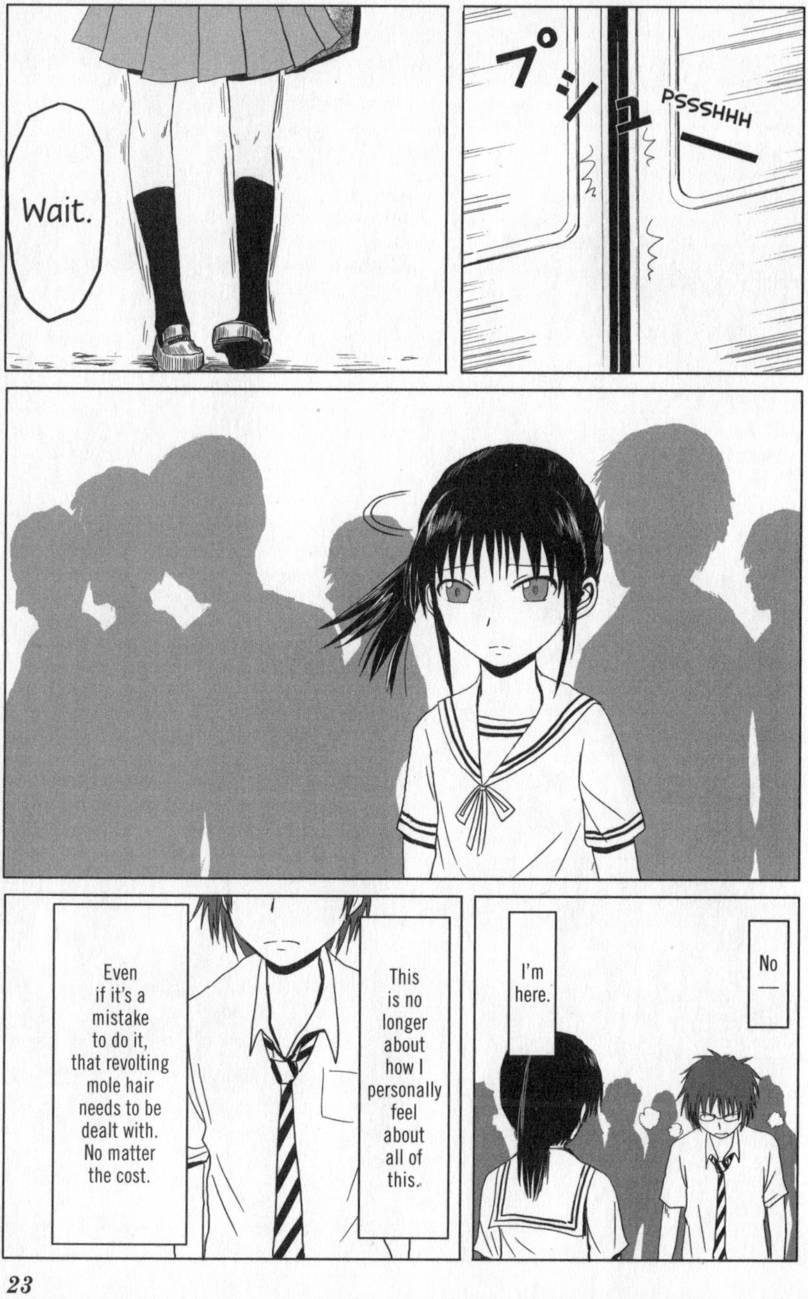
プシュー
PSSSHHH
Wait.
No —
I'm here.
This is no longer about how I personally feel about all of this.
Even if it's a mistake to do it, that revolting mole hair needs to be dealt with. No matter the cost.

You've got a hair growing from your mole.

Hehehe...

Pfft—

24

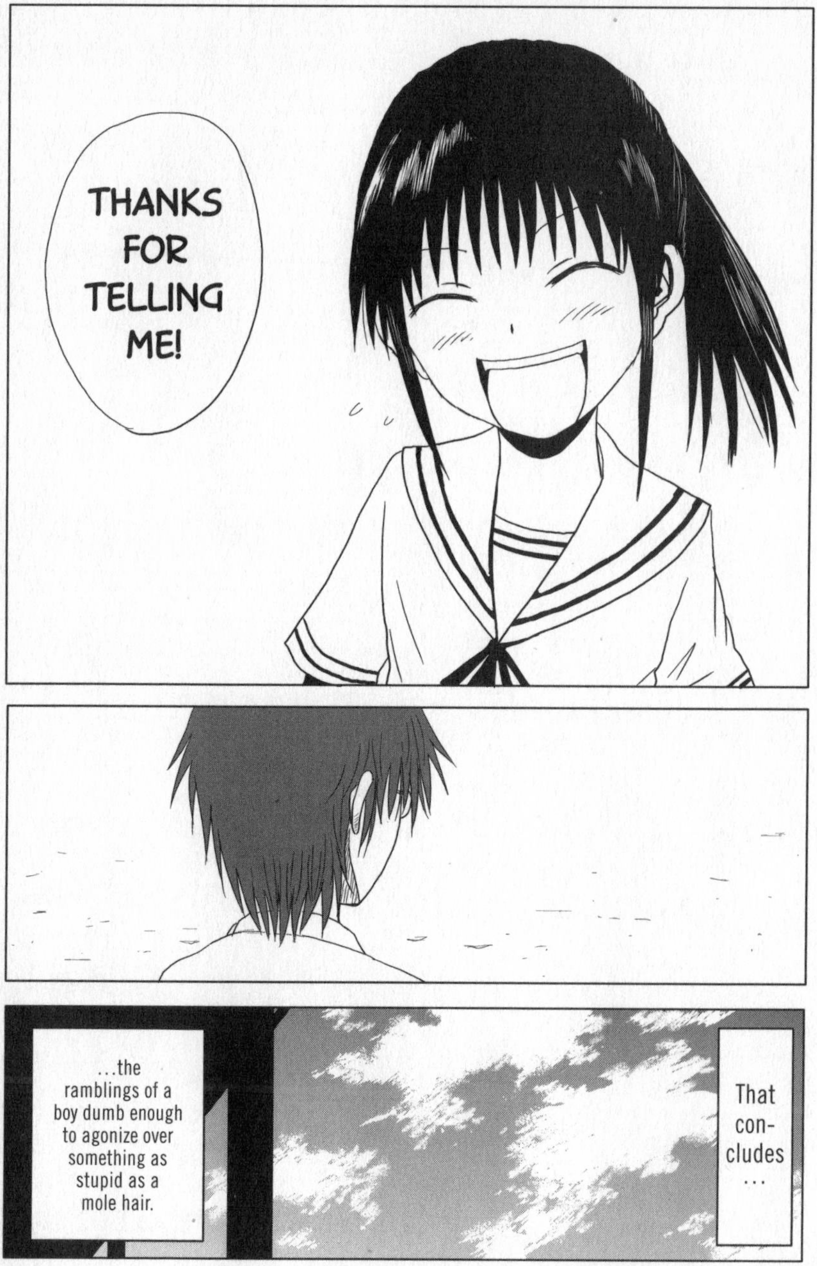
THANKS FOR TELLING ME!
That con- cludes …
…the ramblings of a boy dumb enough to agonize over something as stupid as a mole hair.

the

daily

lives

of

$\boxed{2}$ high school boys

chapter 19:
high school boys and the cultural festival, pt. 1

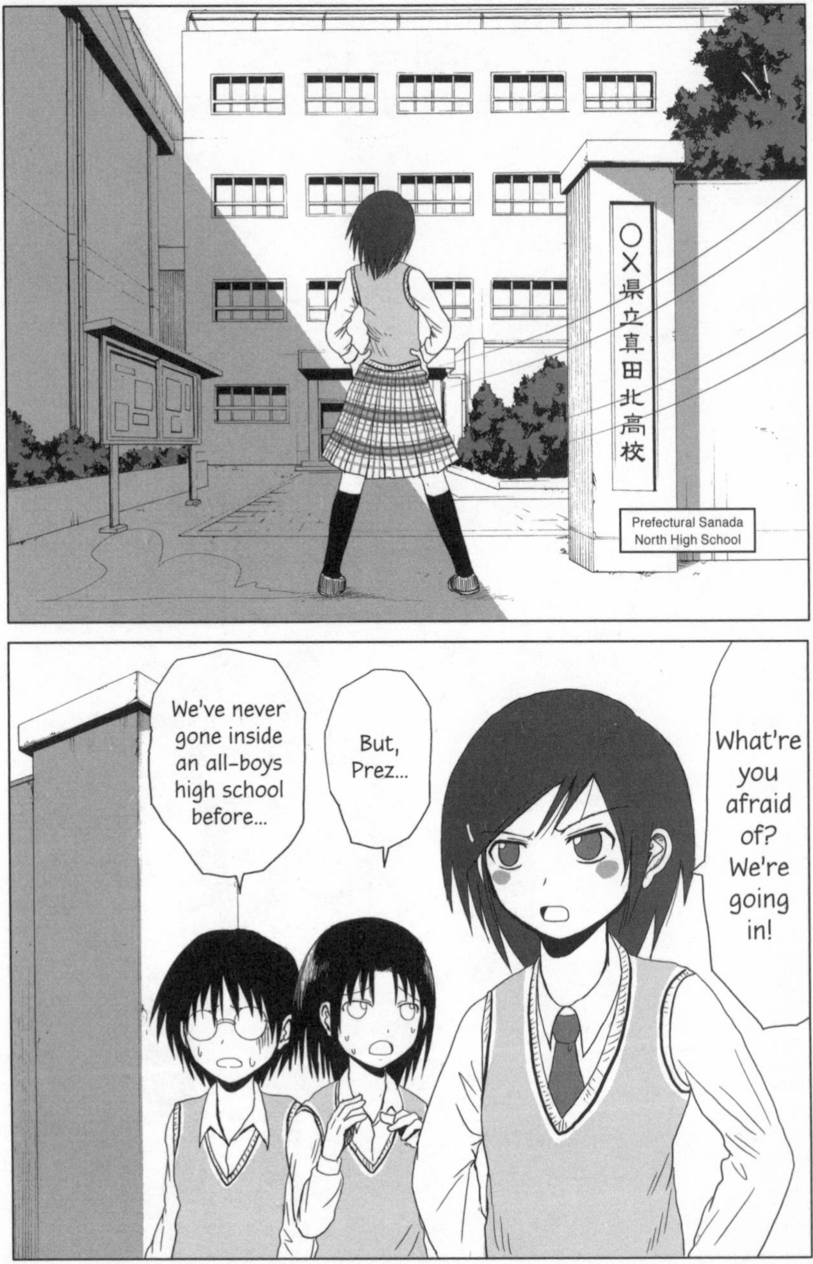
○×県立真田北高校
Prefectural Sanada North High School
What're you afraid of? We're going in!
But, Prez...
We've never gone inside an all-boys high school before...

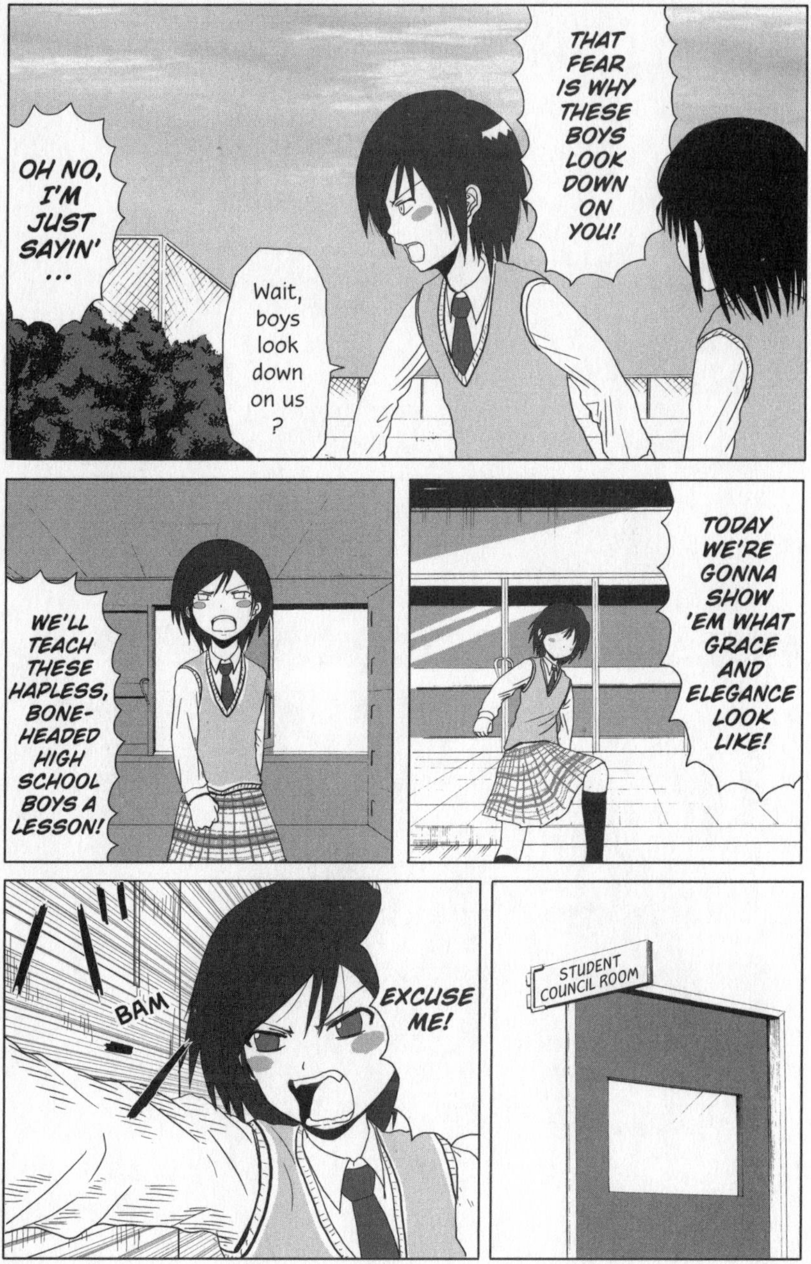
THAT FEAR IS WHY THESE BOYS LOOK DOWN ON YOU!
Wait, boys look down on us?
OH NO, I'M JUST SAYIN'...
TODAY WE'RE GONNA SHOW 'EM WHAT GRACE AND ELEGANCE LOOK LIKE!
WE'LL TEACH THESE HAPLESS, BONE-HEADED HIGH SCHOOL BOYS A LESSON!
STUDENT COUNCIL ROOM
EXCUSE ME!
BAM

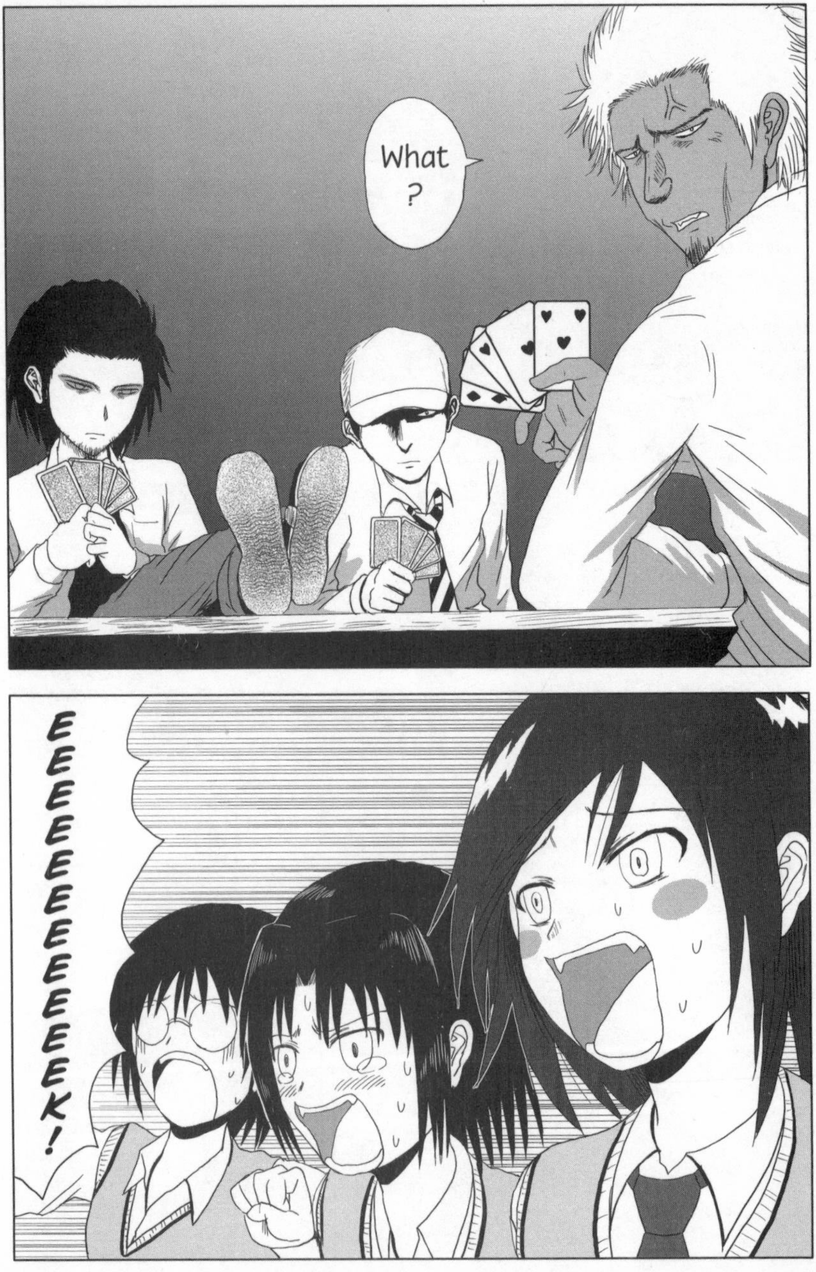
What ?
EEEEEEEEEEEEEEK!

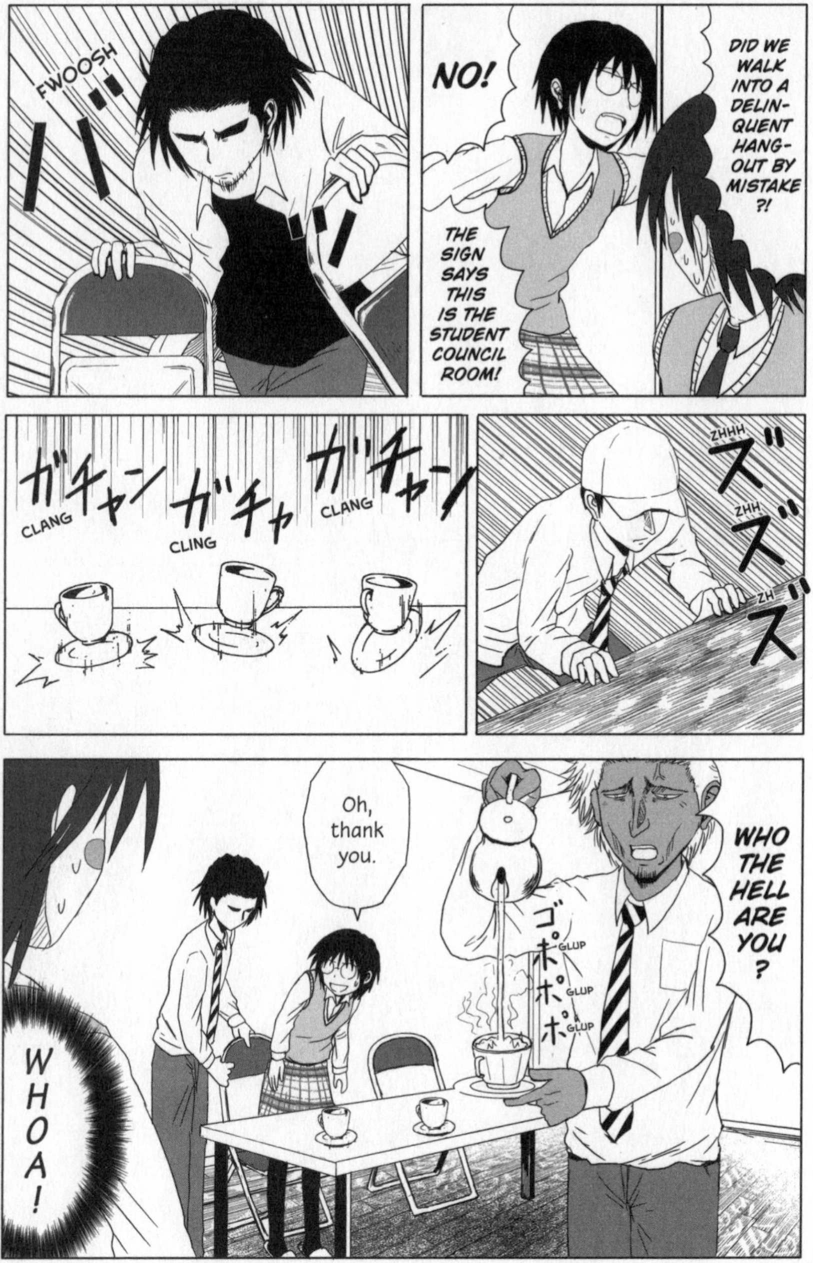
NO!
DID WE WALK INTO A DELIN-QUENT HANG-OUT BY MISTAKE ?!
THE SIGN SAYS THIS IS THE STUDENT COUNCIL ROOM!
FWOOSH
ズ ZHHH
ズ ZHH
ズ ZH
ガチャン CLANG
ガチャ CLING
ガチャーン CLANG
WHO THE HELL ARE YOU ?
Oh, thank you.
ゴポポポ GLUP GLUP GLUP
WHOA!

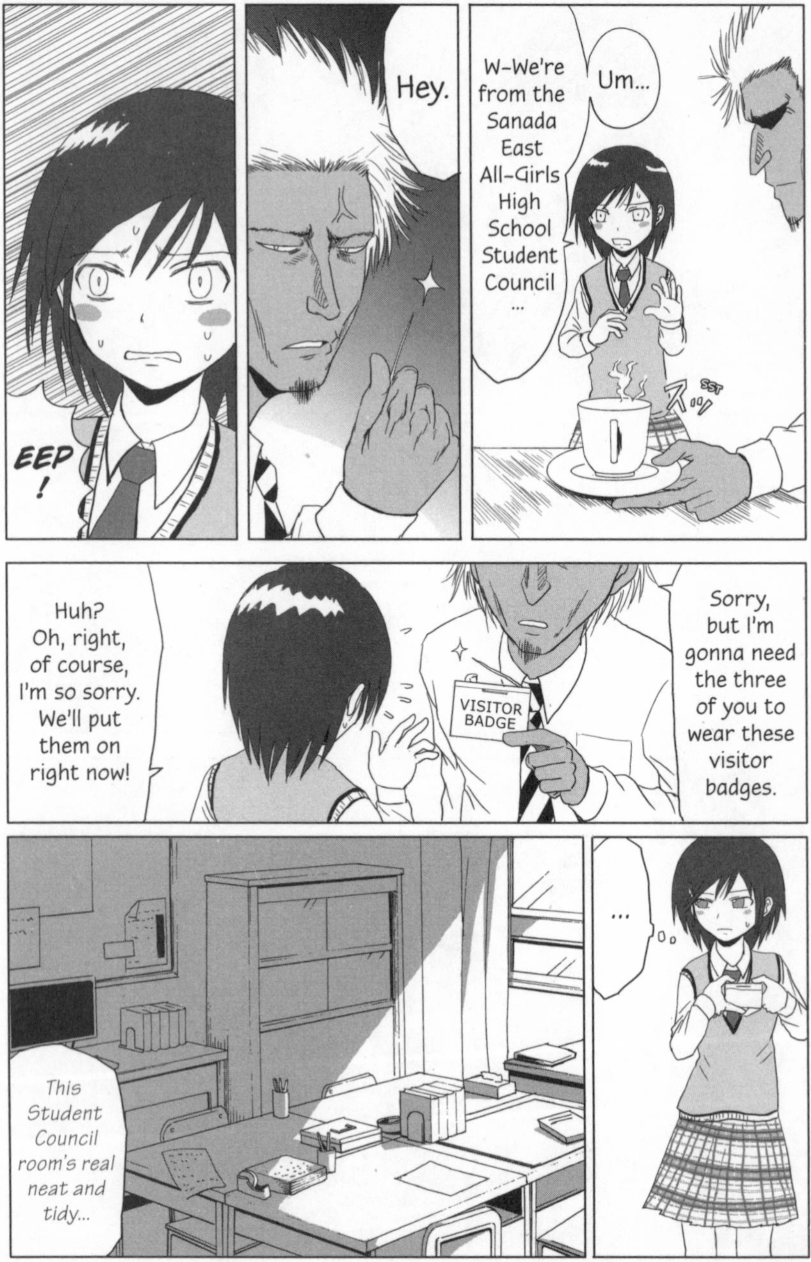
Um...
W-We're from the Sanada East All-Girls High School Student Council ...
SST
Hey.
EEP!
Sorry, but I'm gonna need the three of you to wear these visitor badges.
VISITOR BADGE
Huh? Oh, right, of course, I'm so sorry. We'll put them on right now!
...
This Student Council room's real neat and tidy...

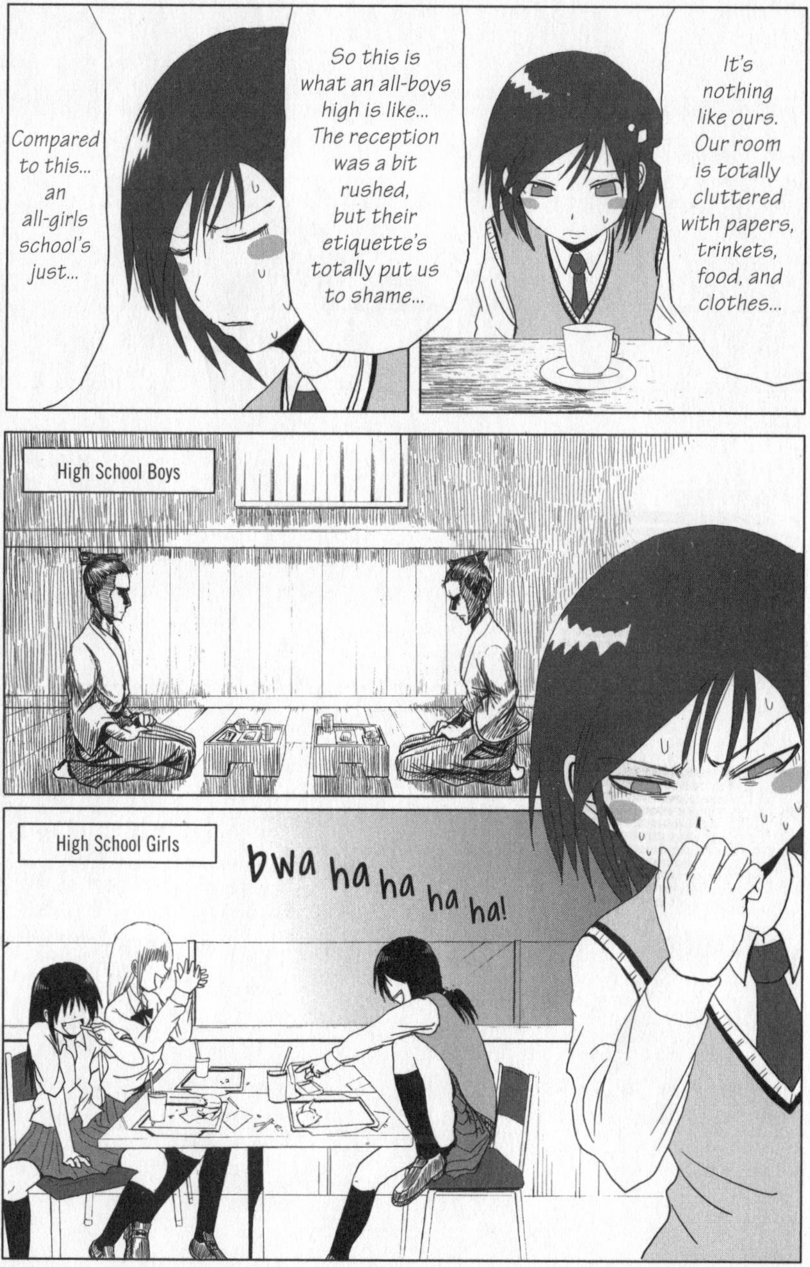
So this is what an all-boys high is like... The reception was a bit rushed, but their etiquette's totally put us to shame...
It's nothing like ours. Our room is totally cluttered with papers, trinkets, food, and clothes...
Compared to this... an all-girls school's just...
High School Boys
High School Girls
bwa ha ha ha ha!

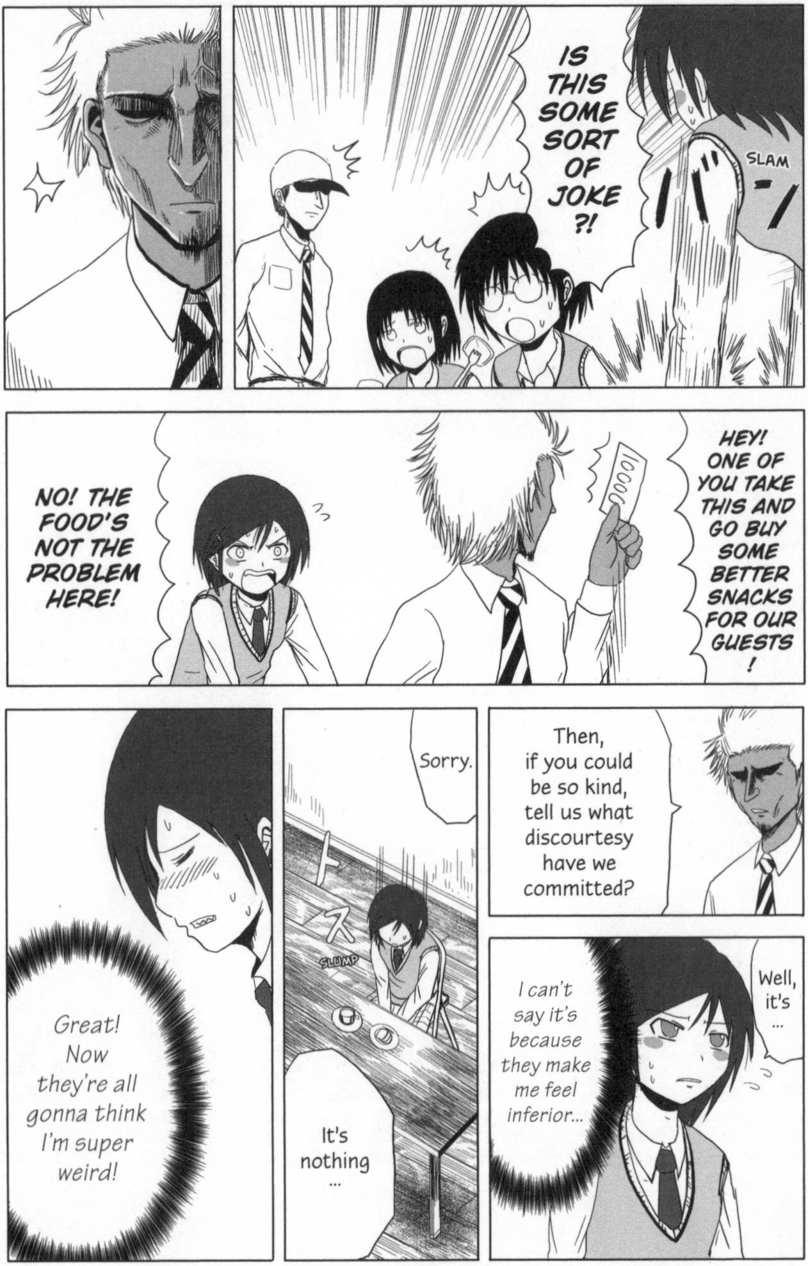
IS THIS SOME SORT OF JOKE?!
SLAM
HEY! ONE OF YOU TAKE THIS AND GO BUY SOME BETTER SNACKS FOR OUR GUESTS!
NO! THE FOOD'S NOT THE PROBLEM HERE!
Then, if you could be so kind, tell us what discourtesy have we committed?
Well, it's ...
I can't say it's because they make me feel inferior...
Sorry.
SLUMP
It's nothing ...
Great! Now they're all gonna think I'm super weird!

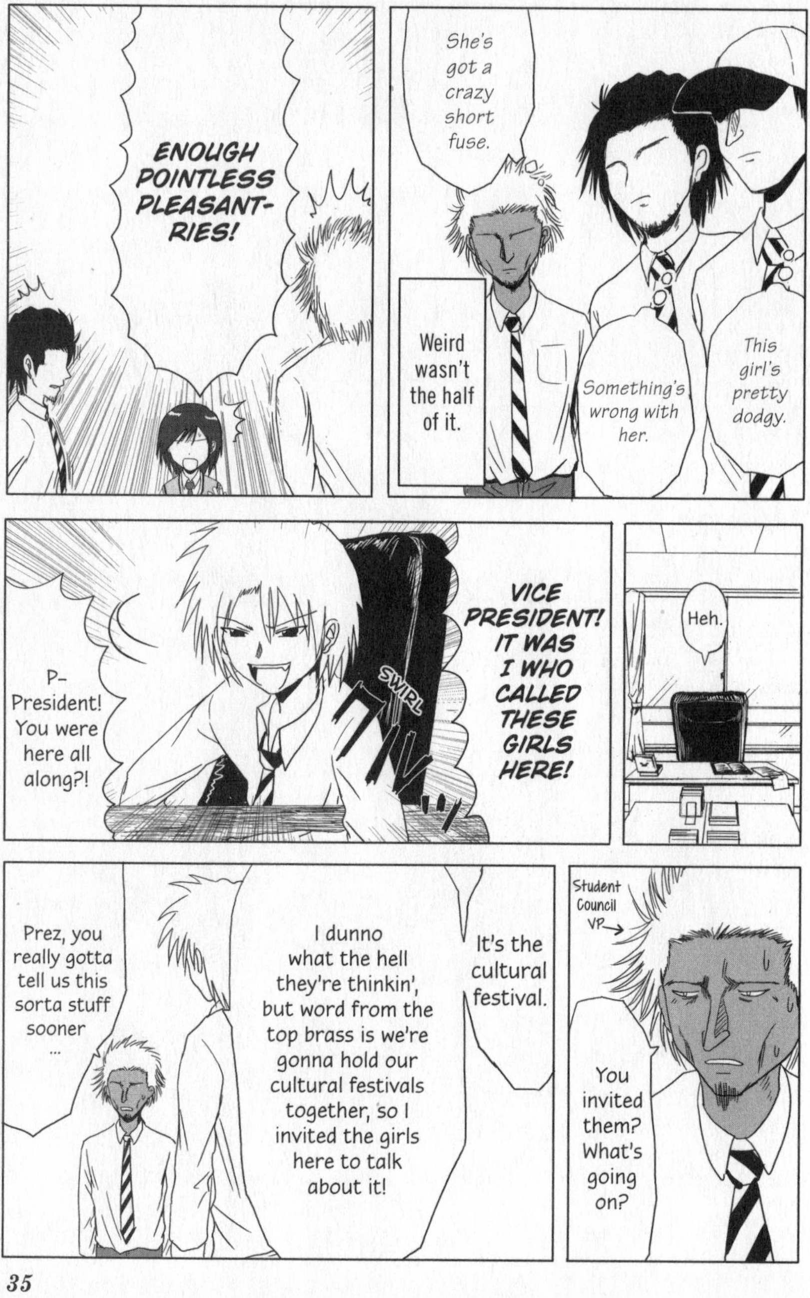
She's got a crazy short fuse.
This girl's pretty dodgy.
Something's wrong with her.
Weird wasn't the half of it.
ENOUGH POINTLESS PLEASANT-RIES!
Heh.
VICE PRESIDENT! IT WAS I WHO CALLED THESE GIRLS HERE!
SWIRL
P-President! You were here all along?!
Student Council VP
You invited them? What's going on?
It's the cultural festival.
I dunno what the hell they're thinkin', but word from the top brass is we're gonna hold our cultural festivals together, so I invited the girls here to talk about it!
Prez, you really gotta tell us this sorta stuff sooner ...

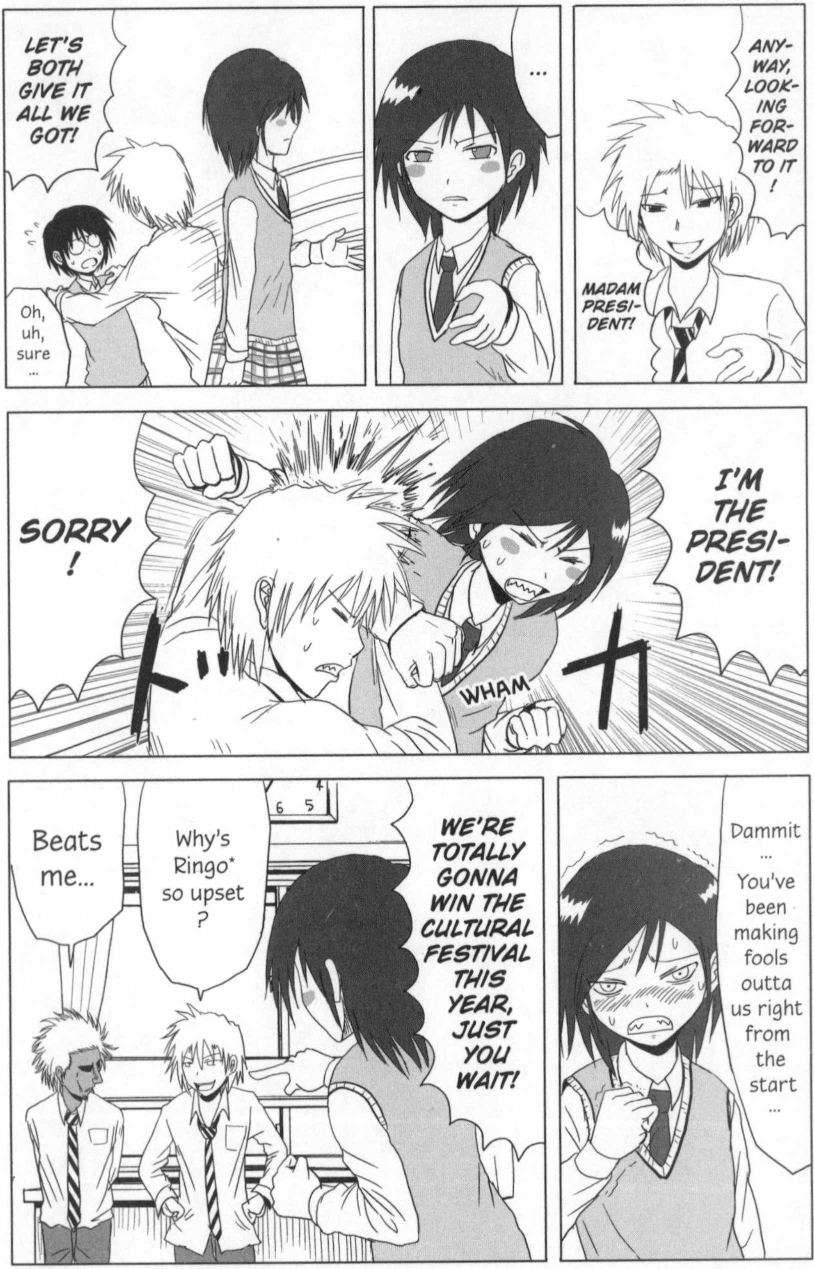
ANYWAY, LOOKING FORWARD TO IT!
MADAM PRESIDENT!
...
LET'S BOTH GIVE IT ALL WE GOT!
Oh, uh, sure ...
I'M THE PRESIDENT!
SORRY!
ドカ
WHAM
Dammit ... You've been making fools outta us right from the start ...
WE'RE TOTALLY GONNA WIN THE CULTURAL FESTIVAL THIS YEAR, JUST YOU WAIT!
Why's Ringo* so upset?
Beats me...

*Japanese word for apple. Alludes to her red cheeks.

chapter 20:
high school boys and the cultural festival, pt. 2

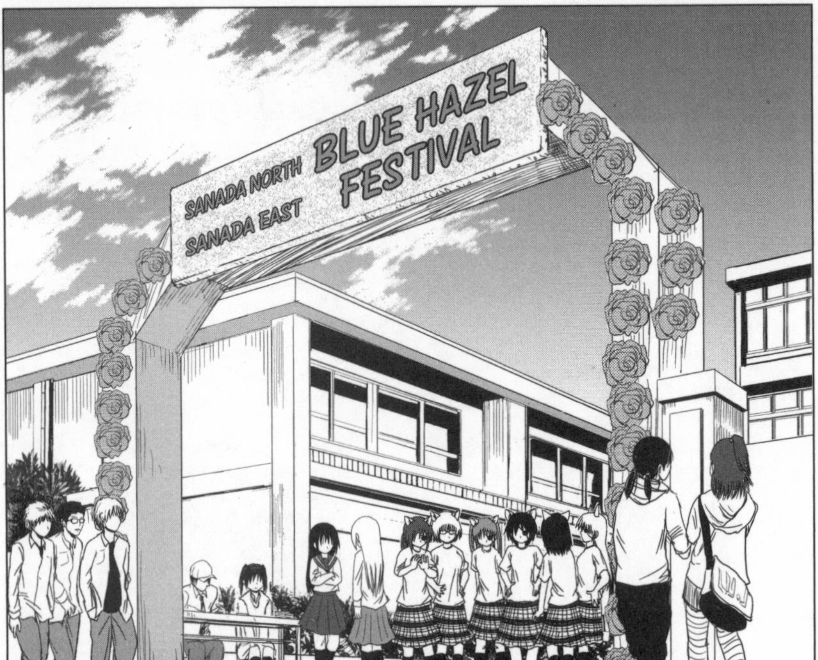
SANADA NORTH
SANADA EAST
BLUE HAZEL FESTIVAL

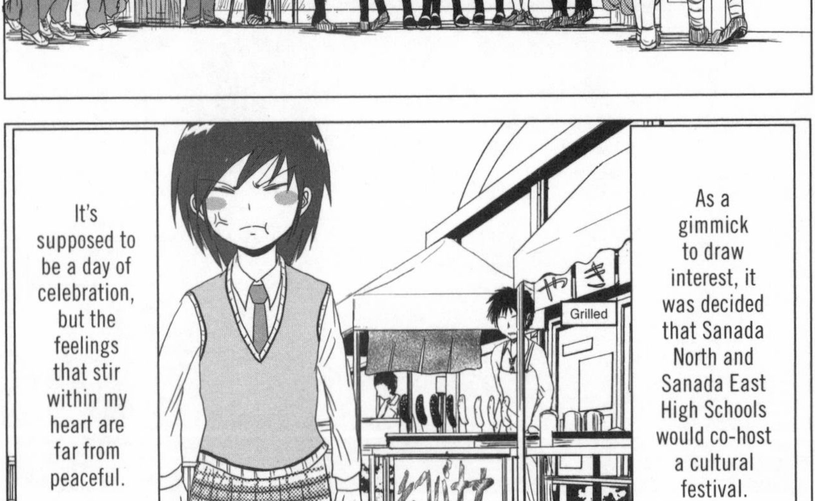
As a gimmick to draw interest, it was decided that Sanada North and Sanada East High Schools would co-host a cultural festival.
やき
Grilled
Chocolate-Covered Bananas
It's supposed to be a day of celebration, but the feelings that stir within my heart are far from peaceful.

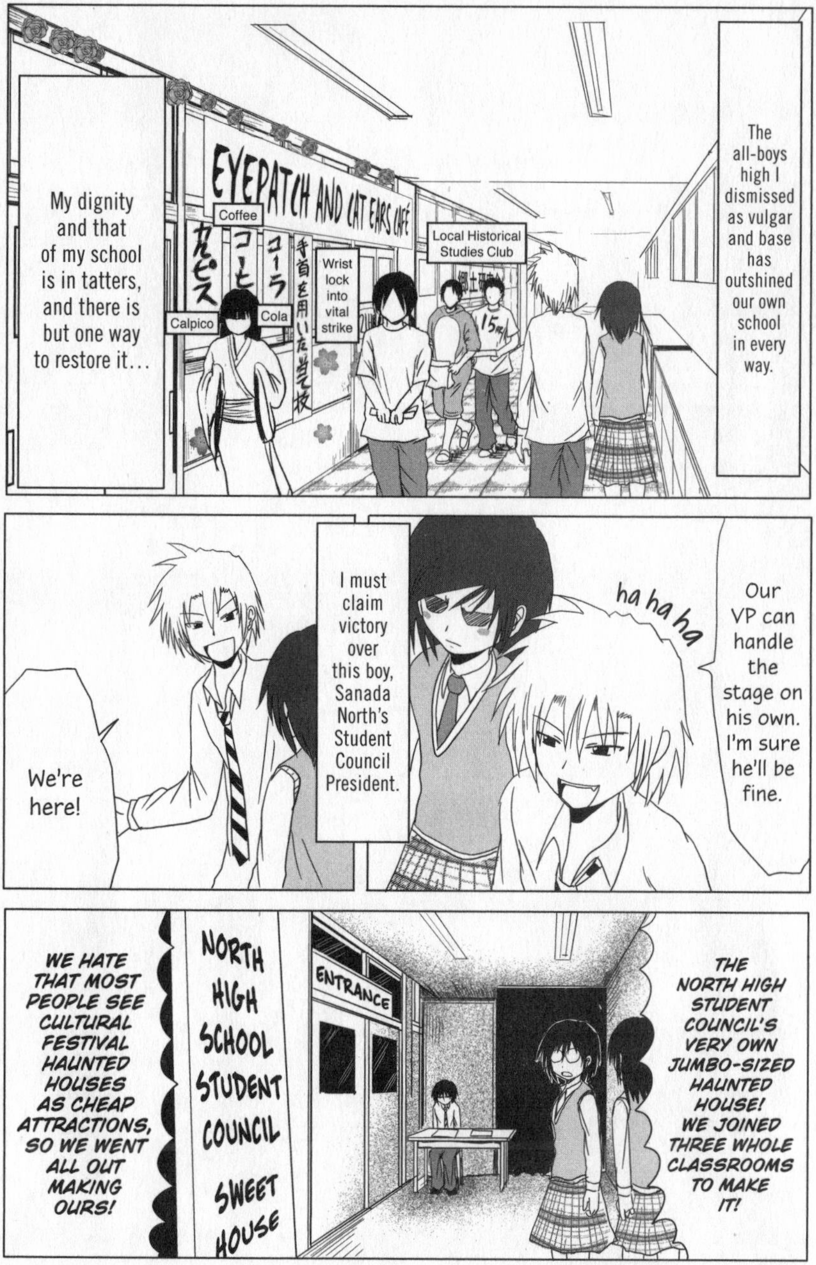
The all-boys high I dismissed as vulgar and base has outshined our own school in every way.
Local Historical Studies Club
EYEPATCH AND CAT EARS CAFÉ
Wrist lock into vital strike
コーラ
Cola
コーヒー
Coffee
カルピス
Calpico
My dignity and that of my school is in tatters, and there is but one way to restore it...
Our VP can handle the stage on his own. I'm sure he'll be fine.
ha ha ha
I must claim victory over this boy, Sanada North's Student Council President.
We're here!
THE NORTH HIGH STUDENT COUNCIL'S VERY OWN JUMBO-SIZED HAUNTED HOUSE! WE JOINED THREE WHOLE CLASSROOMS TO MAKE IT!
ENTRANCE
NORTH HIGH SCHOOL STUDENT COUNCIL SWEET HOUSE
WE HATE THAT MOST PEOPLE SEE CULTURAL FESTIVAL HAUNTED HOUSES AS CHEAP ATTRACTIONS, SO WE WENT ALL OUT MAKING OURS!

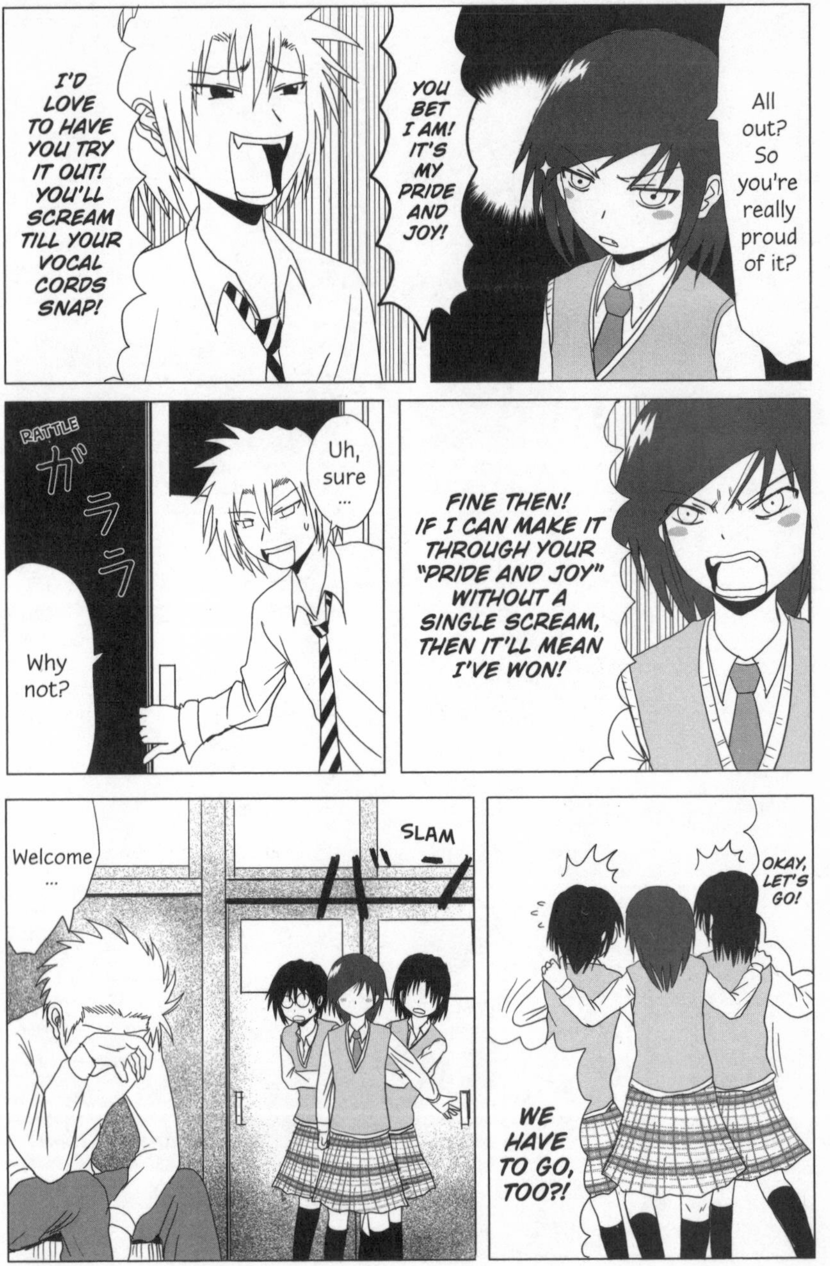

All out? So you're really proud of it?
YOU BET I AM! IT'S MY PRIDE AND JOY!
I'D LOVE TO HAVE YOU TRY IT OUT! YOU'LL SCREAM TILL YOUR VOCAL CORDS SNAP!
FINE THEN! IF I CAN MAKE IT THROUGH YOUR "PRIDE AND JOY" WITHOUT A SINGLE SCREAM, THEN IT'LL MEAN I'VE WON!
Uh, sure ...
RATTLE
ガララ
Why not?
OKAY, LET'S GO!
WE HAVE TO GO, TOO?!
SLAM
バー
Welcome ...

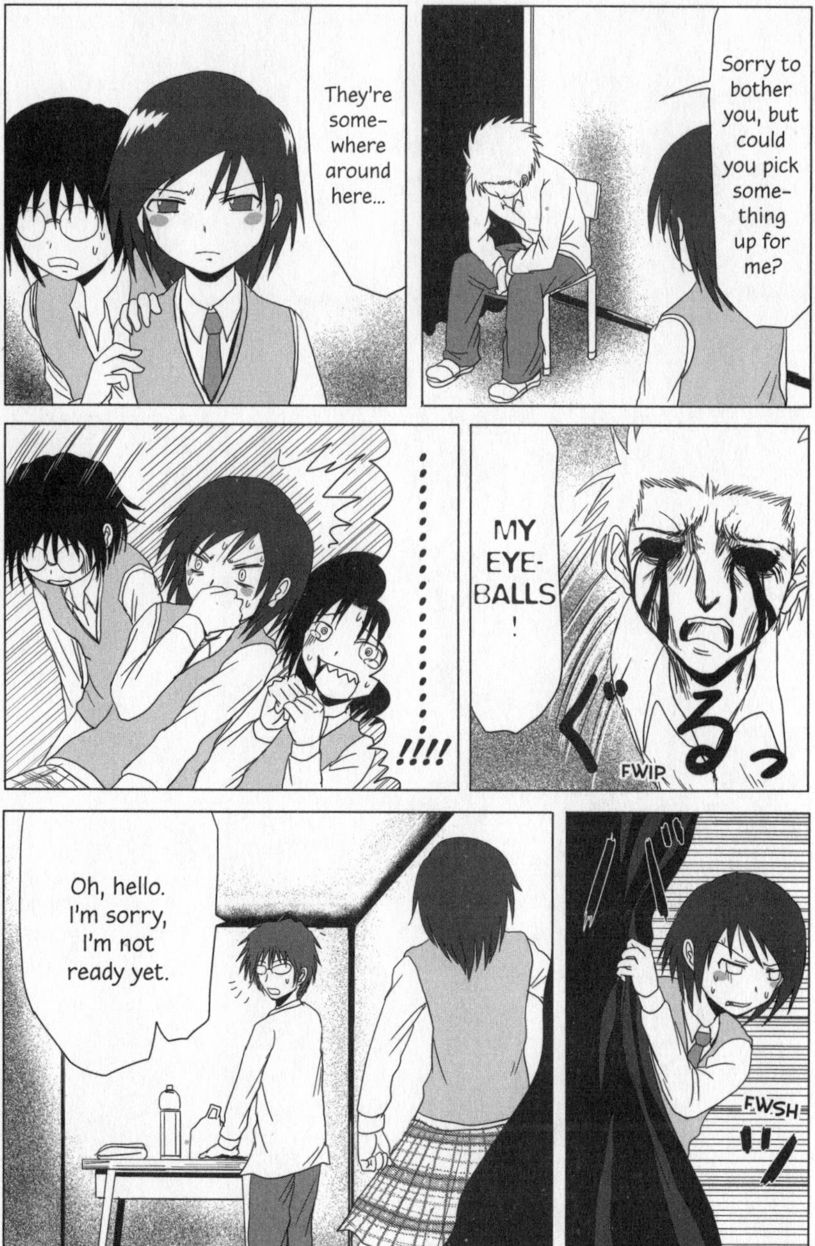
Sorry to bother you, but could you pick some-thing up for me?
They're some-where around here...
MY EYE-BALLS!
ぐるっ
FWIP
..........!!!!
F.W.SH
ッ
Oh, hello. I'm sorry, I'm not ready yet.

...!!

DASH

THUNK

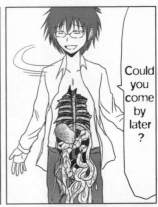

Could you come by later?

FRSH

DIE! DIE! DIE!

My head! Give me back my head!

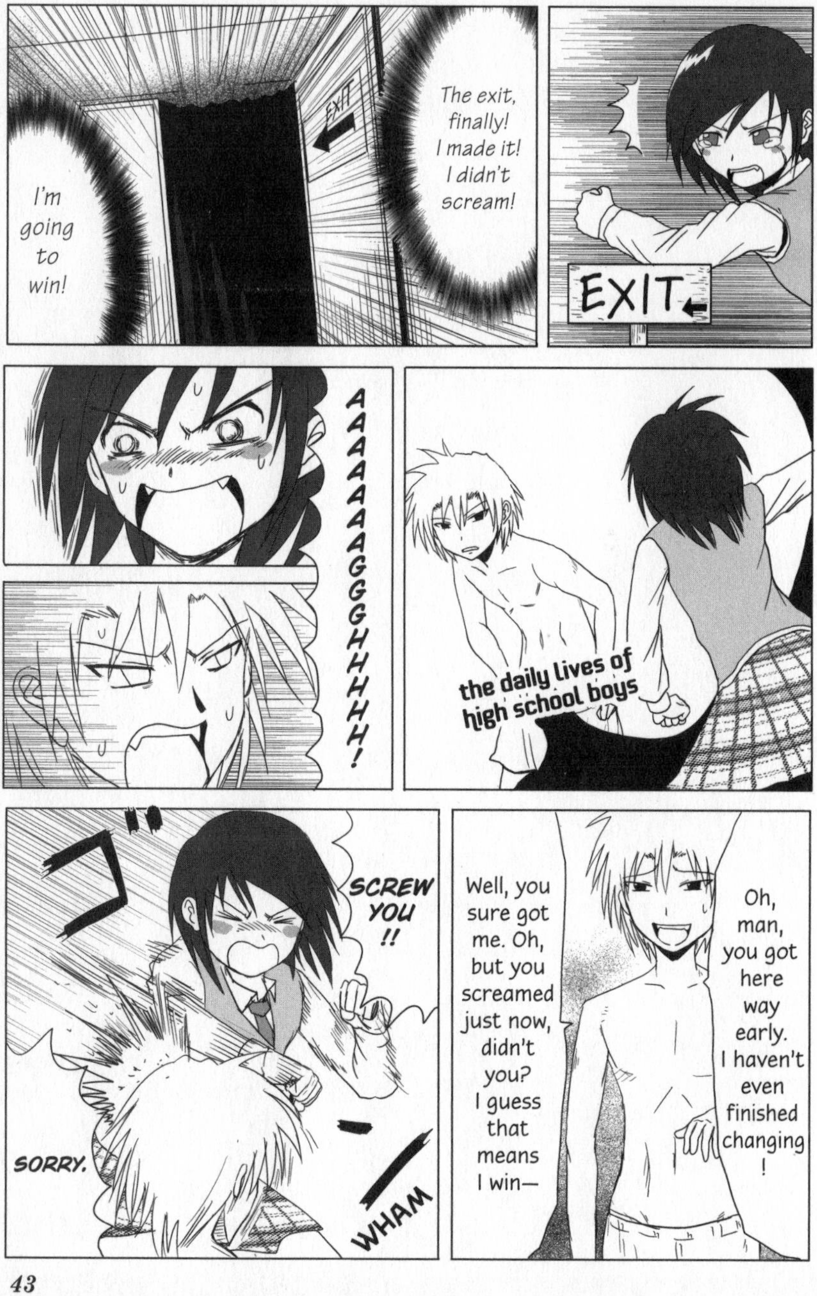
EXIT
The exit, finally! I made it! I didn't scream!
I'm going to win!
the daily lives of high school boys
AAAAAAAGGGHHHHH!
Oh, man, you got here way early. I haven't even finished changing!
Well, you sure got me. Oh, but you screamed just now, didn't you? I guess that means I win—
SCREW YOU!!
SORRY.
WHAM

the

daily

lives

of

2 high school boys

chapter 21:
high school boys and the cultural festival, pt. 3

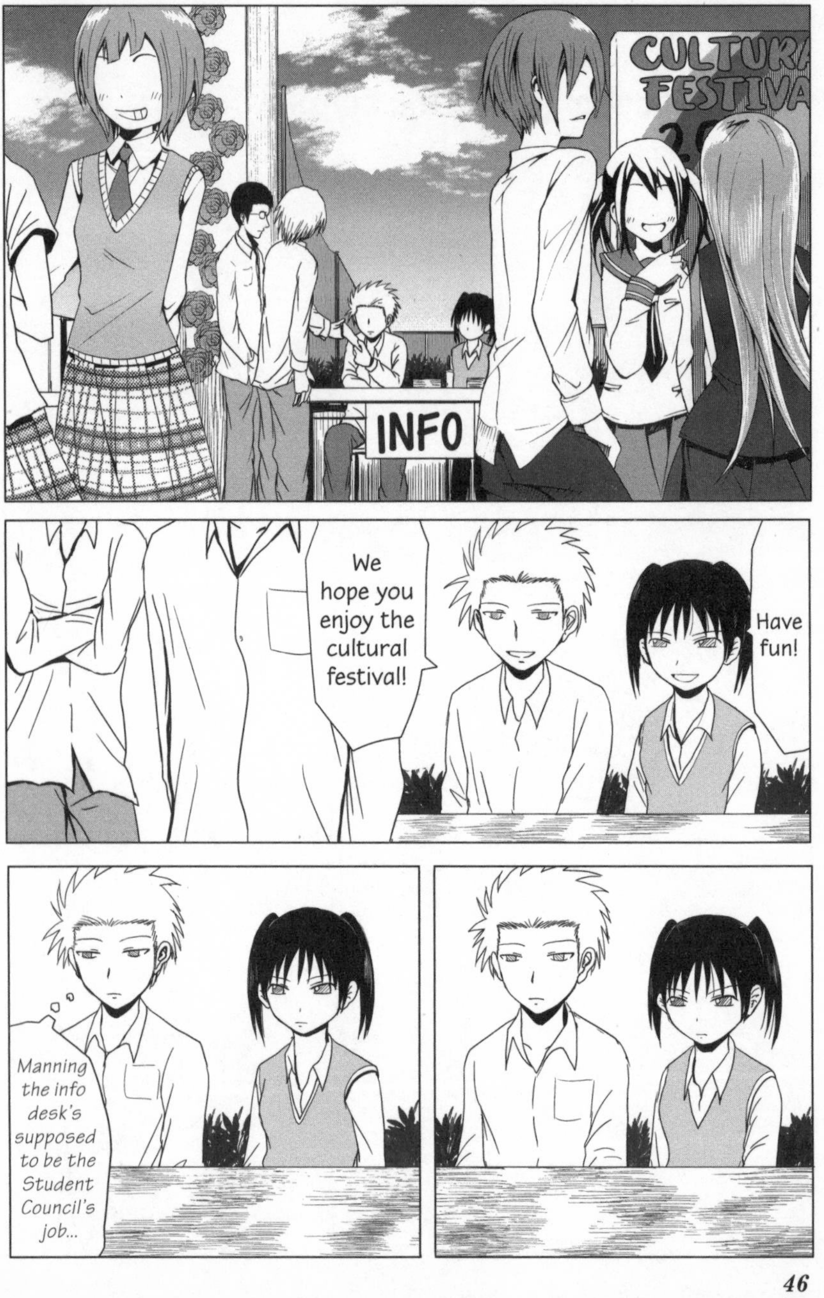
CULTURA
FESTIVA
INFO
Have fun!
We hope you enjoy the cultural festival!
Manning the info desk's supposed to be the Student Council's job...

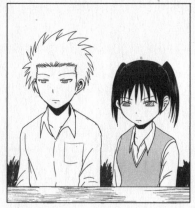

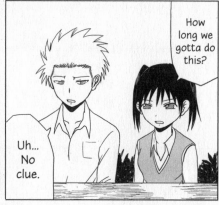

How long we gotta do this?
Uh... No clue.
Look, there's a maid. She's running around.
Oh, yeah.
Crazy that she can wear an outfit like that.
Seri-ously? Anyone can wear an outfit like that.
You can even dance in it.
I see ...
No, no, see, unlike you guys, us girls don't think anything about wearing a maid outfit.
I see.

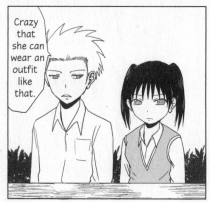

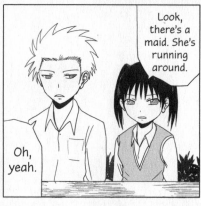

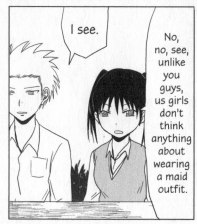

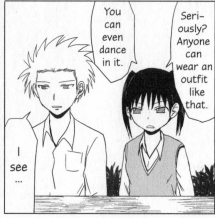

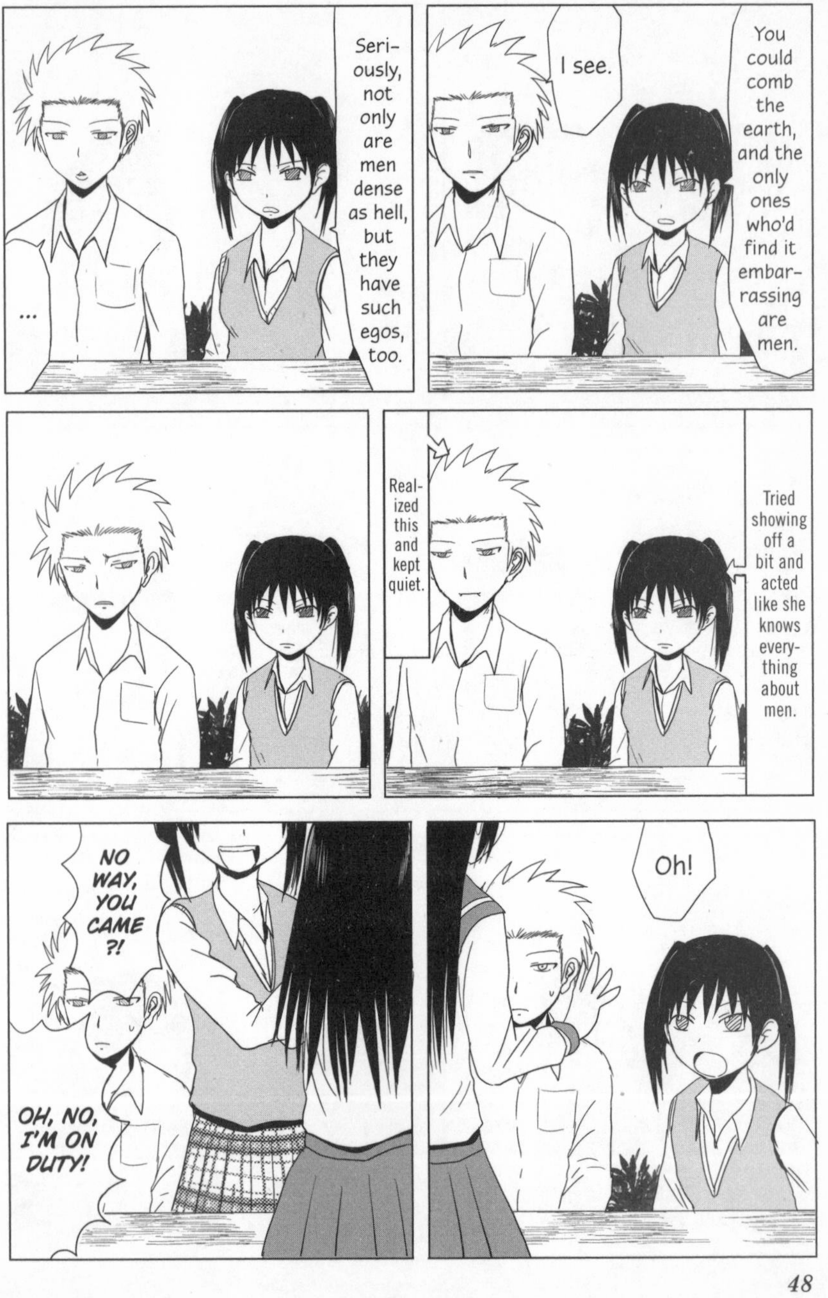
You could comb the earth, and the only ones who'd find it embarrassing are men.
I see.
Seriously, not only are men dense as hell, but they have such egos, too.
...
Tried showing off a bit and acted like she knows everything about men.
Realized this and kept quiet.
Oh!
NO WAY, YOU CAME?!
OH, NO, I'M ON DUTY!

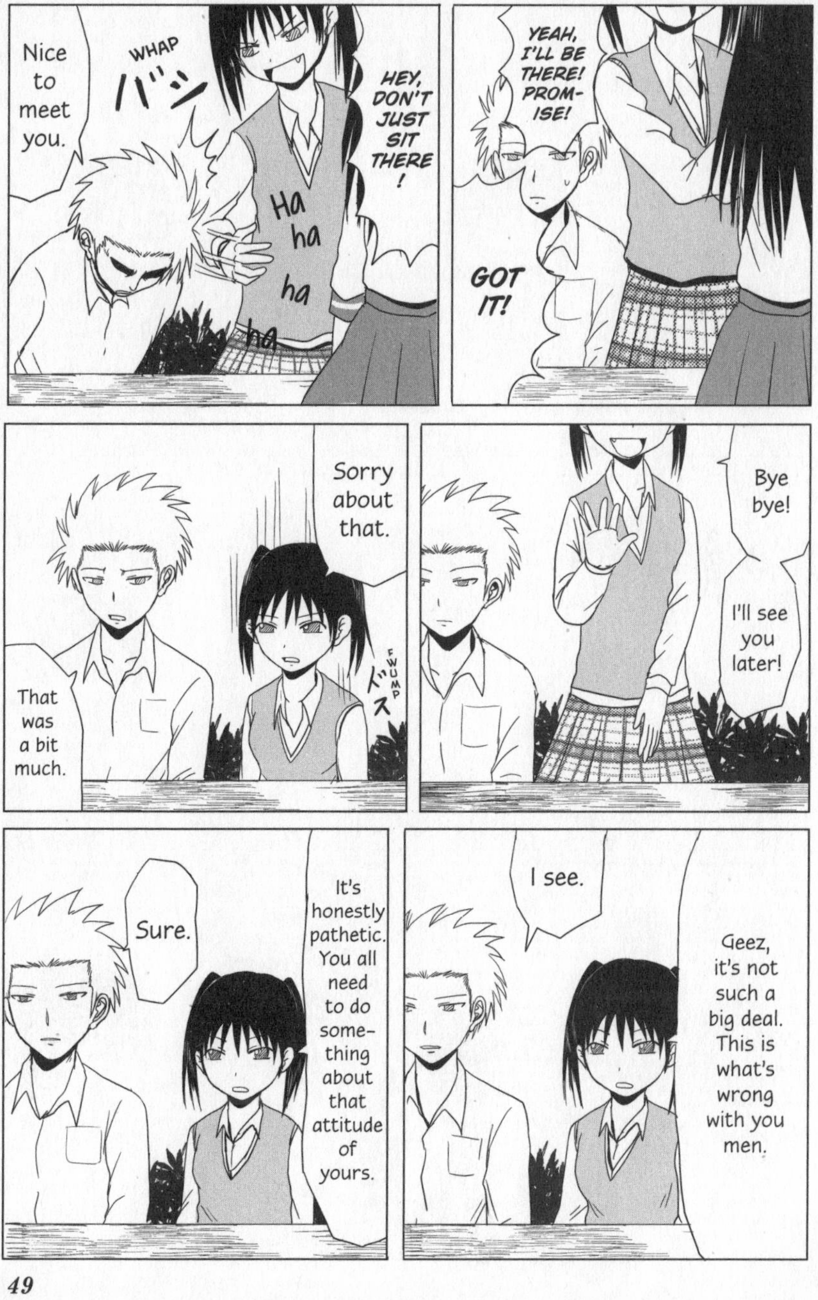
YEAH, I'LL BE THERE! PROMISE!
GOT IT!
HEY, DON'T JUST SIT THERE!
WHAP
バッ
Nice to meet you.
Ha ha ha ha
Bye bye!
I'll see you later!
Sorry about that.
FWUMP
ドス
That was a bit much.
Geez, it's not such a big deal. This is what's wrong with you men.
I see.
It's honestly pathetic. You all need to do some-thing about that attitude of yours.
Sure.

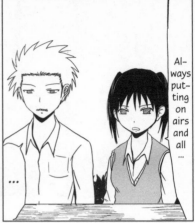

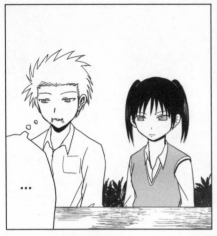

Al-ways put-ting on airs and all ...
...
...
'Scuse me a mo-ment.
Hello? It's Yoshi-take.
Can you take over for me at the info desk?
10 minutes later.
Is some-thing the matter?
I'M SO SORRY! I GOT CARRIED AWAY!
Huh?

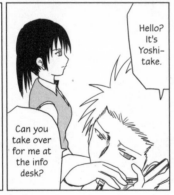

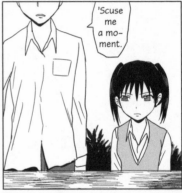

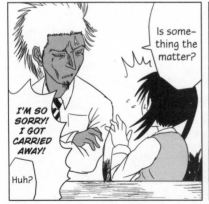

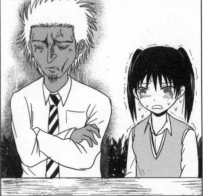

chapter 22:
high school boys and the cultural festival. pt. 4

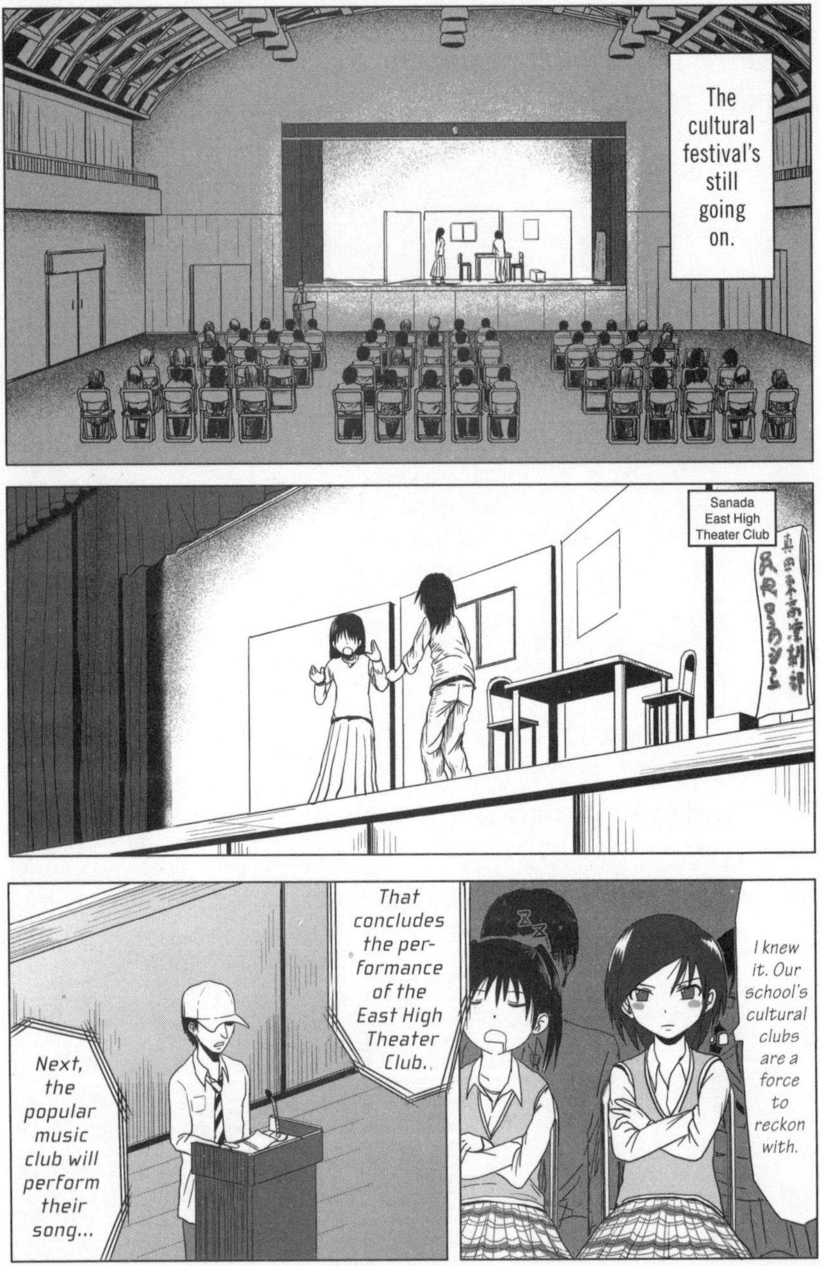
The cultural festival's still going on.
Sanada East High Theater Club
I knew it. Our school's cultural clubs are a force to reckon with.
That concludes the performance of the East High Theater Club.
Next, the popular music club will perform their song...

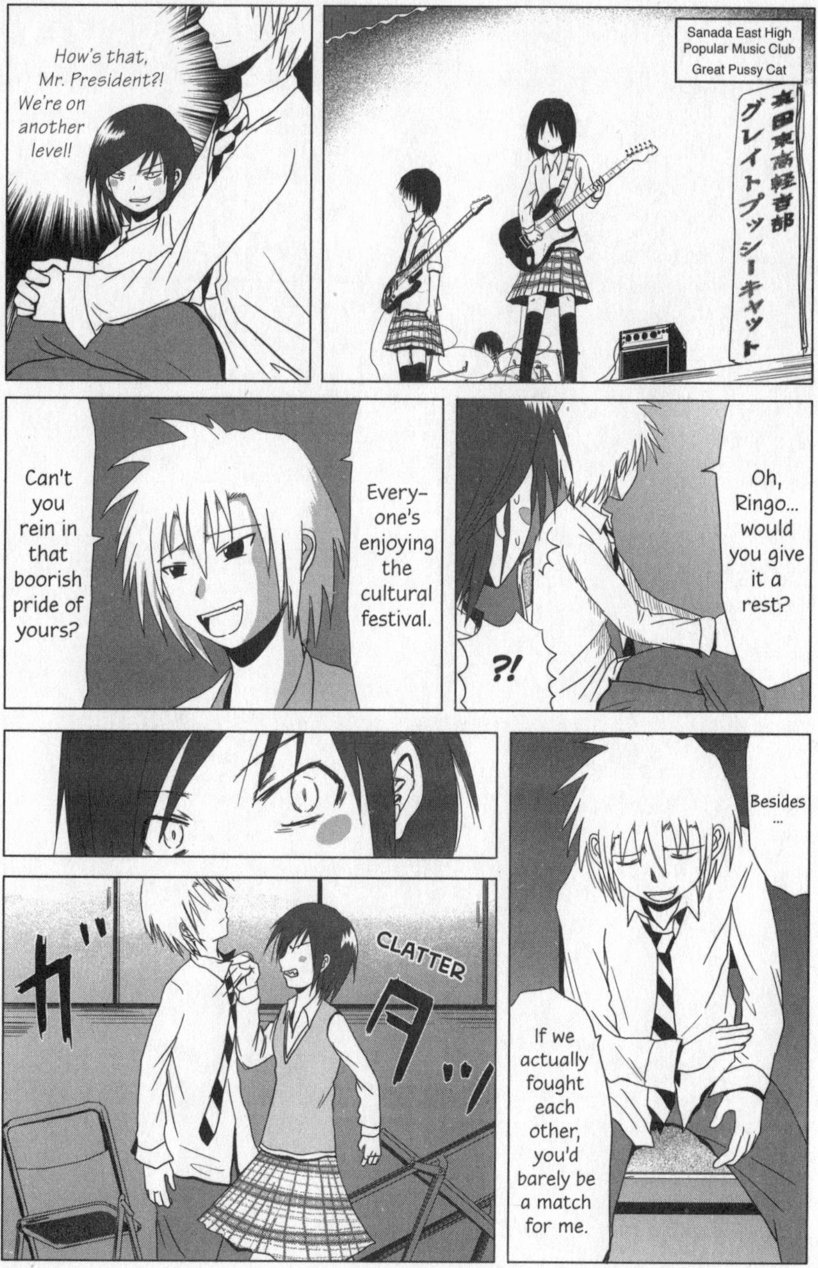
Sanada East High
Popular Music Club
Great Pussy Cat
真田東高軽音部
グレイトプッシーキャット
How's that, Mr. President?! We're on another level!
Oh, Ringo... would you give it a rest?
?!
Every-one's enjoying the cultural festival.
Can't you rein in that boorish pride of yours?
Besides ...
If we actually fought each other, you'd barely be a match for me.
ガ
CLATTER
タッ

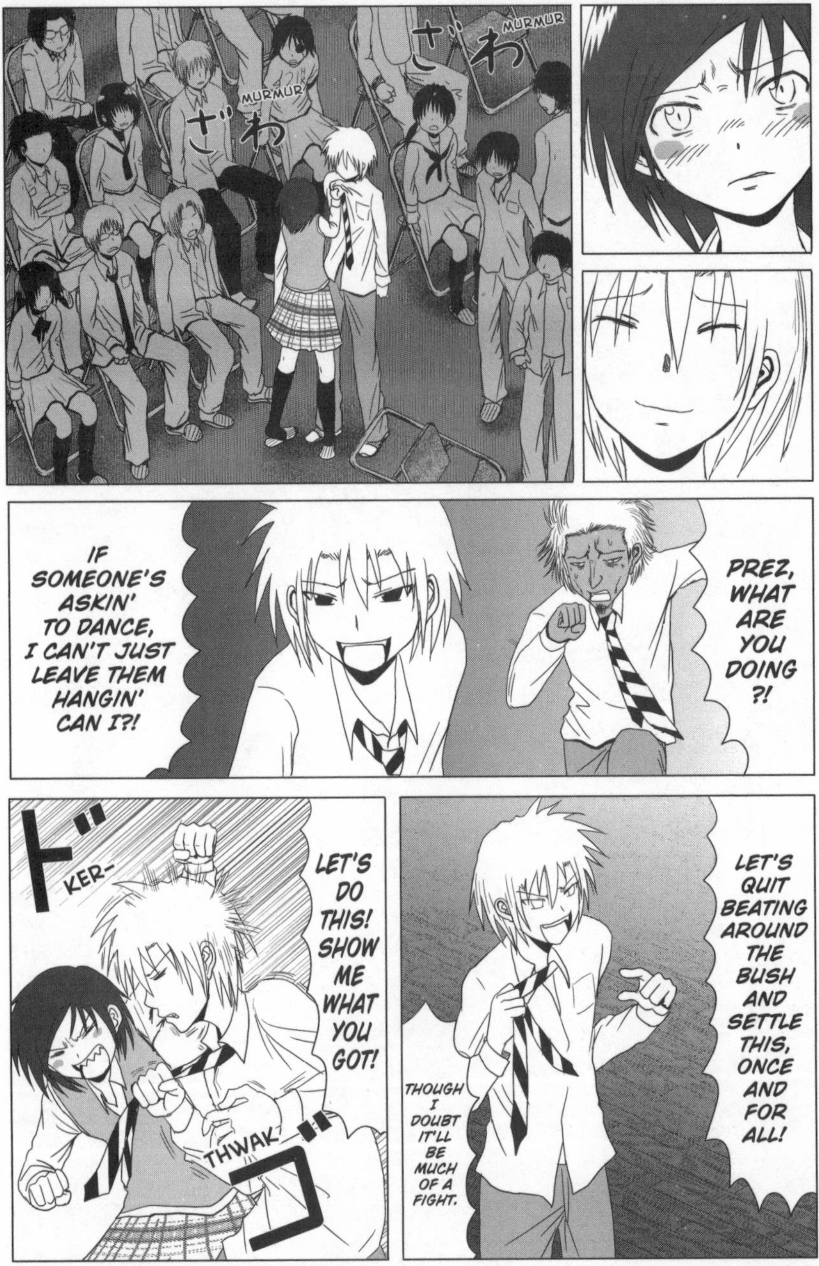
ざわ
MURMUR
ざわ
MURMUR
PREZ, WHAT ARE YOU DOING?!
IF SOMEONE'S ASKIN' TO DANCE, I CAN'T JUST LEAVE THEM HANGIN' CAN I?!
LET'S QUIT BEATING AROUND THE BUSH AND SETTLE THIS, ONCE AND FOR ALL!
THOUGH I DOUBT IT'LL BE MUCH OF A FIGHT.
ド
KER-
LET'S DO THIS! SHOW ME WHAT YOU GOT!
THWAK
ゴ

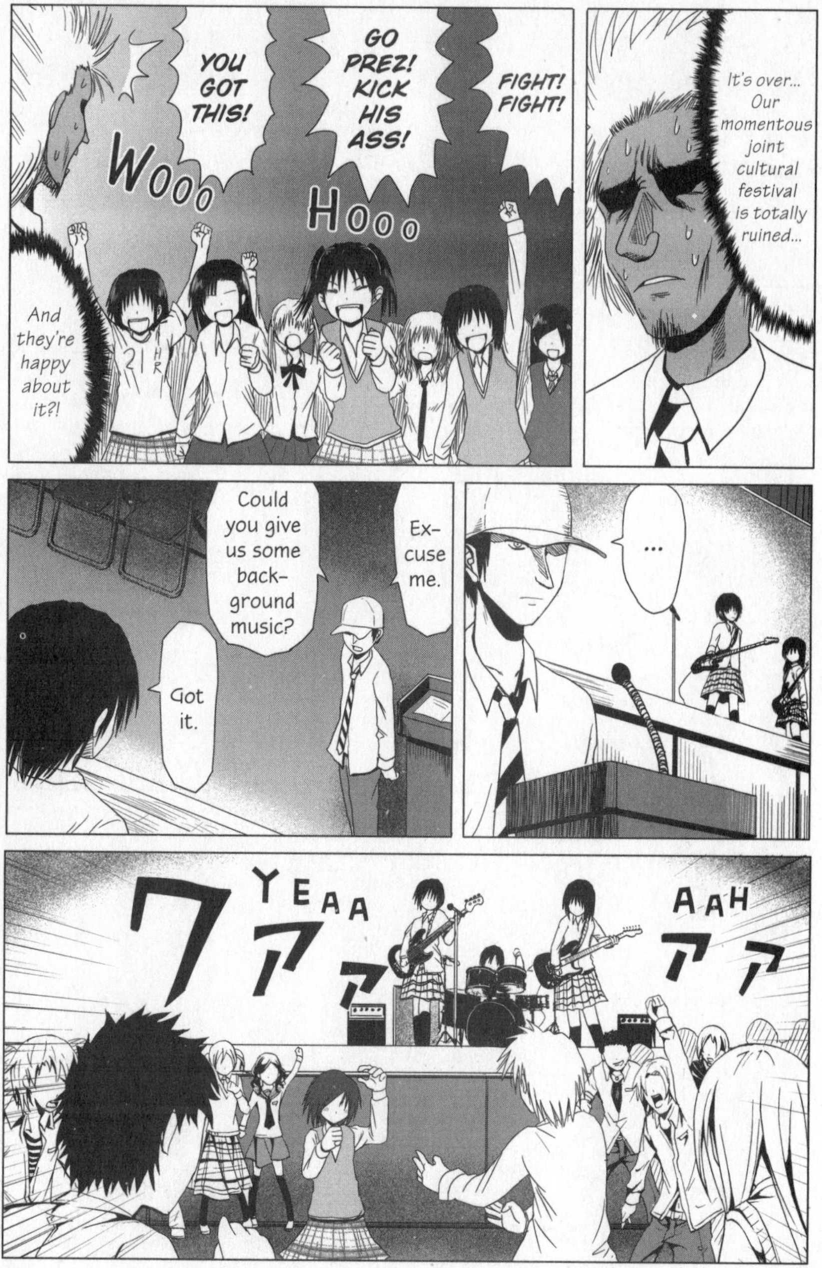
It's over... Our momentous joint cultural festival is totally ruined...
FIGHT! FIGHT!
GO PREZ! KICK HIS ASS!
YOU GOT THIS!
Wooo
Hooo
And they're happy about it?!
...
Ex-cuse me.
Could you give us some back-ground music?
Got it.
アア
AAH
ワァァ
YEAA

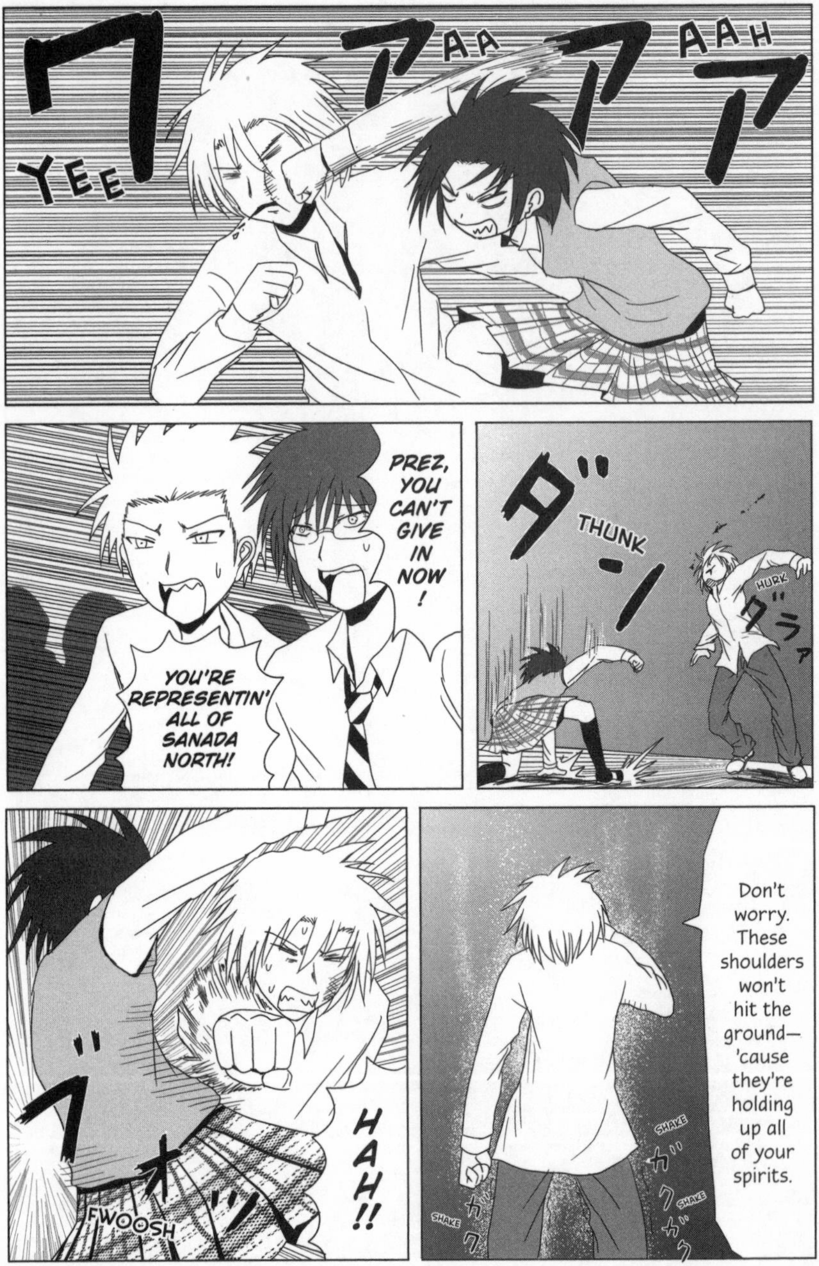
ワアアア
YEE
AA
AAH
ダーン
THUNK
グラァ
HURK
PREZ, YOU CAN'T GIVE IN NOW!
YOU'RE REPRESENTIN' ALL OF SANADA NORTH!
Don't worry. These shoulders won't hit the ground—'cause they're holding up all of your spirits.
SHAKE
SHAKE
SHAKE
HAH!!
FWOOSH

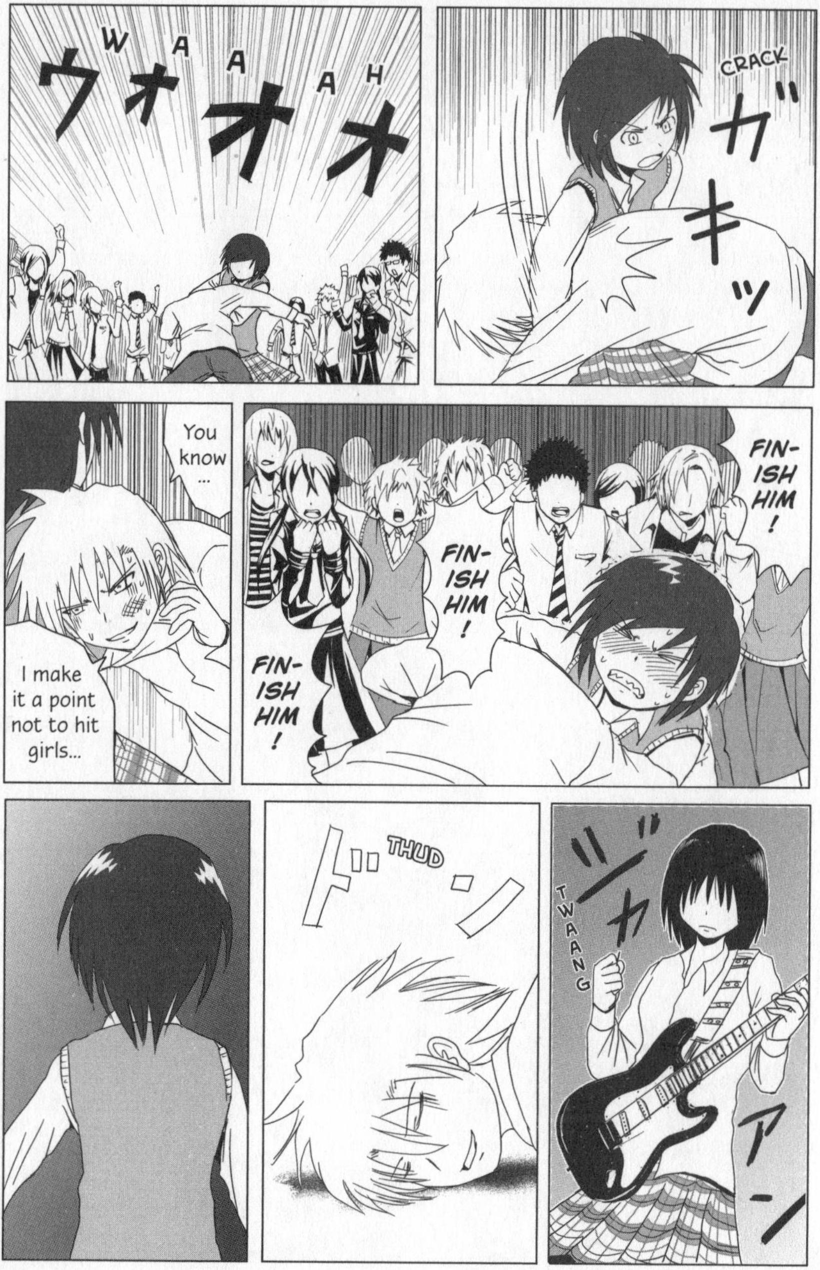
CRACK
ガキッ
WAAAAH
ウォオオ
FIN-ISH HIM!
FIN-ISH HIM!
FIN-ISH HIM!
You know ...
I make it a point not to hit girls...
TWAANG
THUD
ドーン

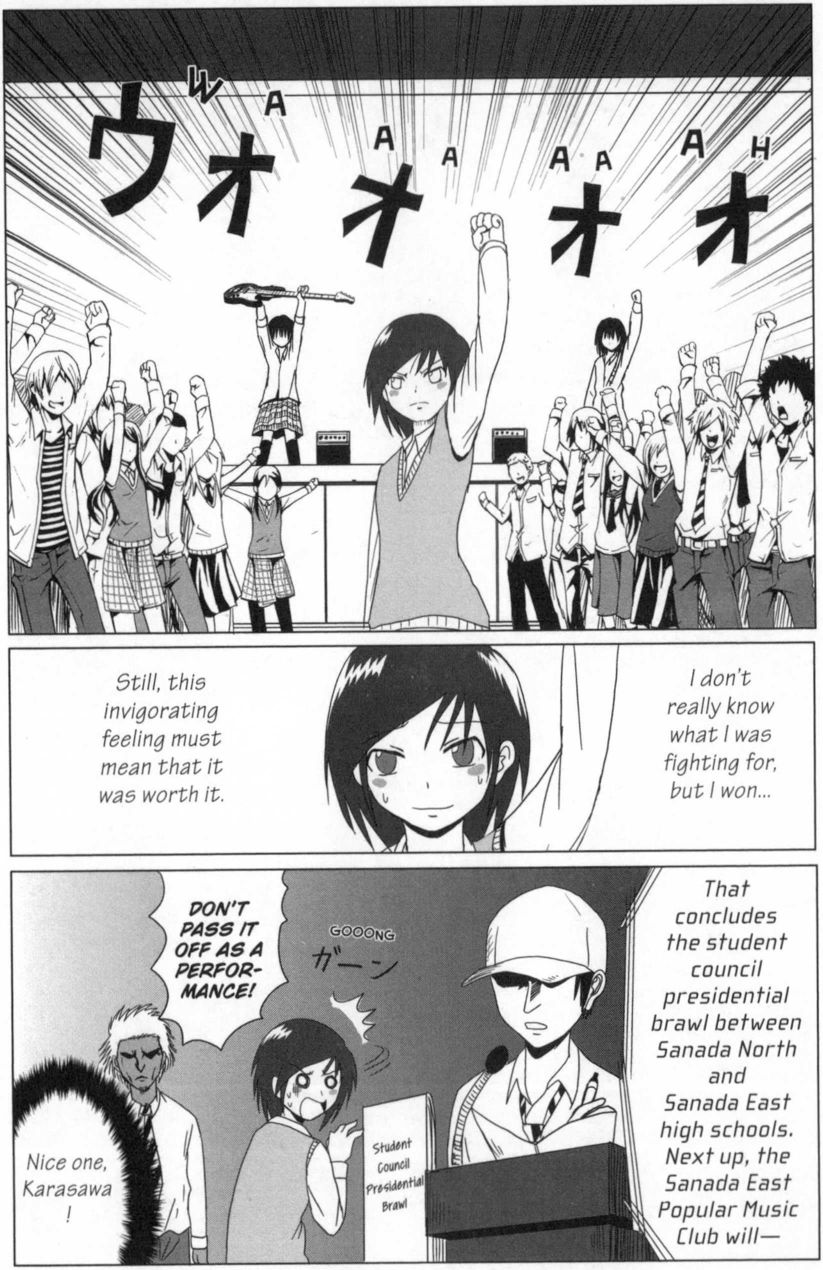
WAAAAAAAH
ウォオオオ
I don't really know what I was fighting for, but I won...
Still, this invigorating feeling must mean that it was worth it.
That concludes the student council presidential brawl between Sanada North and Sanada East high schools. Next up, the Sanada East Popular Music Club will—
Student Council Presidential Brawl
GOOONG
ガーン
DON'T PASS IT OFF AS A PERFORMANCE!
Nice one, Karasawa!

chapter 23:
high school boys and eavesdropping

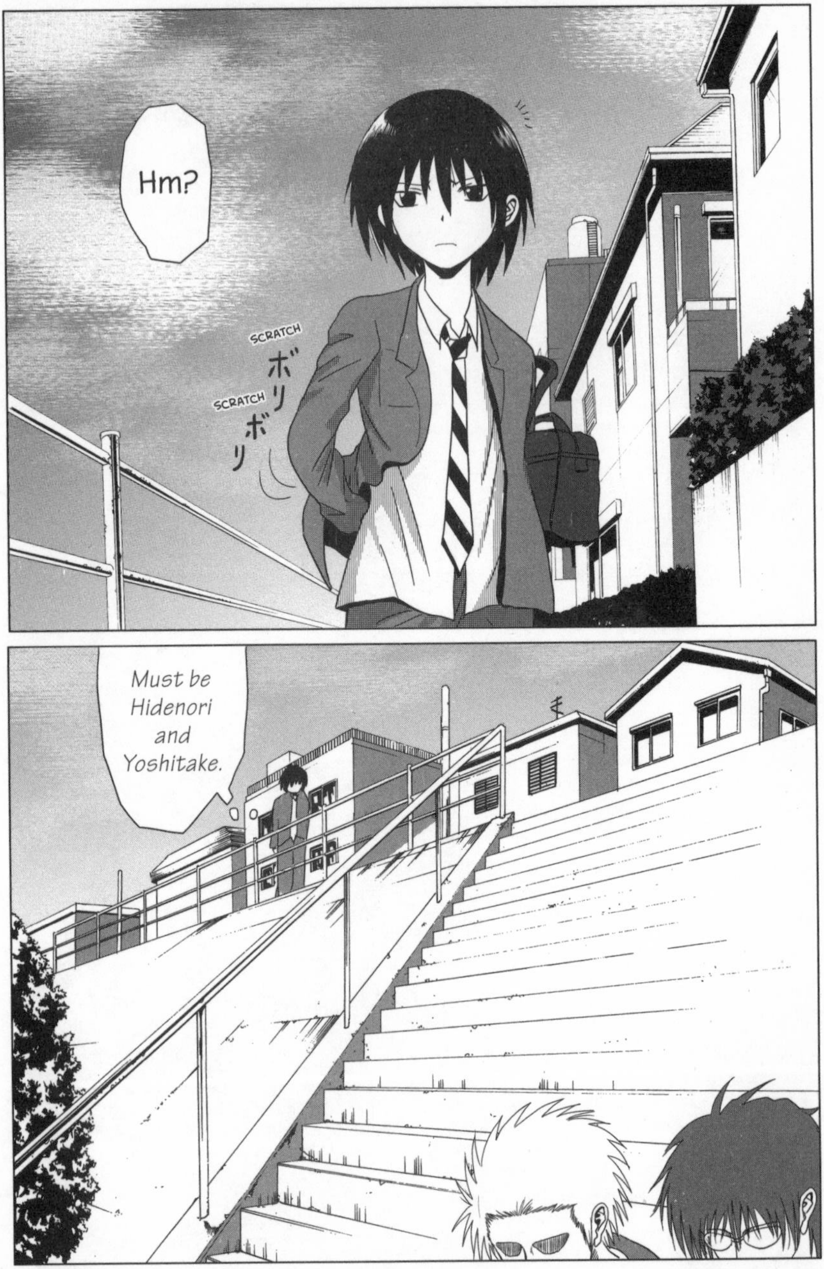
Hm?
SCRATCH
ボリ
SCRATCH
ボリ
Must be Hidenori and Yoshitake.

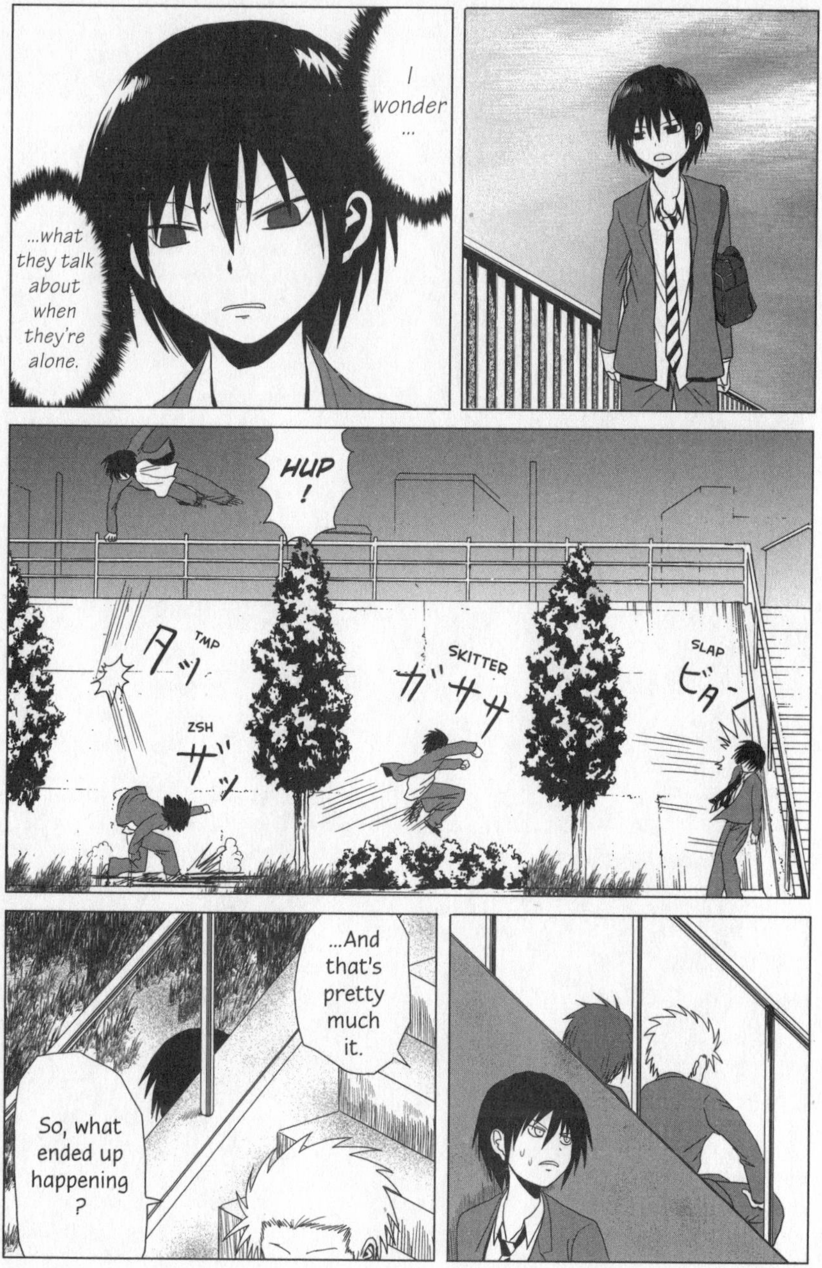
I wonder...
...what they talk about when they're alone.
HUP!
SLAP
ビターン
SKITTER
ガササ
ZSH
ザッ
TMP
タッ
...And that's pretty much it.
So, what ended up happening?

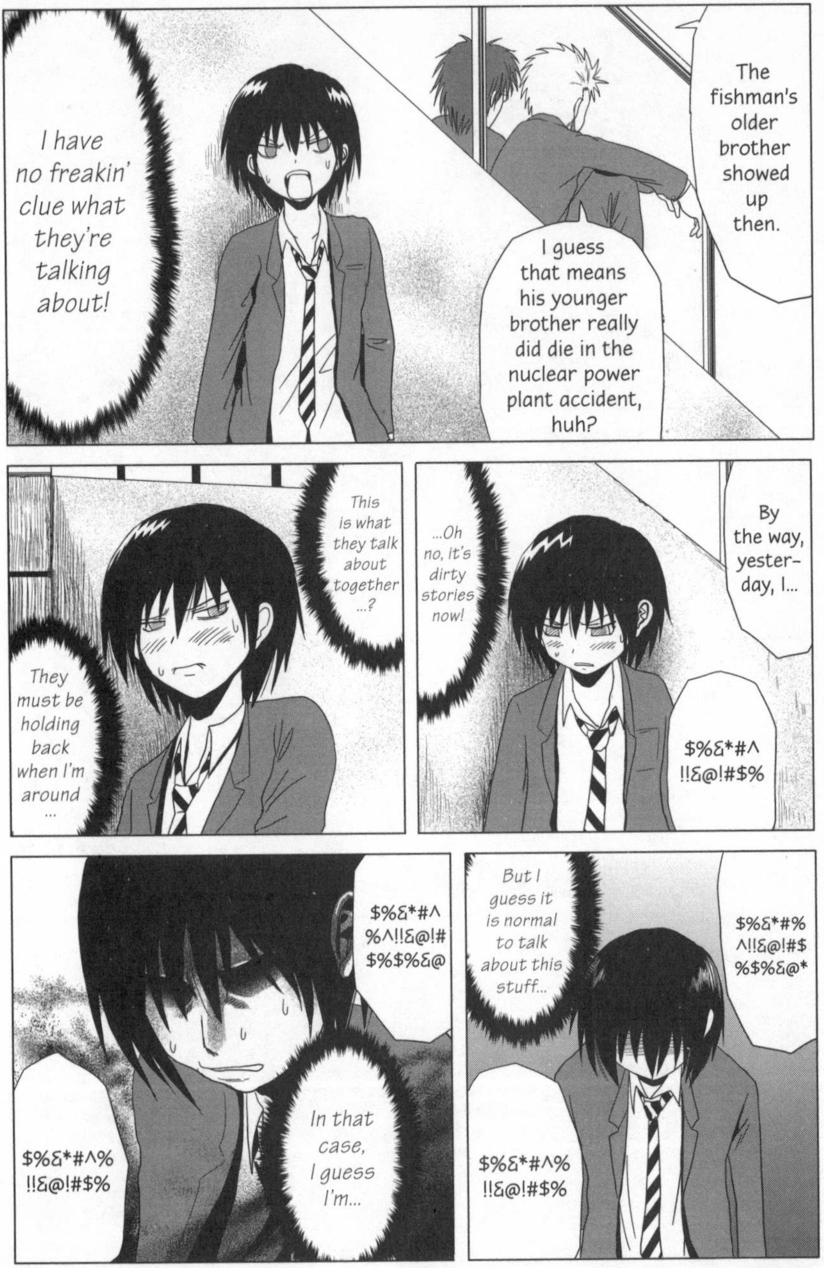
The fishman's older brother showed up then.
I guess that means his younger brother really did die in the nuclear power plant accident, huh?
I have no freakin' clue what they're talking about!
By the way, yester-day, I...
$%&*#^ !!&@!#$%
...Oh no, it's dirty stories now!
This is what they talk about together ...?
They must be holding back when I'm around ...
$%&*#% ^!!&@!#$ %$%&@*
But I guess it is normal to talk about this stuff...
$%&*#^% !!&@!#$%
$%&*#^ %^!!&@!# $%$%&@
In that case, I guess I'm...
$%&*#^% !!&@!#$%

*The Democratic Party of Japan (DPJ).

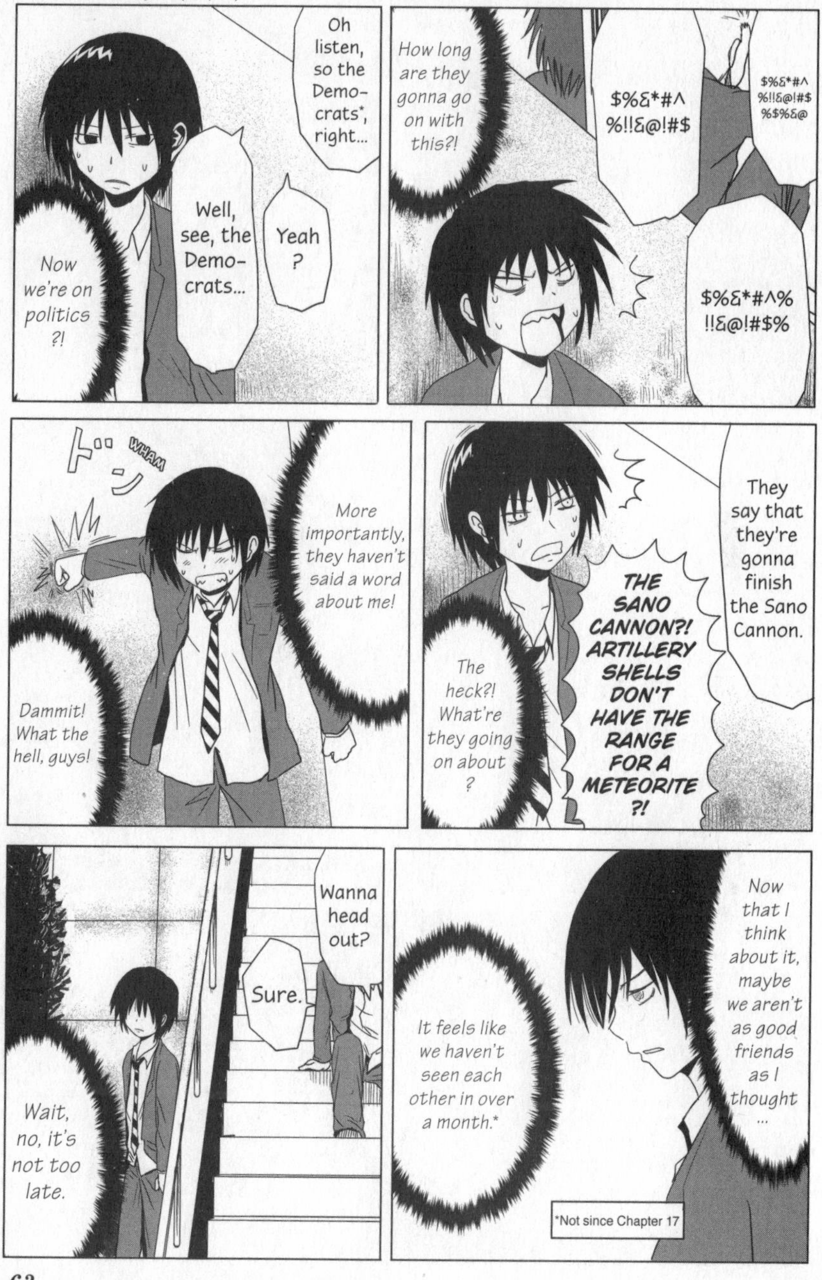
$%&*#^ %!!&@!#$ %$%&@
$%&*#^ %!!&@!#$
How long are they gonna go on with this?!
$%&*#^% !!&@!#$%
Oh listen, so the Demo-crats*, right...
Yeah?
Well, see, the Demo-crats...
Now we're on politics?!
They say that they're gonna finish the Sano Cannon.
THE SANO CANNON?! ARTILLERY SHELLS DON'T HAVE THE RANGE FOR A METEORITE?!
The heck?! What're they going on about?
More importantly, they haven't said a word about me!
ドン
WHAM
Dammit! What the hell, guys!
Now that I think about it, maybe we aren't as good friends as I thought...
It feels like we haven't seen each other in over a month.*
*Not since Chapter 17
Wanna head out?
Sure.
Wait, no, it's not too late.

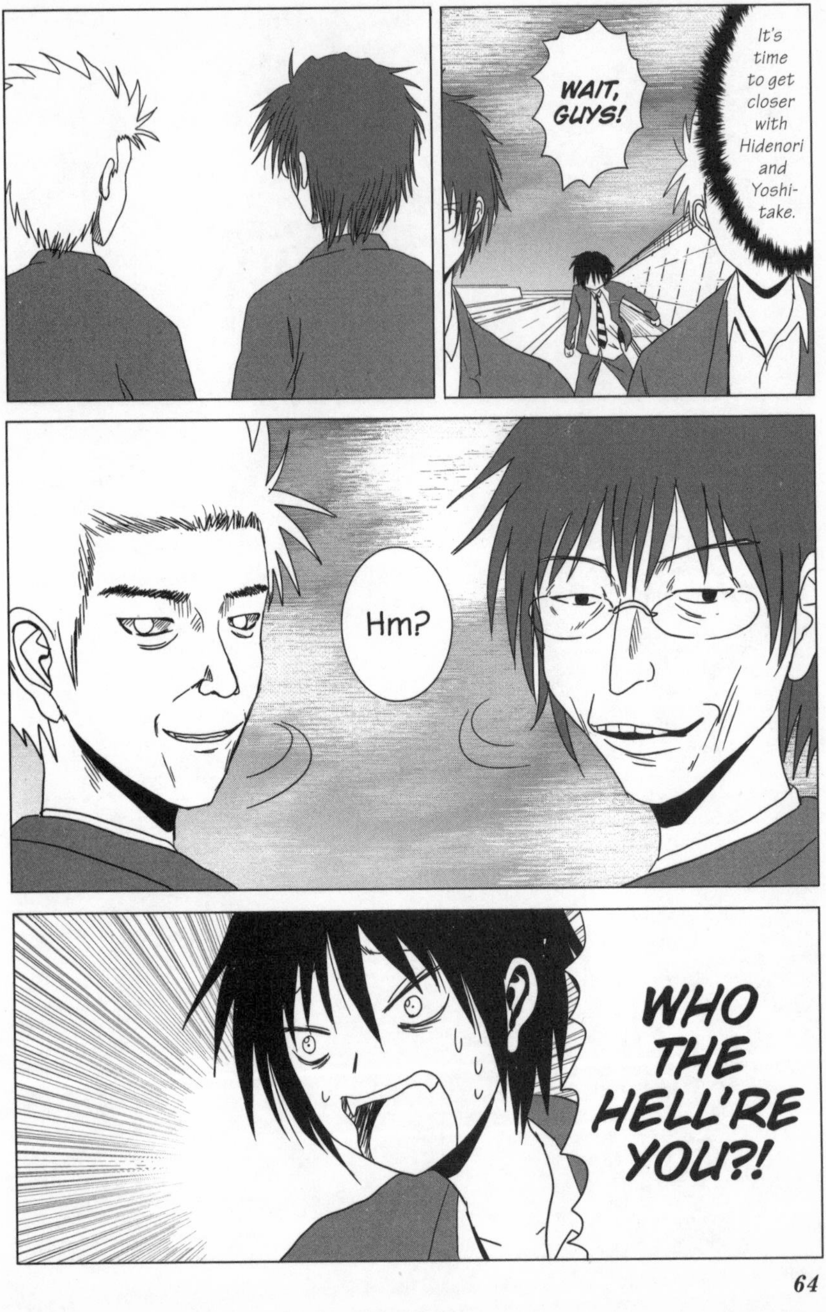
It's time to get closer with Hidenori and Yoshi-take.
WAIT, GUYS!
Hm?
WHO THE HELL'RE YOU?!

chapter 24:
high school boys and seniority

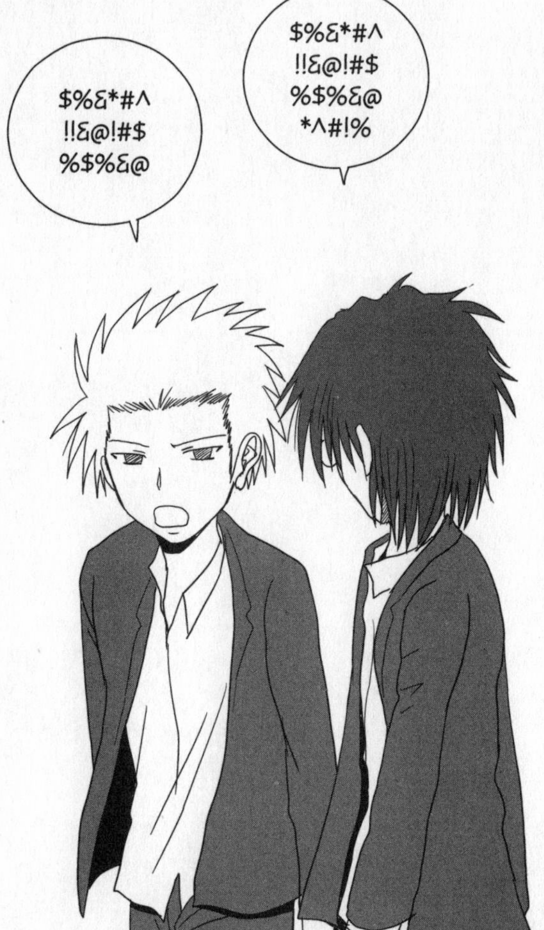
$%ꜫ*#^ !!ꜫ@!#$ %$%ꜫ@ *^#!%
$%ꜫ*#^ !!ꜫ@!#$ %$%ꜫ@

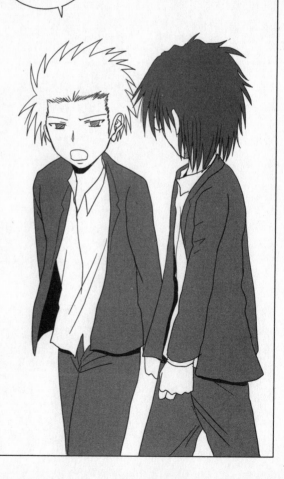

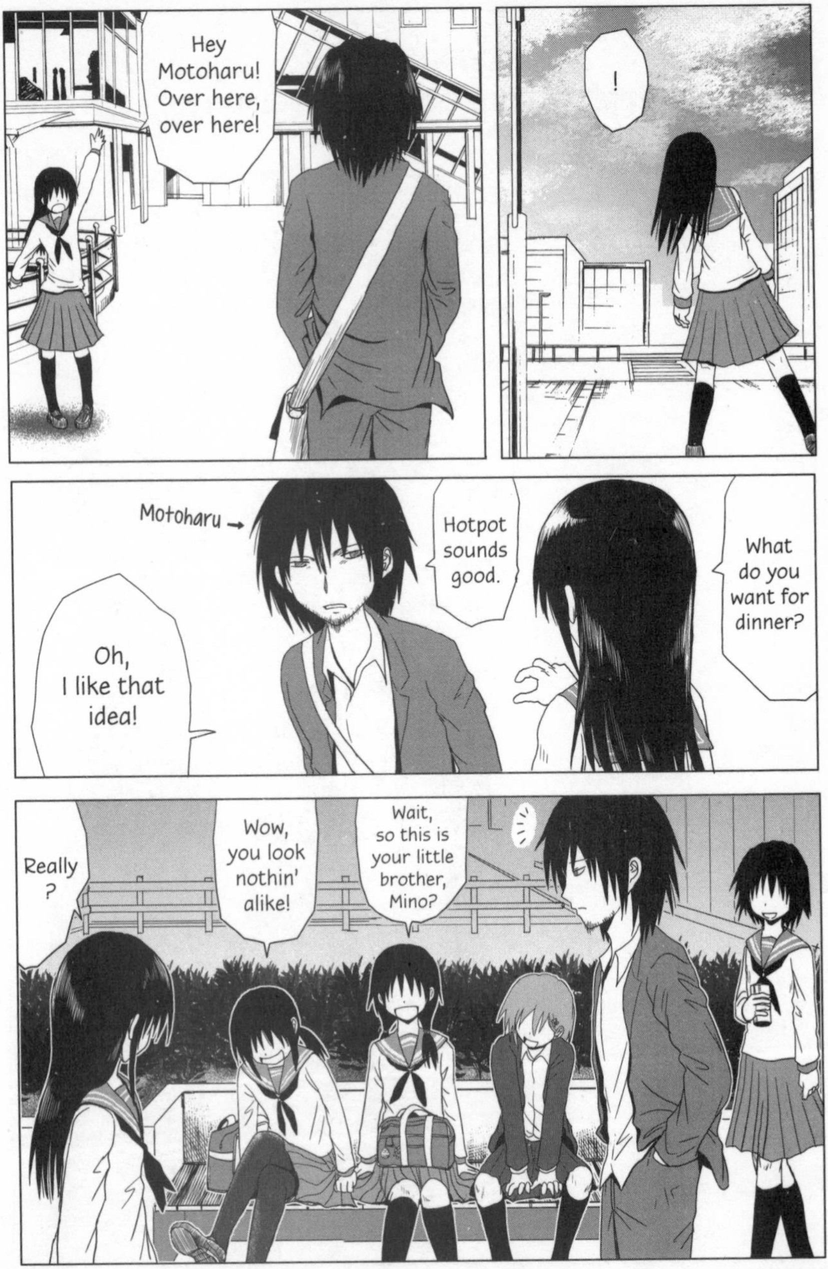
!
Hey Motoharu! Over here, over here!
What do you want for dinner?
Hotpot sounds good.
Motoharu →
Oh, I like that idea!
Wait, so this is your little brother, Mino?
Wow, you look nothin' alike!
Really?

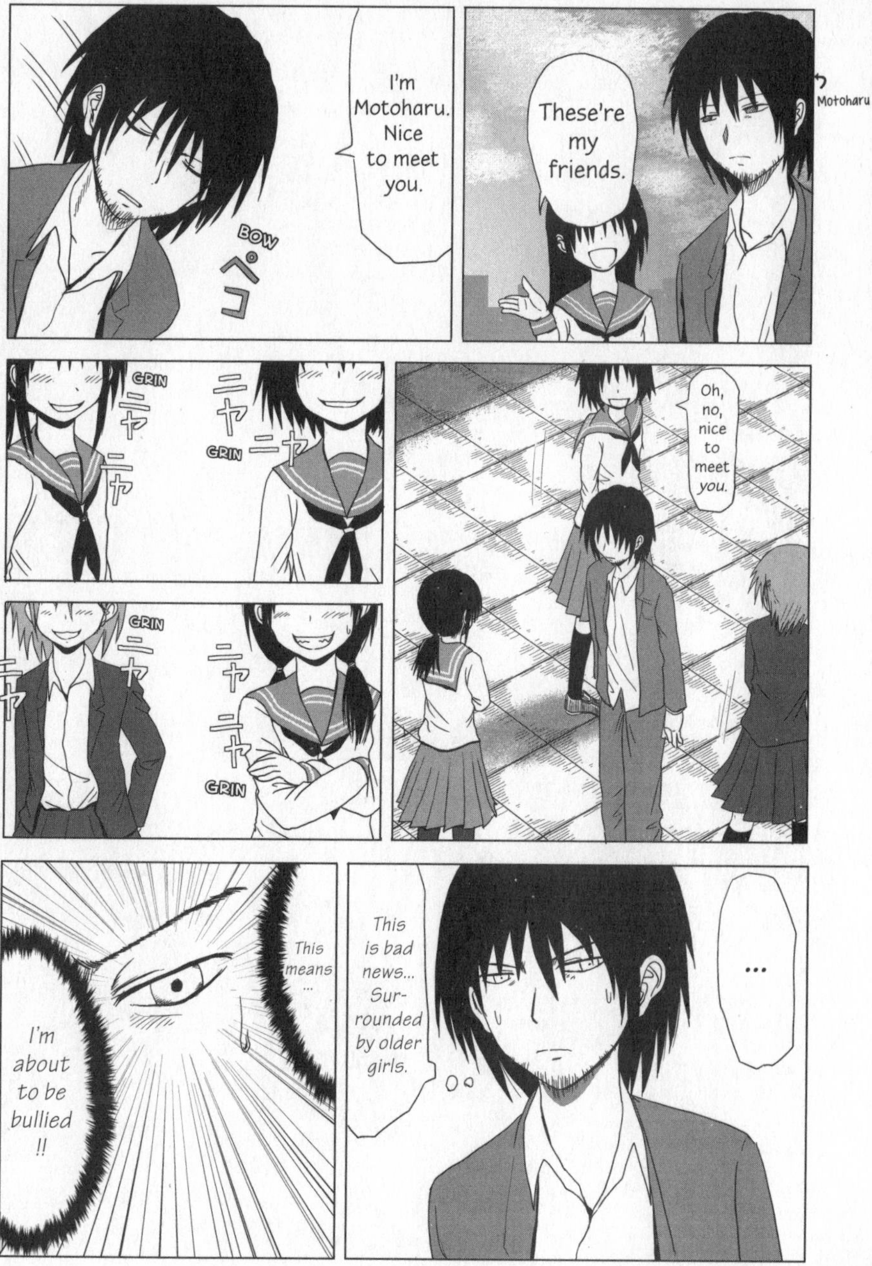

Motoharu
These're my friends.
I'm Motoharu. Nice to meet you.
BOW
ペコ
Oh, no, nice to meet you.
GRIN
ニヤ
ニヤ
GRIN
ニヤ
ニヤ
GRIN
ニヤ
ニヤ
ニヤ
ニヤ
GRIN
...
This is bad news... Surrounded by older girls.
This means ...
I'm about to be bullied !!

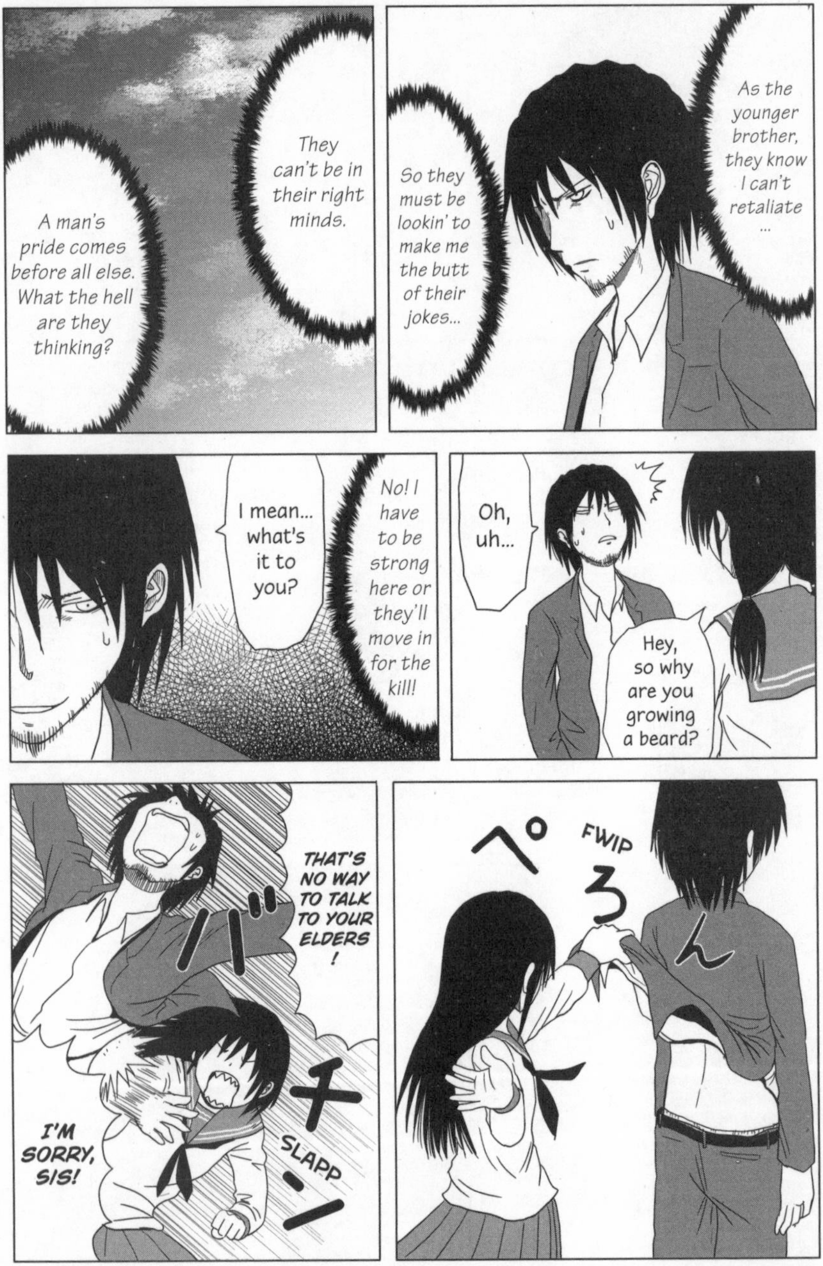
As the younger brother, they know I can't retaliate ...
So they must be lookin' to make me the butt of their jokes...
They can't be in their right minds.
A man's pride comes before all else. What the hell are they thinking?
Oh, uh...
Hey, so why are you growing a beard?
No! I have to be strong here or they'll move in for the kill!
I mean... what's it to you?
FWIP
ぺろん
THAT'S NO WAY TO TALK TO YOUR ELDERS !
バチーン
SLAPP
I'M SORRY, SIS!

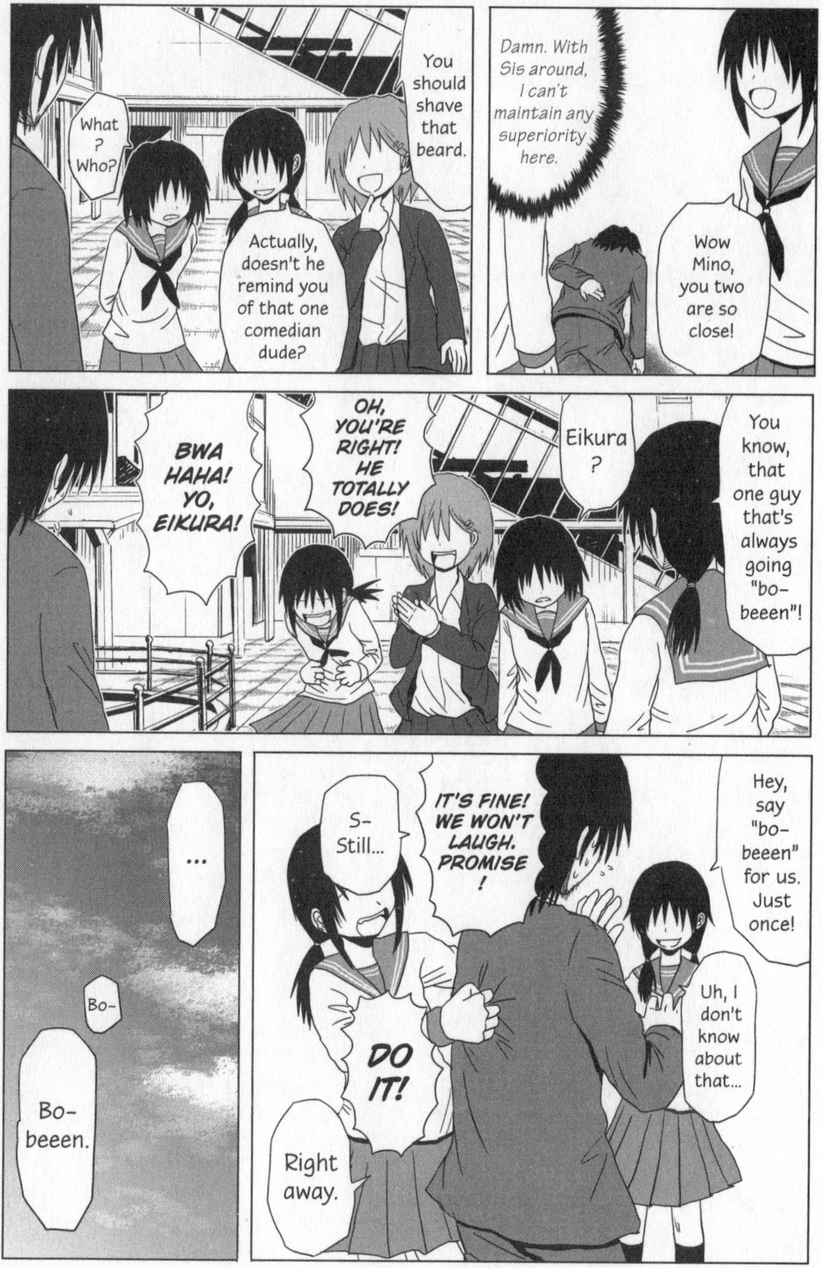
Wow Mino, you two are so close!
Damn. With Sis around, I can't maintain any superiority here.
You should shave that beard.
Actually, doesn't he remind you of that one comedian dude?
What? Who?
You know, that one guy that's always going "bo-beeen"!
Eikura?
OH, YOU'RE RIGHT! HE TOTALLY DOES!
BWA HAHA! YO, EIKURA!
Hey, say "bo-beeen" for us. Just once!
Uh, I don't know about that...
IT'S FINE! WE WON'T LAUGH. PROMISE!
S-Still...
DO IT!
Right away.
...
Bo-
Bo-beeen.

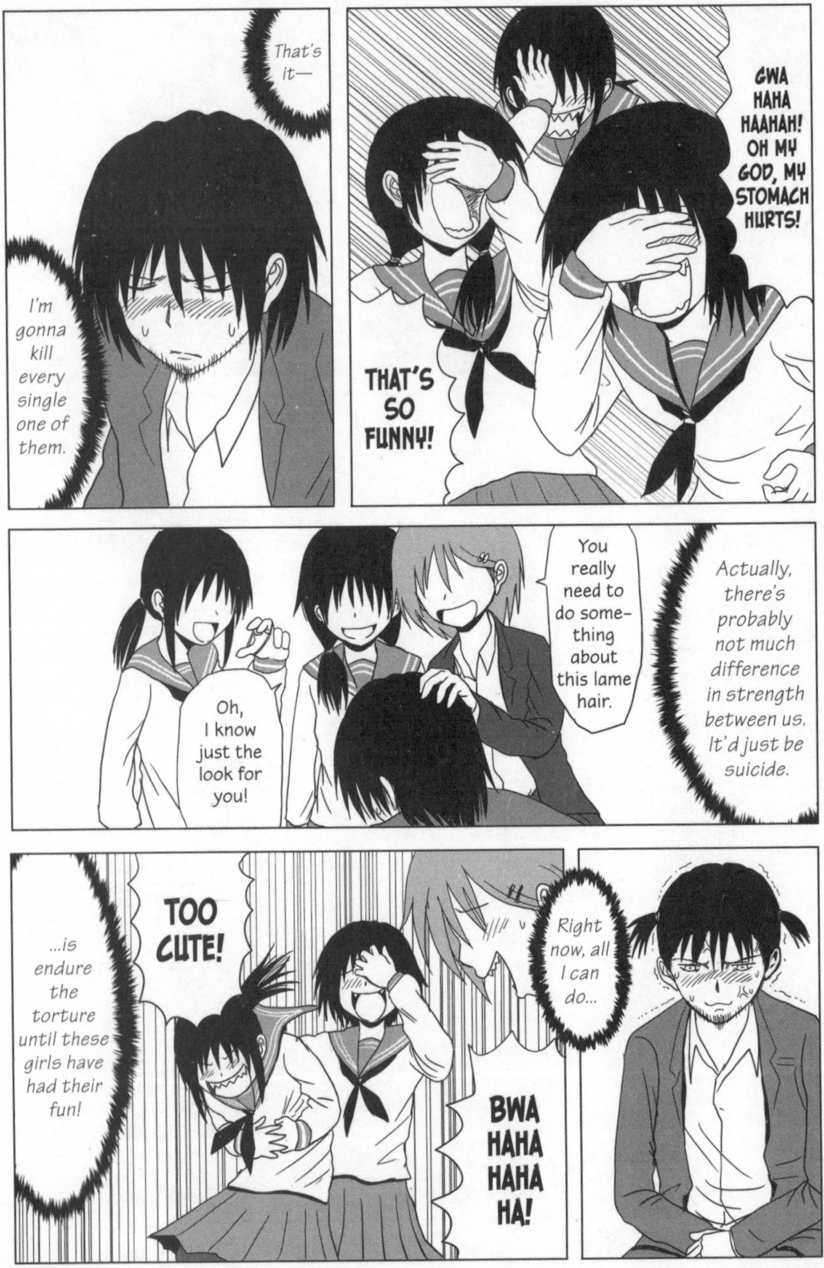
GWA HAHA HAAHAH! OH MY GOD, MY STOMACH HURTS!
THAT'S SO FUNNY!
That's it—
I'm gonna kill every single one of them.
Actually, there's probably not much difference in strength between us. It'd just be suicide.
You really need to do some-thing about this lame hair.
Oh, I know just the look for you!
Right now, all I can do...
TOO CUTE!
...is endure the torture until these girls have had their fun!
BWA HAHA HAHA HA!

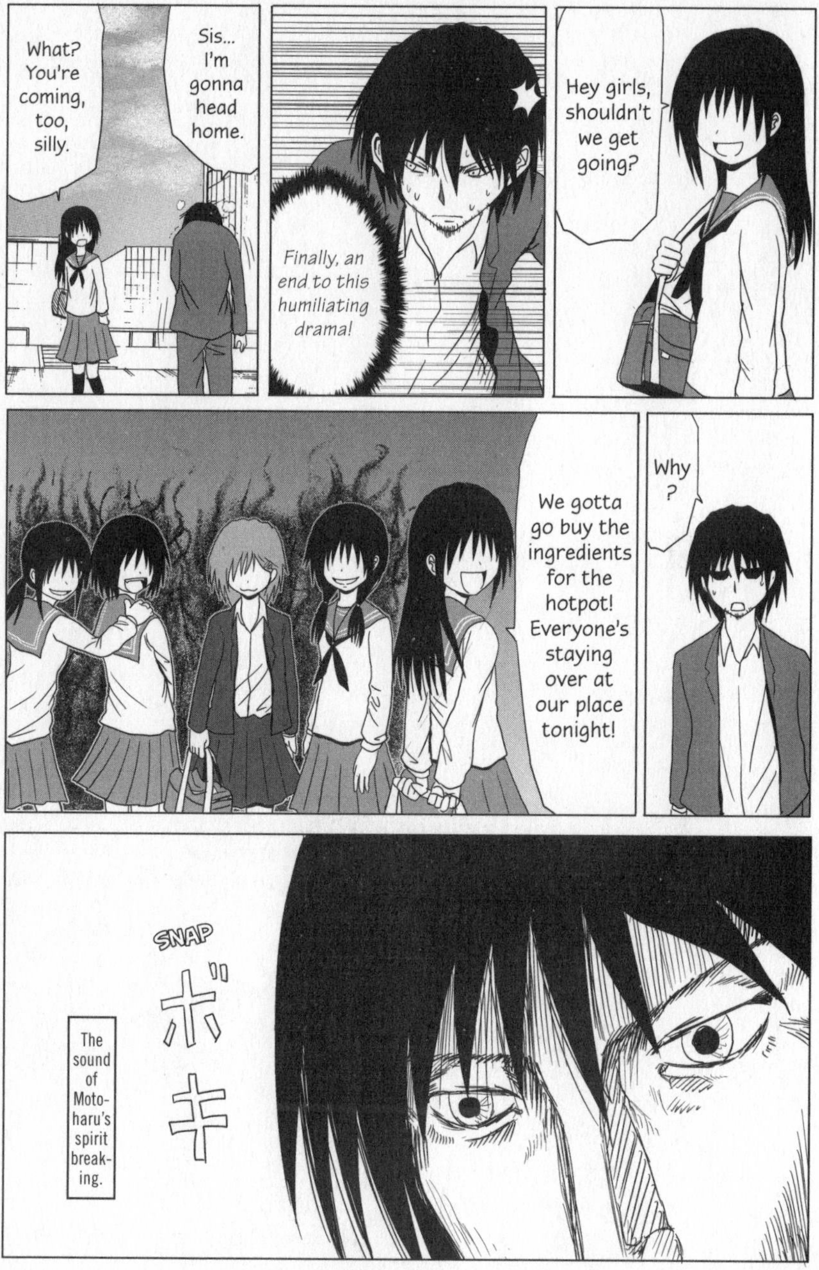
Hey girls, shouldn't we get going?
Finally, an end to this humiliating drama!
Sis... I'm gonna head home.
What? You're coming, too, silly.
Why?
We gotta go buy the ingredients for the hotpot! Everyone's staying over at our place tonight!
SNAP
ボキ
The sound of Moto-haru's spirit break-ing.

Despite the way it looks, drawing
Motoharu's sister is pretty easy.

chapter 25:
high school boys and counseling

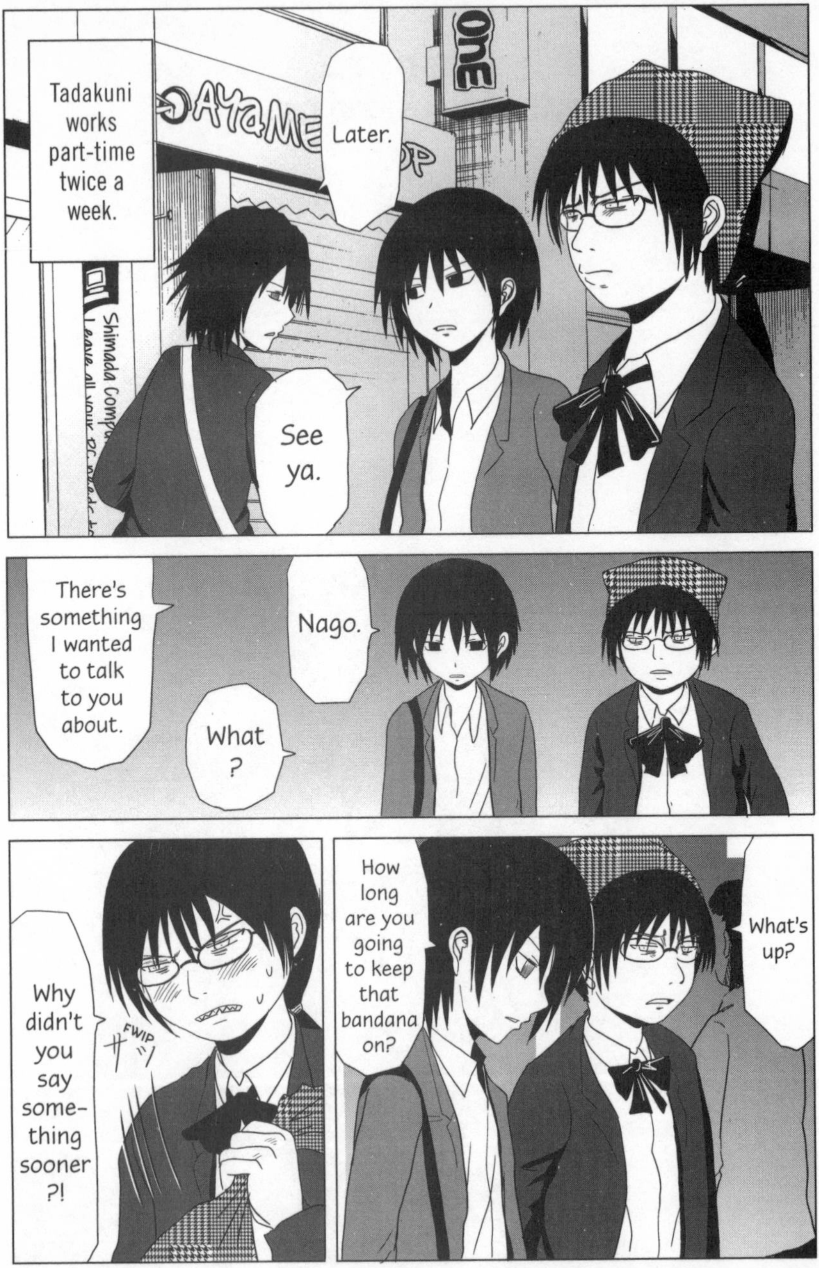
Later.
Tadakuni works part-time twice a week.
See ya.
Nago.
There's something I wanted to talk to you about.
What?
What's up?
How long are you going to keep that bandana on?
Why didn't you say some-thing sooner?!
FWIP

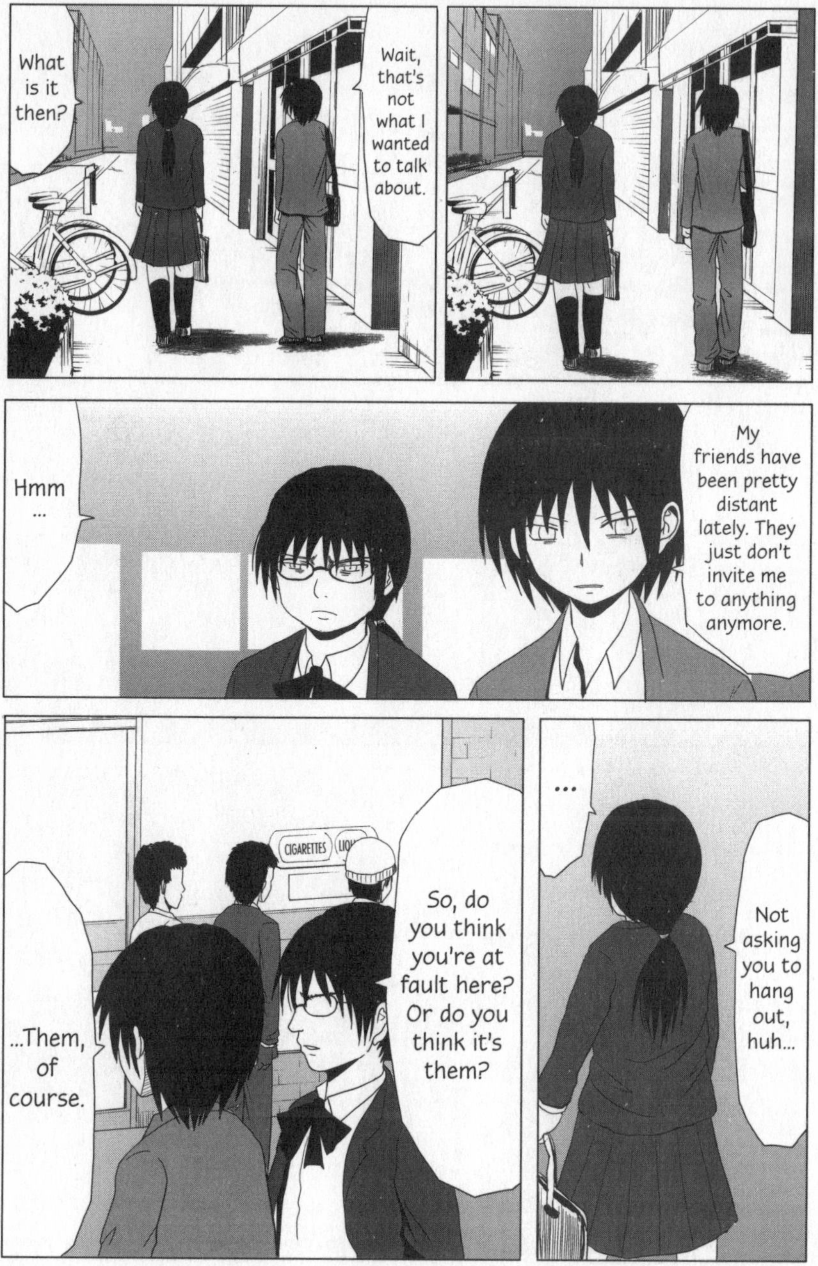
Wait, that's not what I wanted to talk about.
What is it then?
My friends have been pretty distant lately. They just don't invite me to anything anymore.
Hmm ...
Not asking you to hang out, huh...
...
So, do you think you're at fault here? Or do you think it's them?
CIGARETTES
...Them, of course.

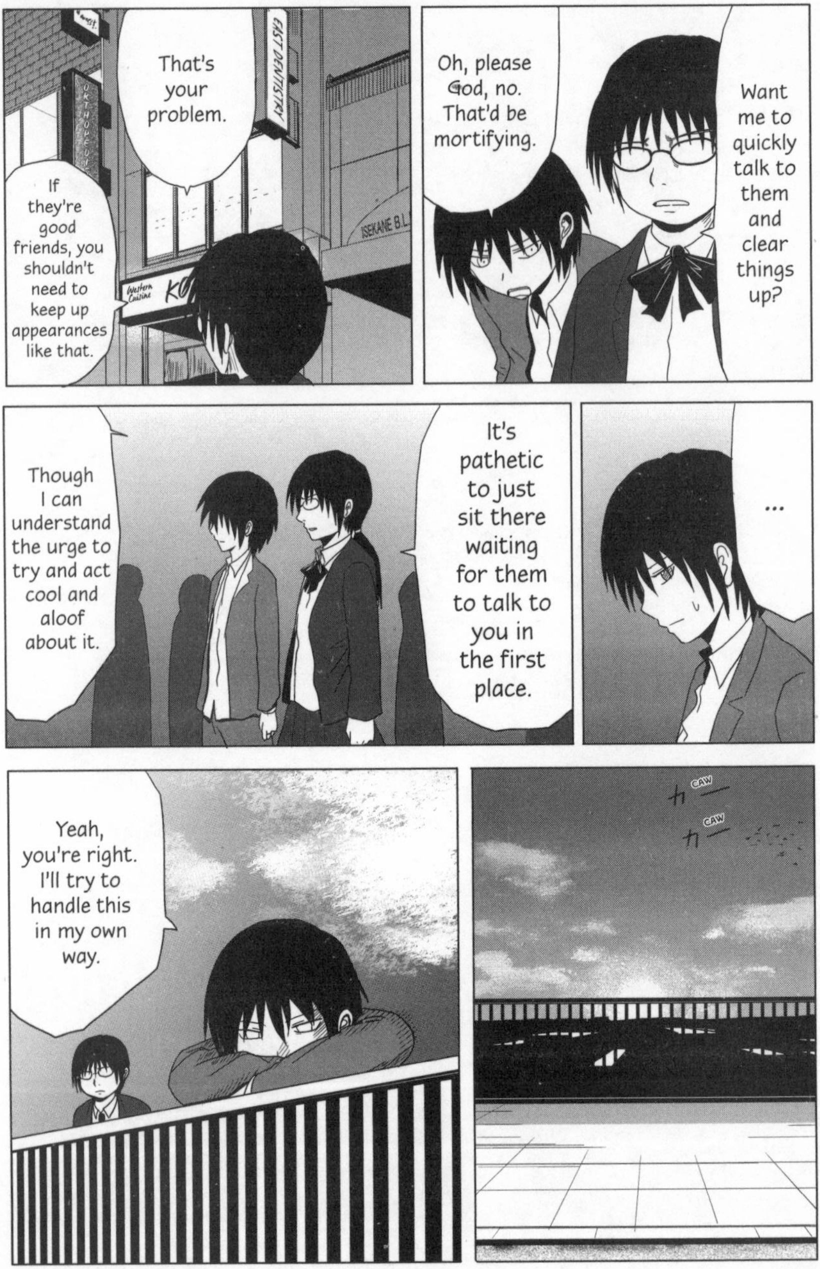
Want me to quickly talk to them and clear things up?
Oh, please God, no. That'd be mortifying.
EAST DENTISTRY
ISEKANE B.L.
Western Cuisine
That's your problem.
If they're good friends, you shouldn't need to keep up appearances like that.
...
It's pathetic to just sit there waiting for them to talk to you in the first place.
Though I can understand the urge to try and act cool and aloof about it.
CAW
CAW
Yeah, you're right. I'll try to handle this in my own way.

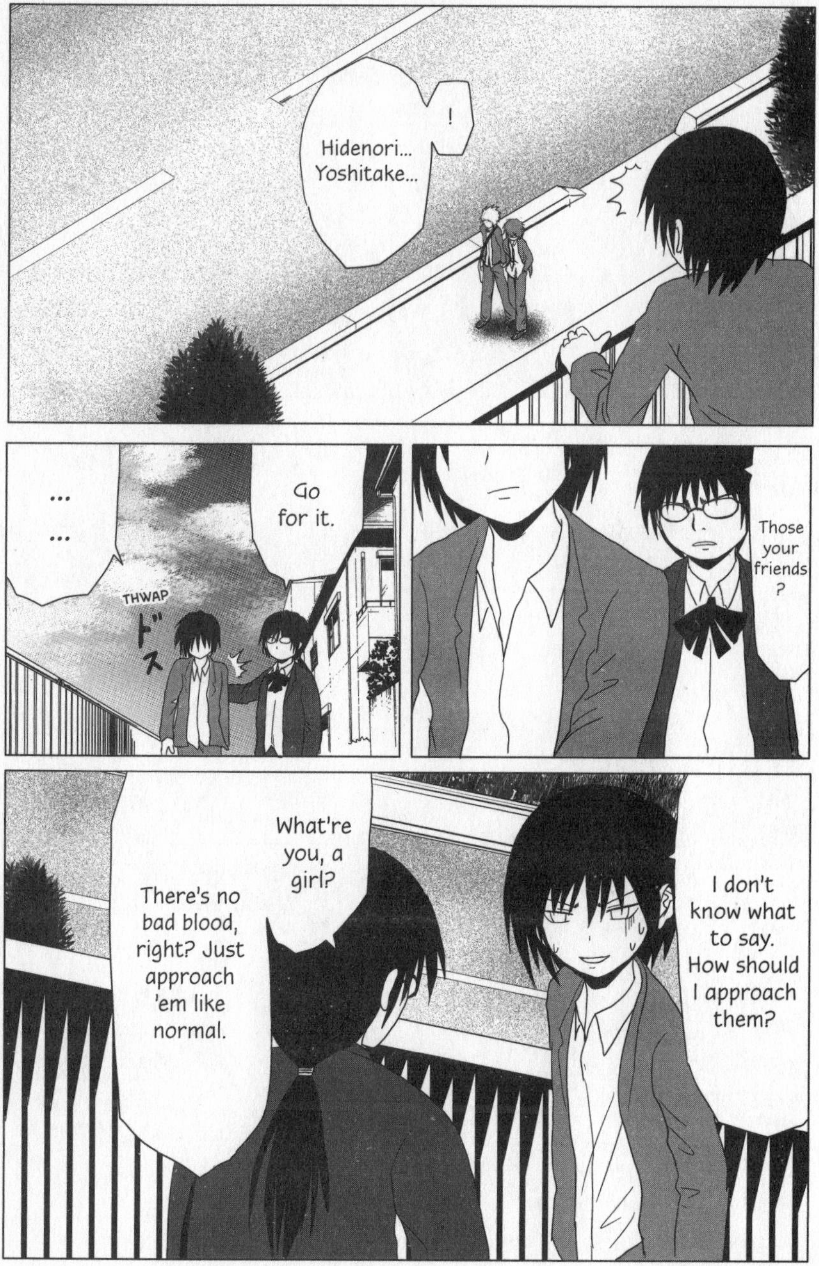
!
Hidenori... Yoshitake...
Those your friends?
Go for it.
... ...
THWAP
ドス
I don't know what to say. How should I approach them?
What're you, a girl?
There's no bad blood, right? Just approach 'em like normal.

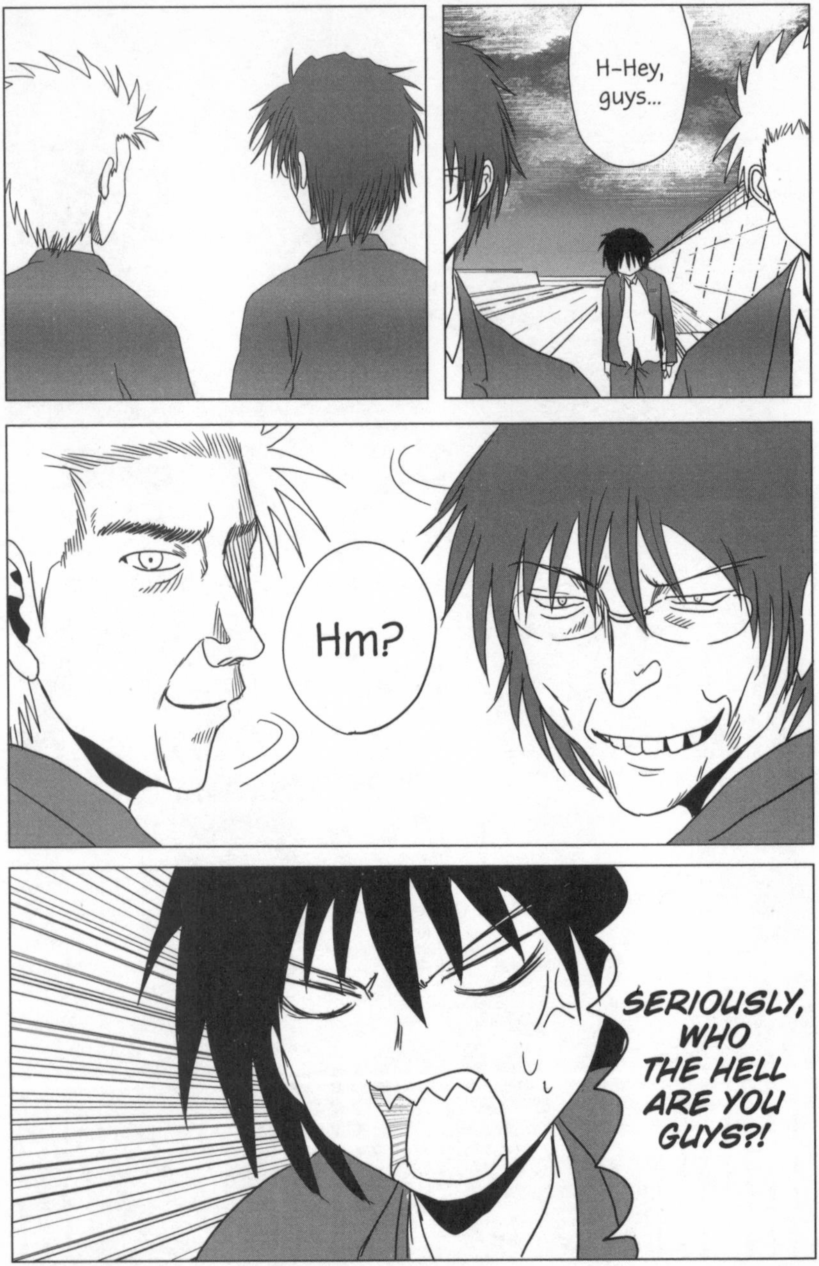
H-Hey, guys...
Hm?
SERIOUSLY, WHO THE HELL ARE YOU GUYS?!

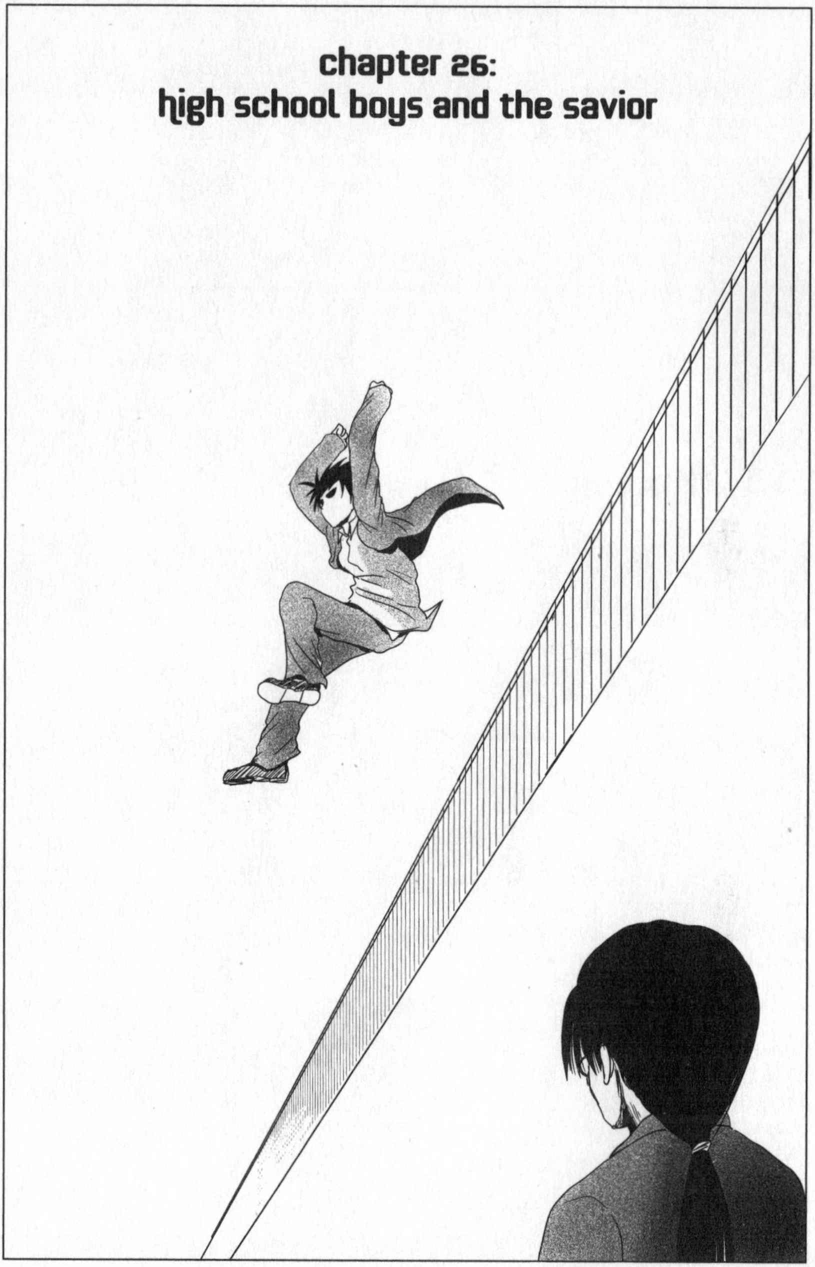
chapter 26:
high school boys and the savior

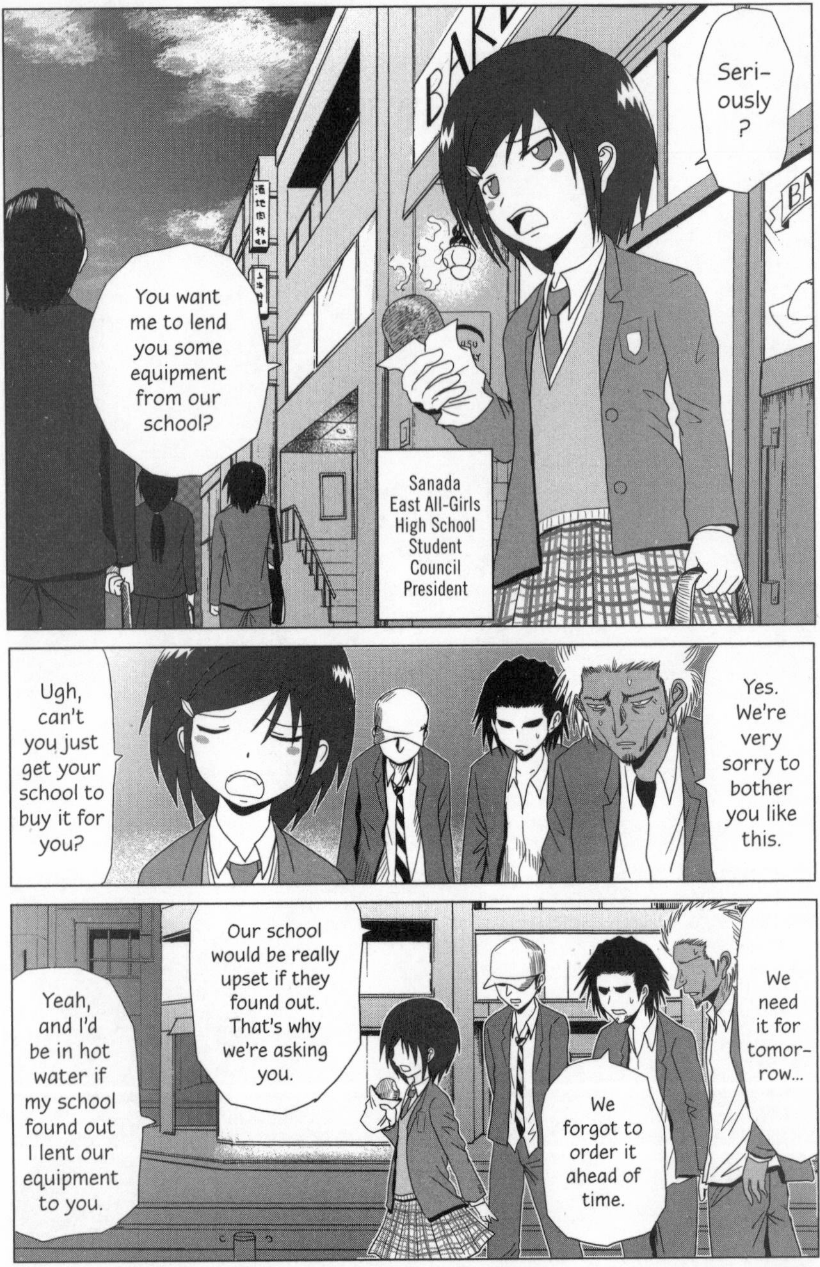
Seri-ously?
You want me to lend you some equipment from our school?
Sanada East All-Girls High School Student Council President
Yes. We're very sorry to bother you like this.
Ugh, can't you just get your school to buy it for you?
We need it for tomorrow...
We forgot to order it ahead of time.
Our school would be really upset if they found out. That's why we're asking you.
Yeah, and I'd be in hot water if my school found out I lent our equipment to you.

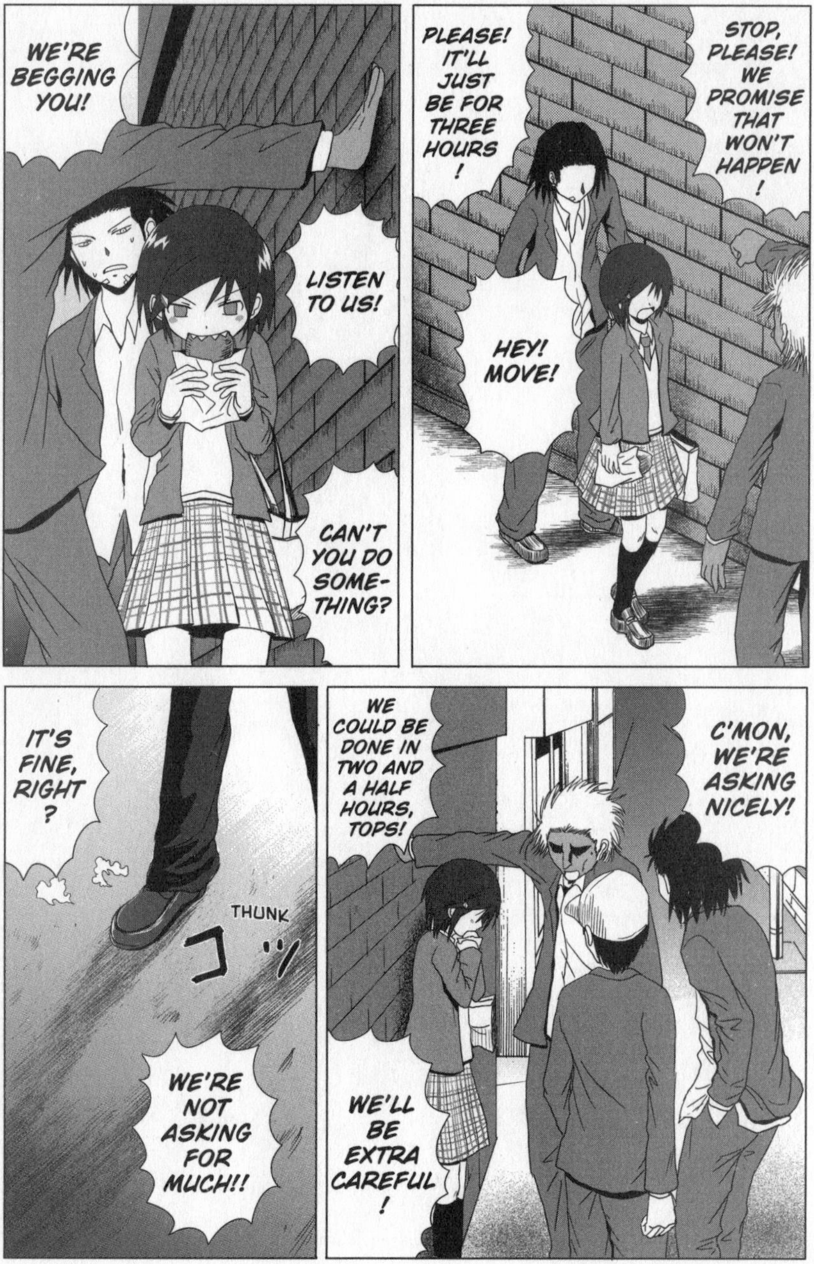
STOP, PLEASE! WE PROMISE THAT WON'T HAPPEN!
PLEASE! IT'LL JUST BE FOR THREE HOURS!
HEY! MOVE!
WE'RE BEGGING YOU!
LISTEN TO US!
CAN'T YOU DO SOME-THING?
C'MON, WE'RE ASKING NICELY!
WE COULD BE DONE IN TWO AND A HALF HOURS, TOPS!
WE'LL BE EXTRA CAREFUL!
IT'S FINE, RIGHT?
THUNK
WE'RE NOT ASKING FOR MUCH!!

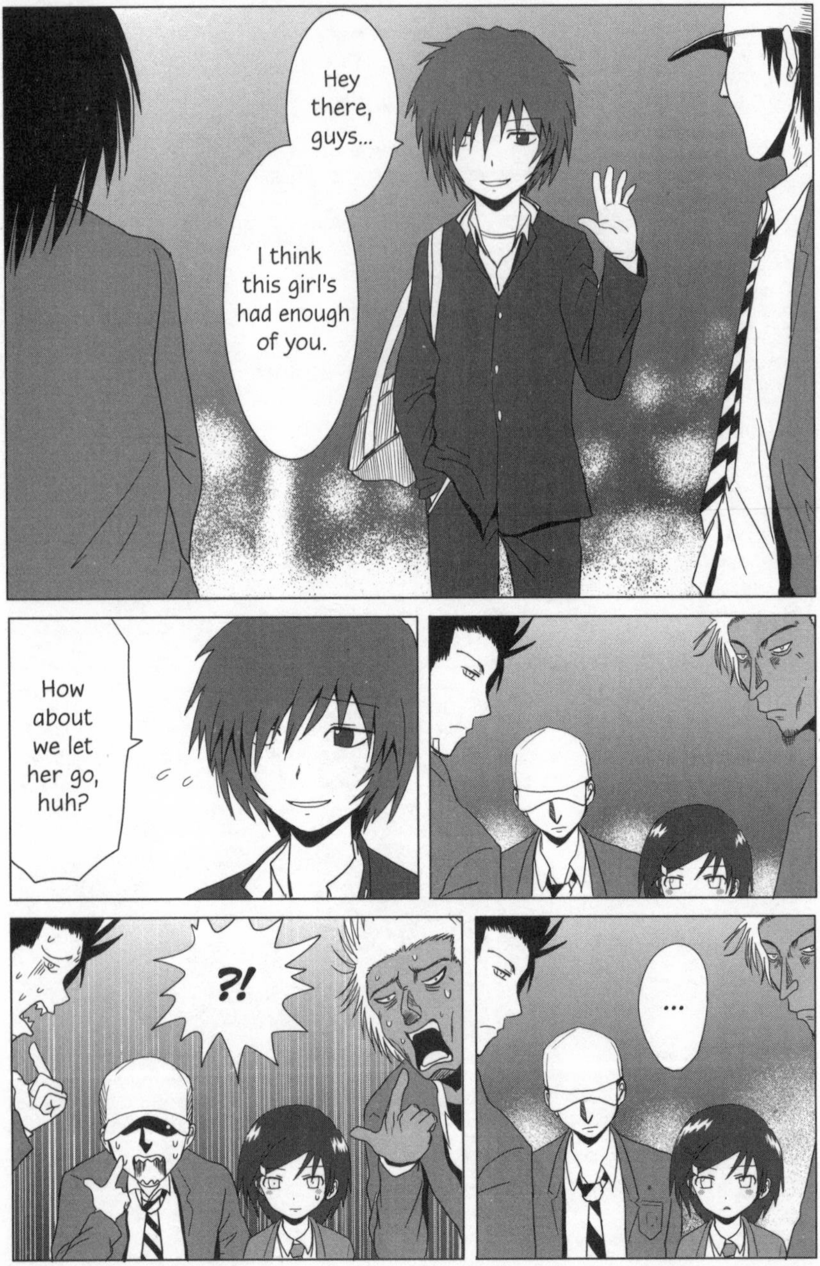
Hey there, guys...
I think this girl's had enough of you.
How about we let her go, huh?
...
?!

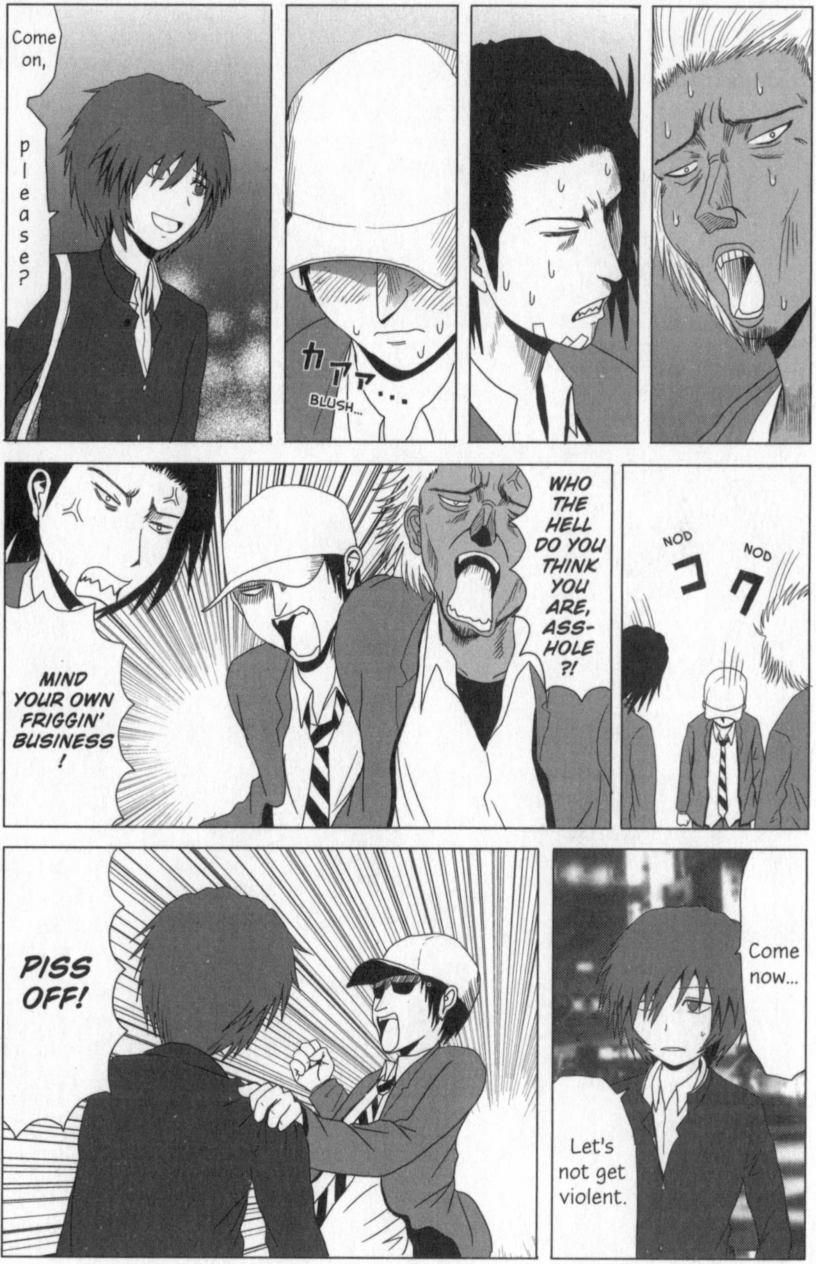

カァァ…
BLUSH...
Come on, please?
NOD
NOD
コク
WHO THE HELL DO YOU THINK YOU ARE, ASS-HOLE?!
MIND YOUR OWN FRIGGIN' BUSINESS!
Come now...
Let's not get violent.
PISS OFF!

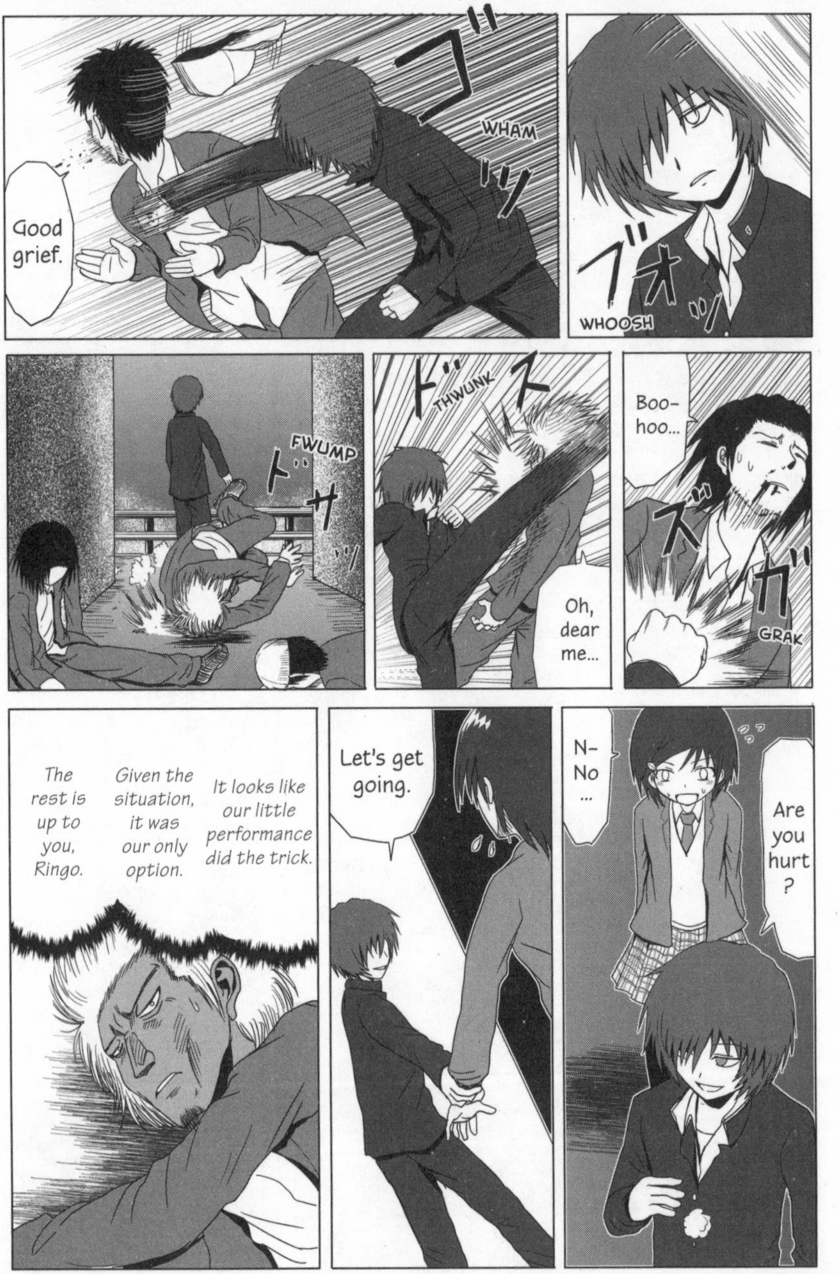
ブオッ
WHOOSH
ゴッ
WHAM
Good grief.
Boo-hoo...
ズガッ
GRAK
ドス
THWUNK
Oh, dear me...
トサッ
FWUMP
Are you hurt?
N-No...
Let's get going.
It looks like our little performance did the trick.
Given the situation, it was our only option.
The rest is up to you, Ringo.

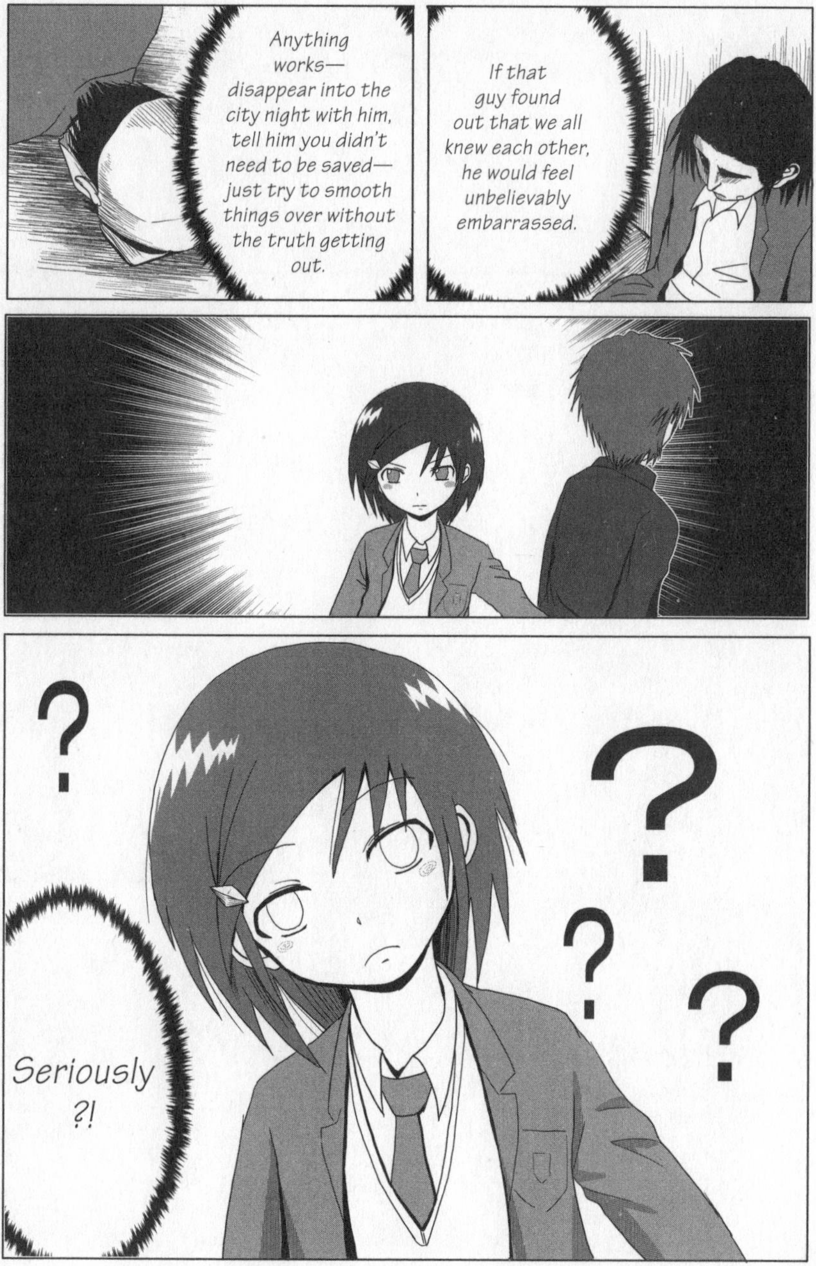
If that guy found out that we all knew each other, he would feel unbelievably embarrassed.
Anything works—disappear into the city night with him, tell him you didn't need to be saved—just try to smooth things over without the truth getting out.
Seriously ?!

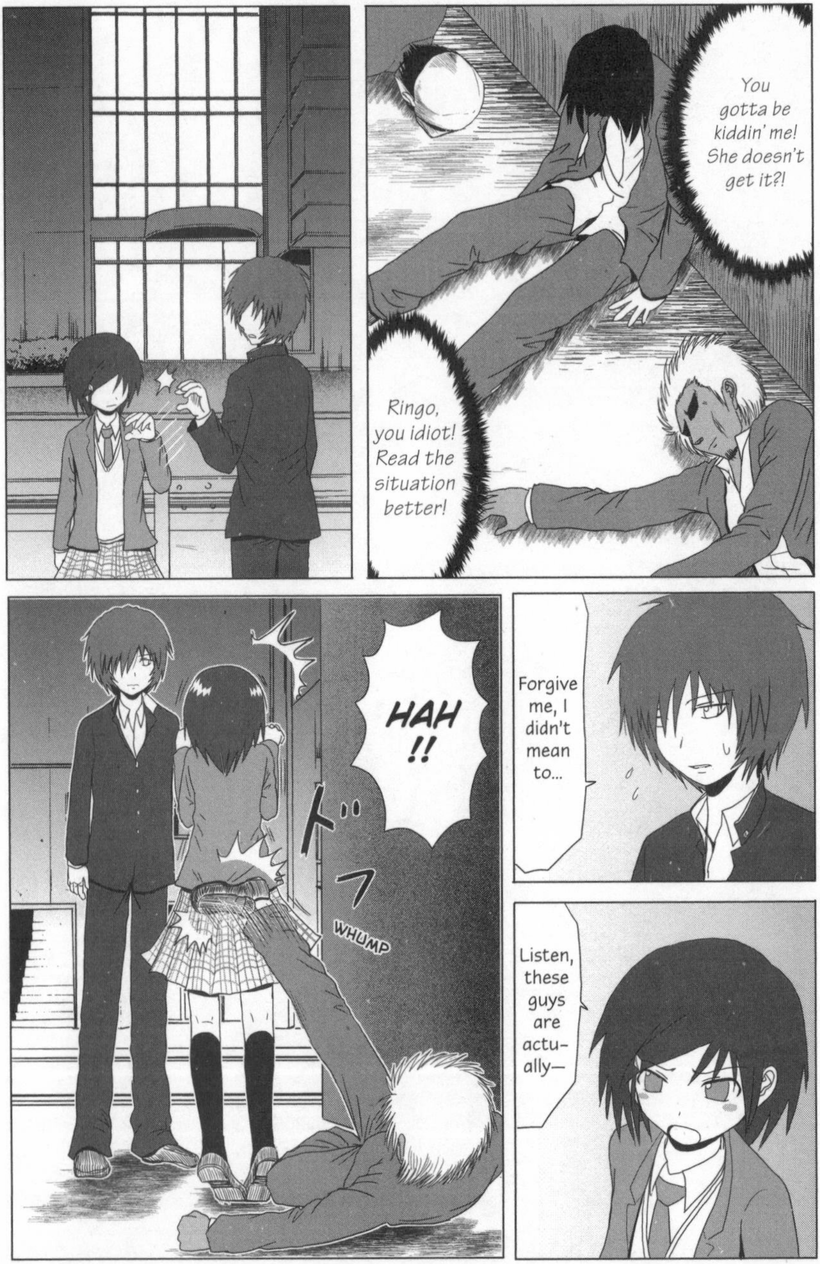
You gotta be kiddin' me! She doesn't get it?!
Ringo, you idiot! Read the situation better!
Forgive me, I didn't mean to...
Listen, these guys are actu-ally—
HAH!!
WHUMP

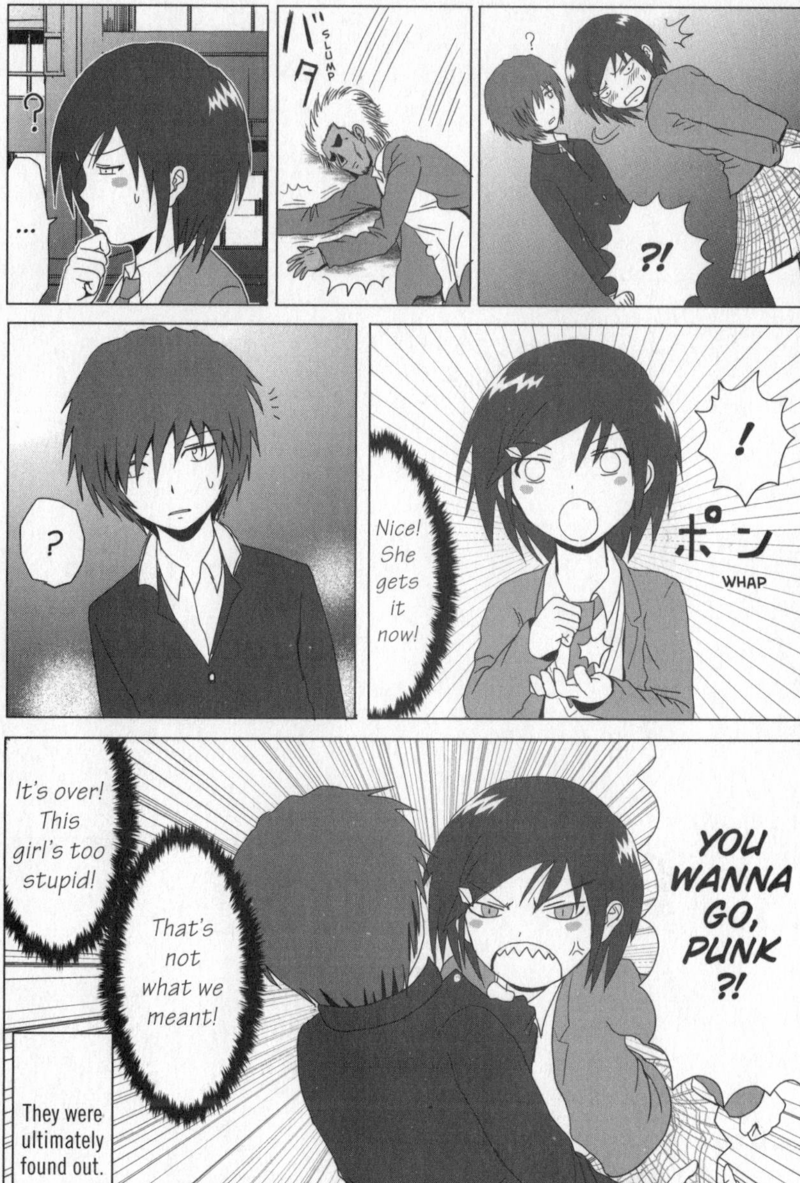
?
?!
バタ
SLUMP
?
...
!
ポン
WHAP
Nice! She gets it now!
?
YOU WANNA GO, PUNK ?!
That's not what we meant!
It's over! This girl's too stupid!
They were ultimately found out.

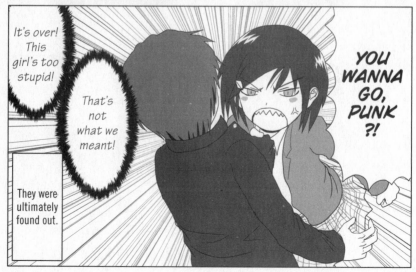

The protagonist finally makes his appearance.

chapter 27:
high school boys and an old friend

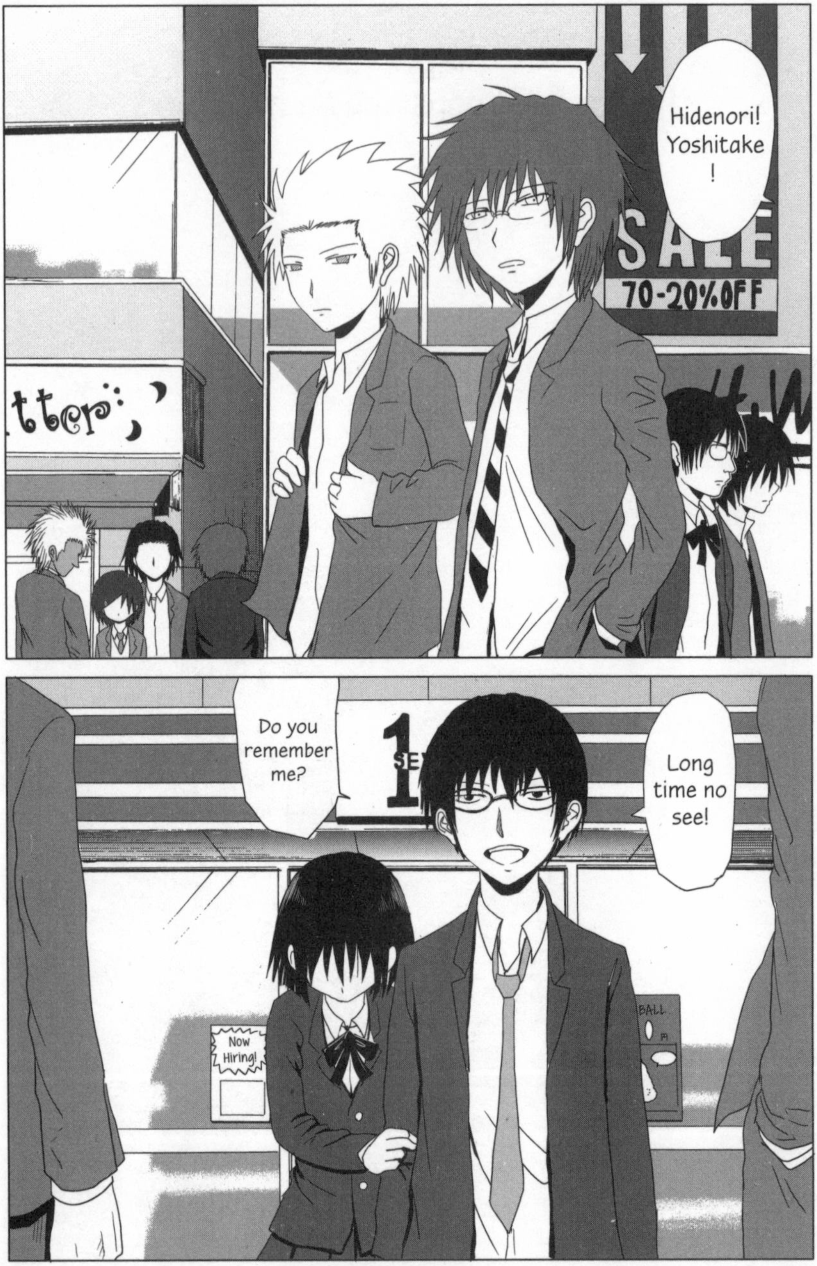
Hidenori! Yoshitake!
SALE
70-20%OFF
Long time no see!
Do you remember me?
Now Hiring!

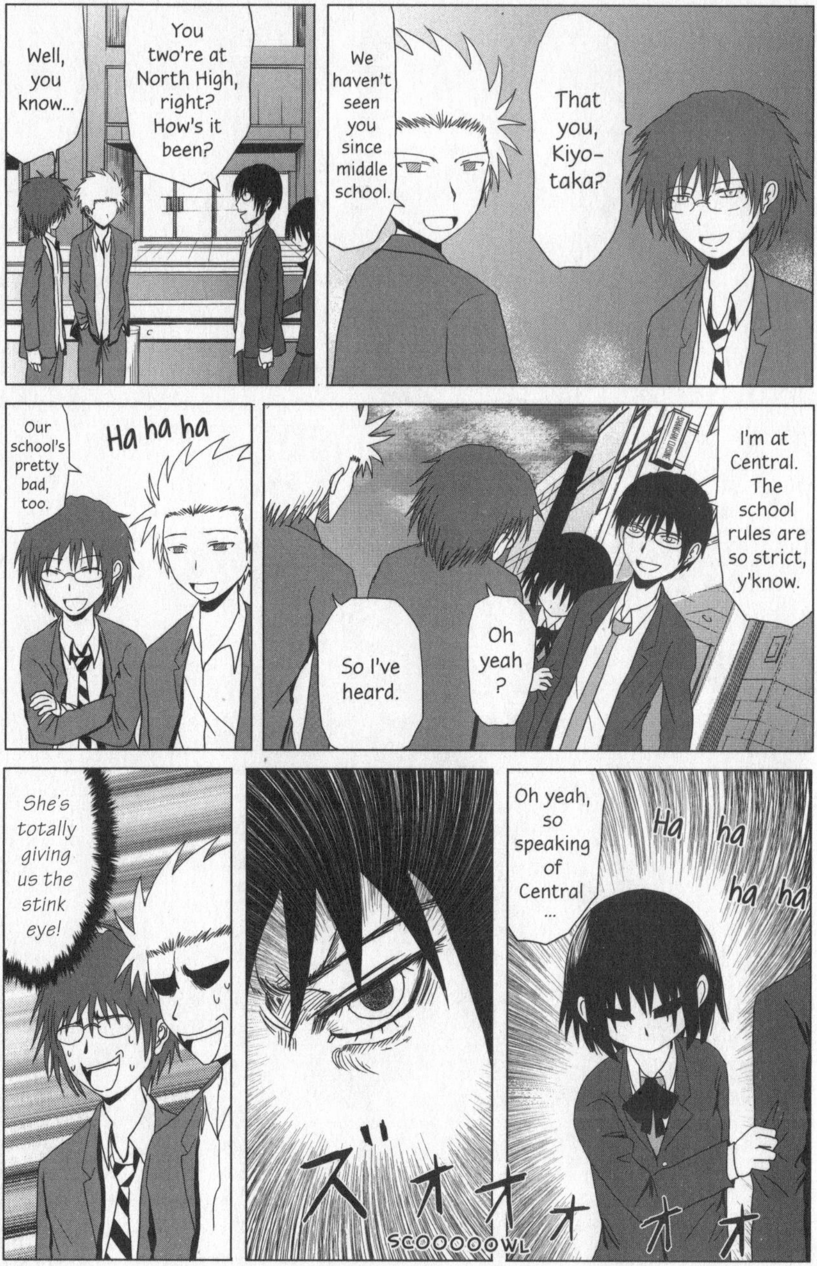
That you, Kiyotaka?
We haven't seen you since middle school.
You two're at North High, right? How's it been?
Well, you know...
I'm at Central. The school rules are so strict, y'know.
Oh yeah?
So I've heard.
Ha ha ha
Our school's pretty bad, too.
Oh yeah, so speaking of Central...
Ha ha ha ha
ズオオオオオ
SCOOOOOWL
She's totally giving us the stink eye!

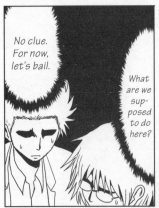

Why, though ?!
I don't know, but you think maybe she's trying to tell us not to ruin her alone time with her boyfriend or something ?
What are we sup- posed to do here?
No clue. For now, let's bail.
We gotta go. See you later.
wcDonad's
Yo, wait up.
HAMBURGER
Wanna grab some food?
C'mon man, take a hint...
Oh, how's Kugihiko doing?
Kugi- hiko? He's good.

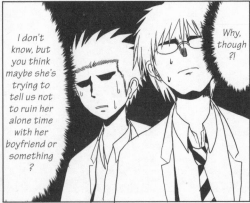

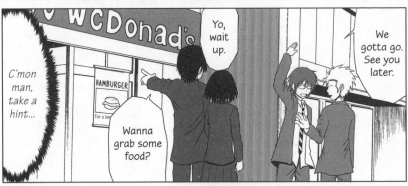

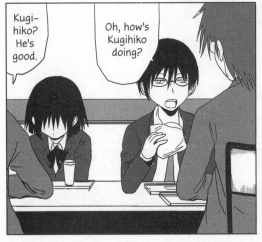

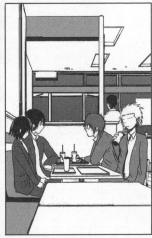

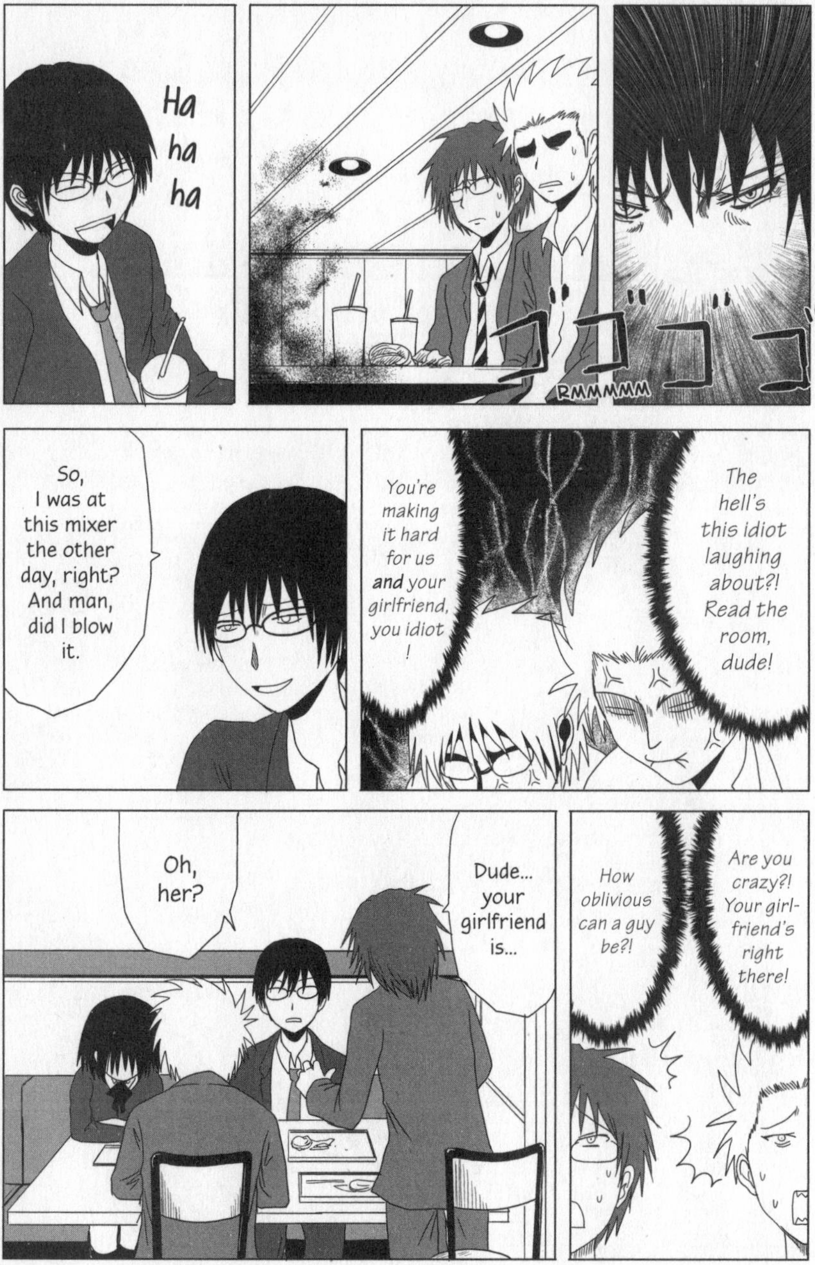
ゴゴゴゴ
RMMMMM
Ha ha ha
The hell's this idiot laughing about?! Read the room, dude!
You're making it hard for us **and** your girlfriend, you idiot!
So, I was at this mixer the other day, right? And man, did I blow it.
Are you crazy?! Your girl-friend's right there!
How oblivious can a guy be?!
Dude... your girlfriend is...
Oh, her?

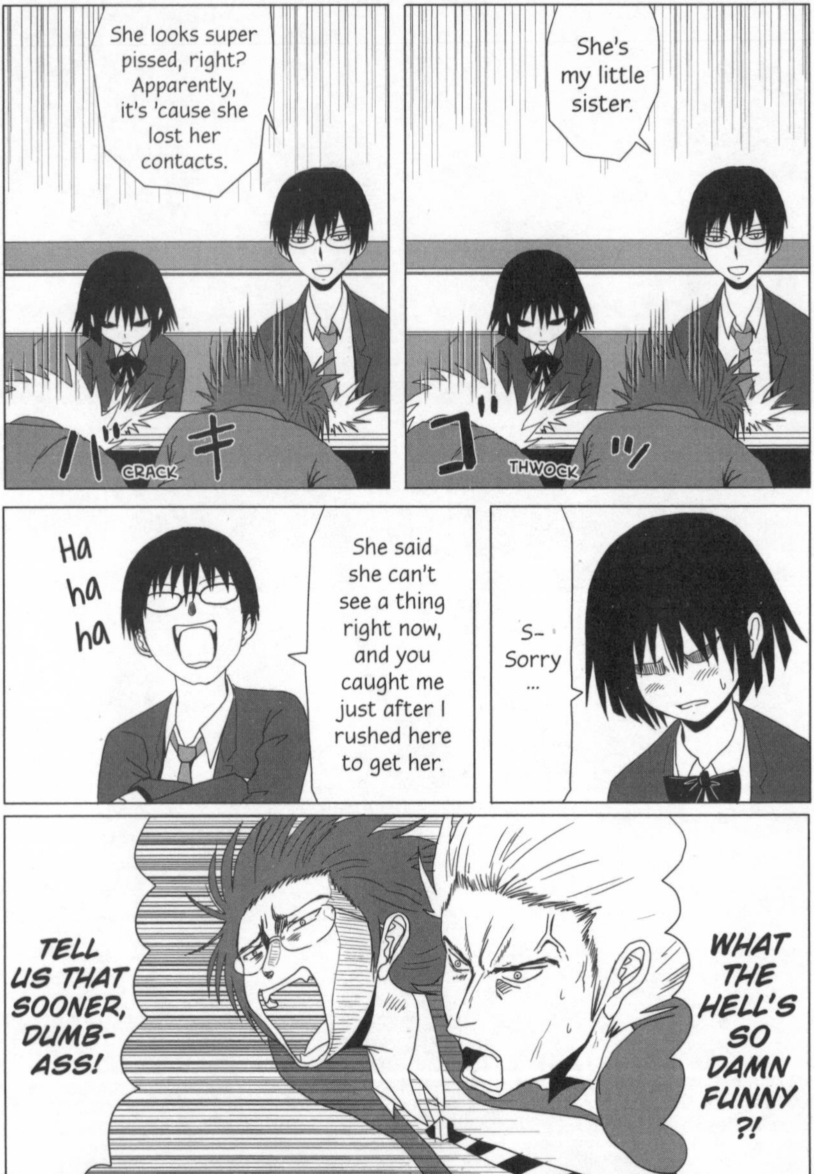
She's my little sister.
ゴッ
THWOCK
She looks super pissed, right? Apparently, it's 'cause she lost her contacts.
バキ
CRACK
S- Sorry ...
Ha ha ha
She said she can't see a thing right now, and you caught me just after I rushed here to get her.
WHAT THE HELL'S SO DAMN FUNNY?!
TELL US THAT SOONER, DUMB-ASS!

chapter 28:
high school boys and live dubbing

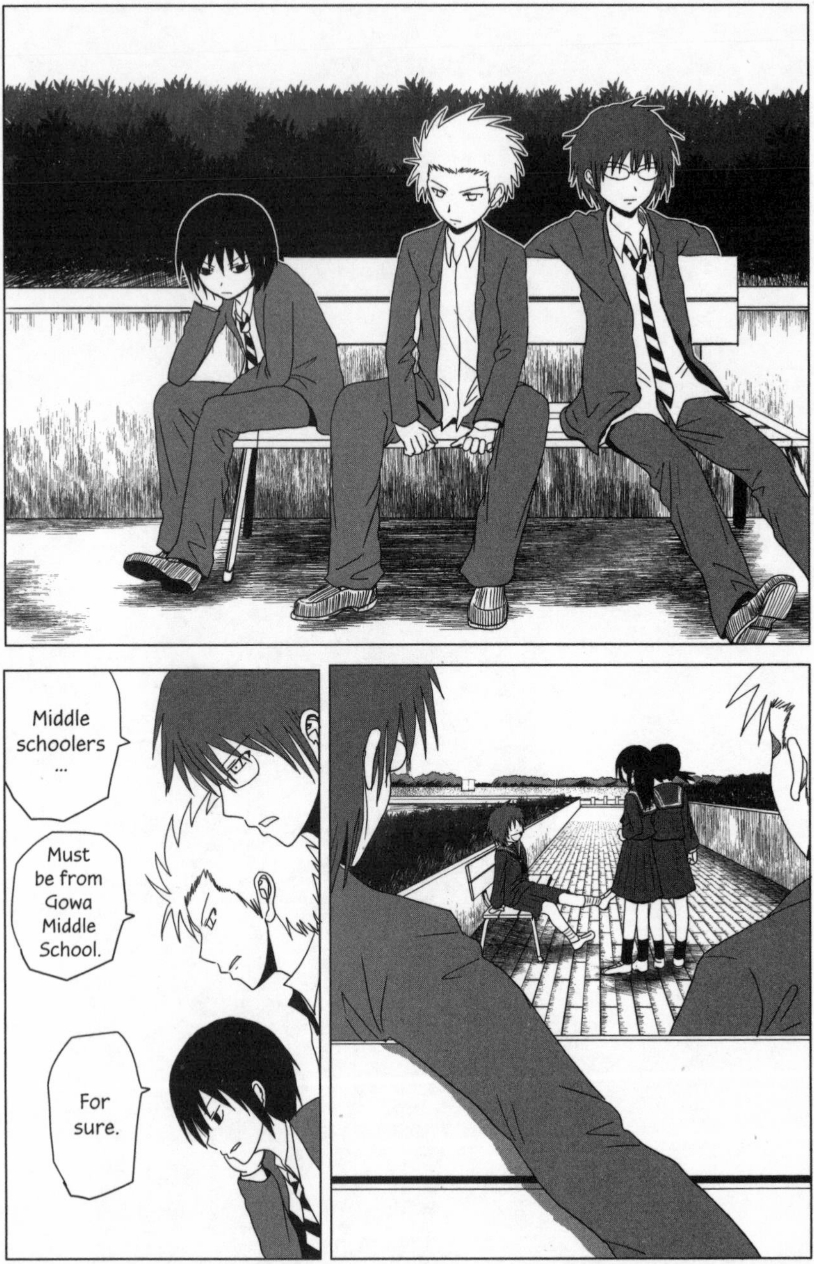
Middle schoolers ...
Must be from Gowa Middle School.
For sure.

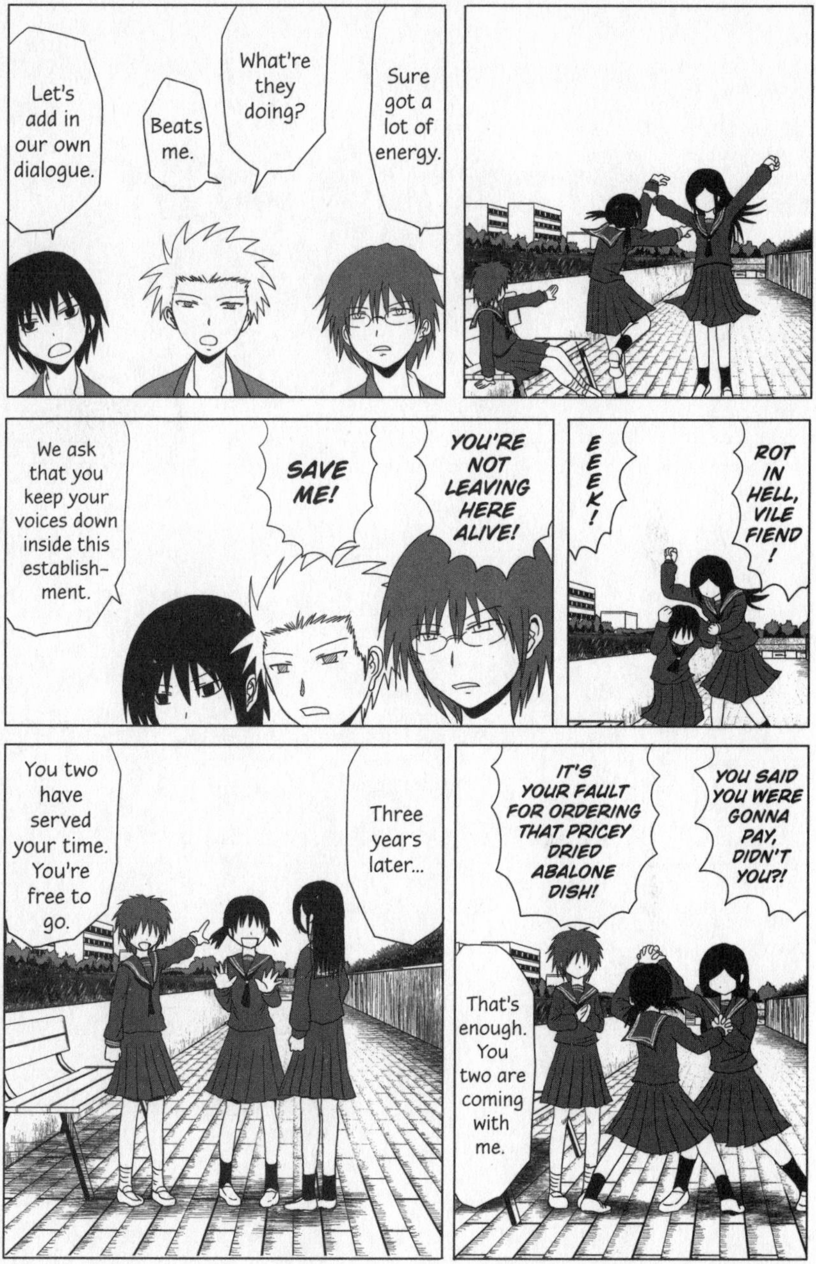
Sure got a lot of energy.
What're they doing?
Beats me.
Let's add in our own dialogue.
ROT IN HELL, VILE FIEND!
EEEK!
YOU'RE NOT LEAVING HERE ALIVE!
SAVE ME!
We ask that you keep your voices down inside this establishment.
YOU SAID YOU WERE GONNA PAY, DIDN'T YOU?!
IT'S YOUR FAULT FOR ORDERING THAT PRICEY DRIED ABALONE DISH!
That's enough. You two are coming with me.
Three years later...
You two have served your time. You're free to go.

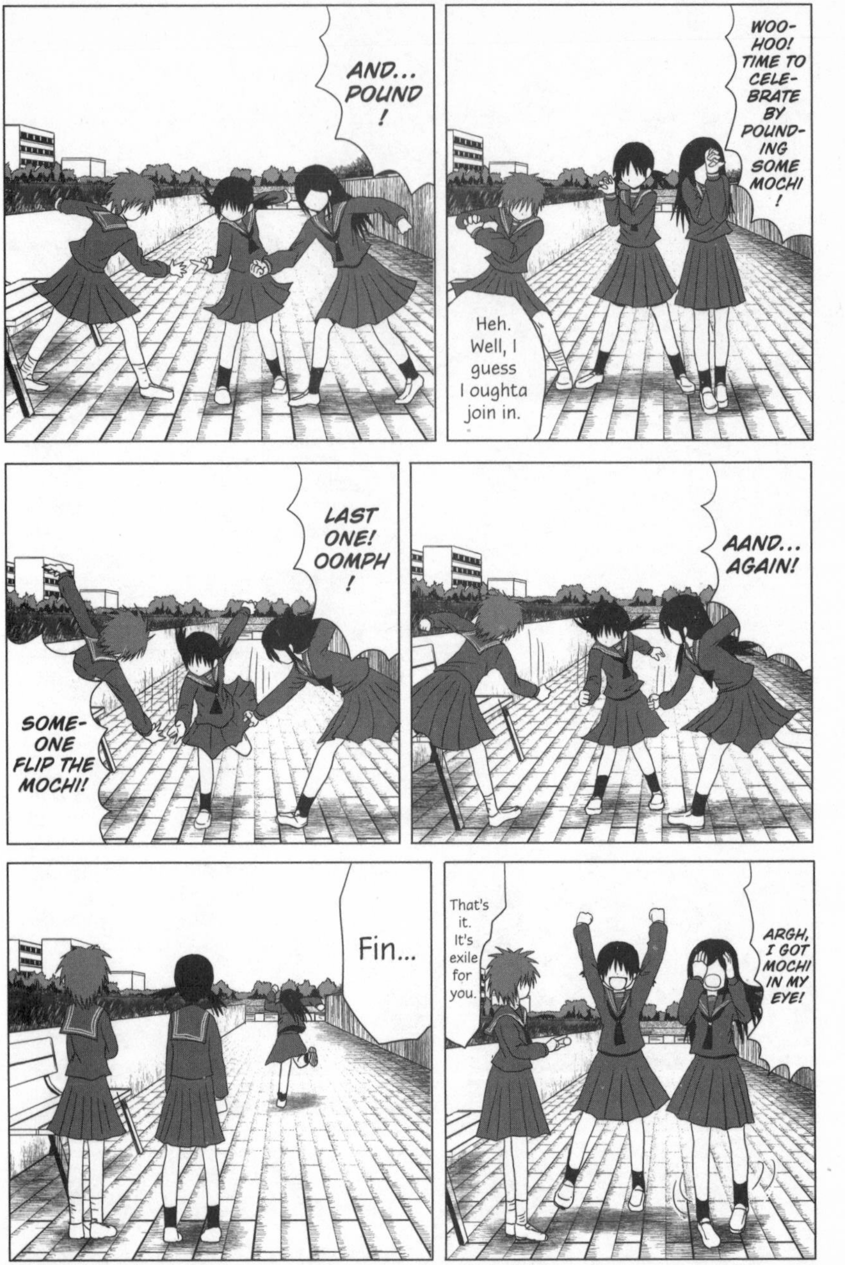
WOO-HOO! TIME TO CELEBRATE BY POUNDING SOME MOCHI!
Heh. Well, I guess I oughta join in.
AND... POUND!
AAND... AGAIN!
LAST ONE! OOMPH!
SOMEONE FLIP THE MOCHI!
ARGH, I GOT MOCHI IN MY EYE!
That's it. It's exile for you.
Fin...

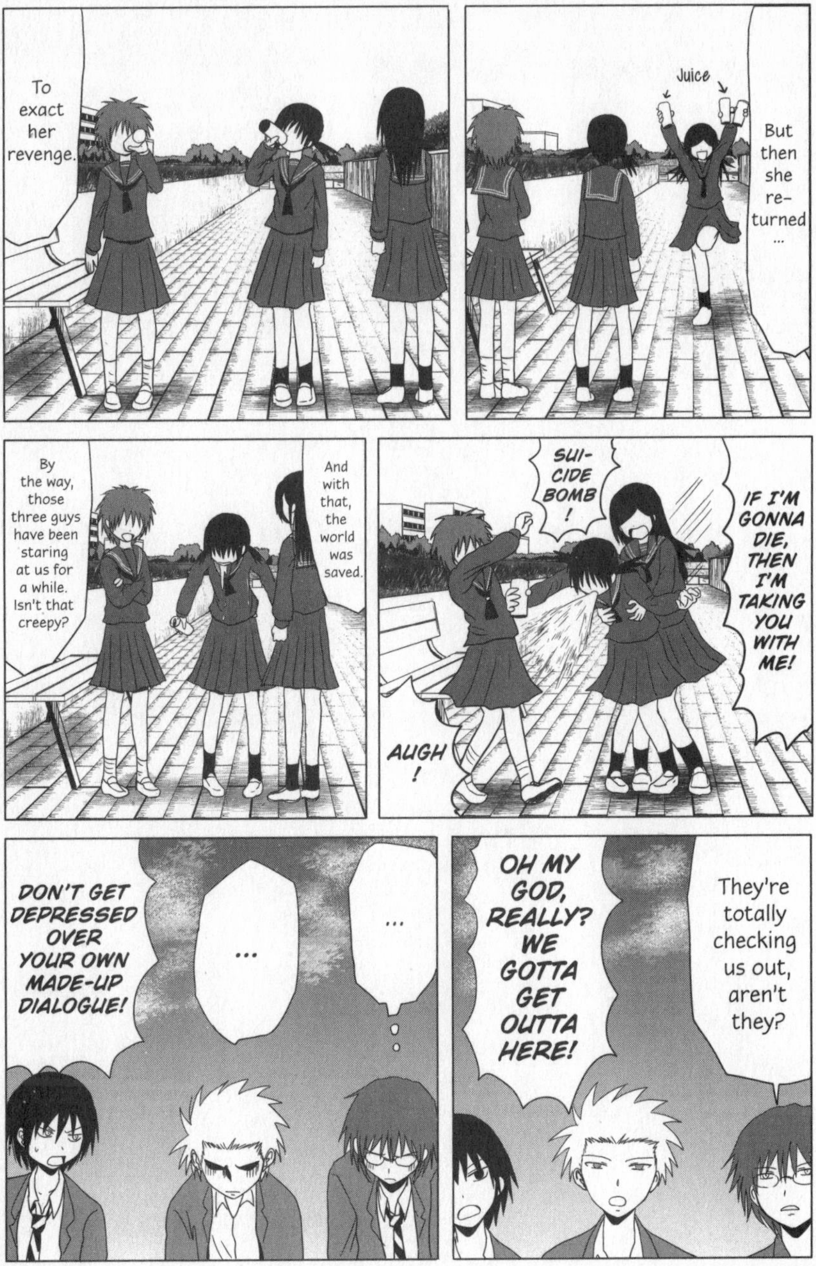
Juice
But then she re-turned ...
To exact her revenge.
IF I'M GONNA DIE, THEN I'M TAKING YOU WITH ME!
SUI-CIDE BOMB!
AUGH!
And with that, the world was saved.
By the way, those three guys have been staring at us for a while. Isn't that creepy?
They're totally checking us out, aren't they?
OH MY GOD, REALLY? WE GOTTA GET OUTTA HERE!
...
...
DON'T GET DEPRESSED OVER YOUR OWN MADE-UP DIALOGUE!

the

daily

lives

of

2 high school boys

chapter 29:
high school boys and a biography of an icon

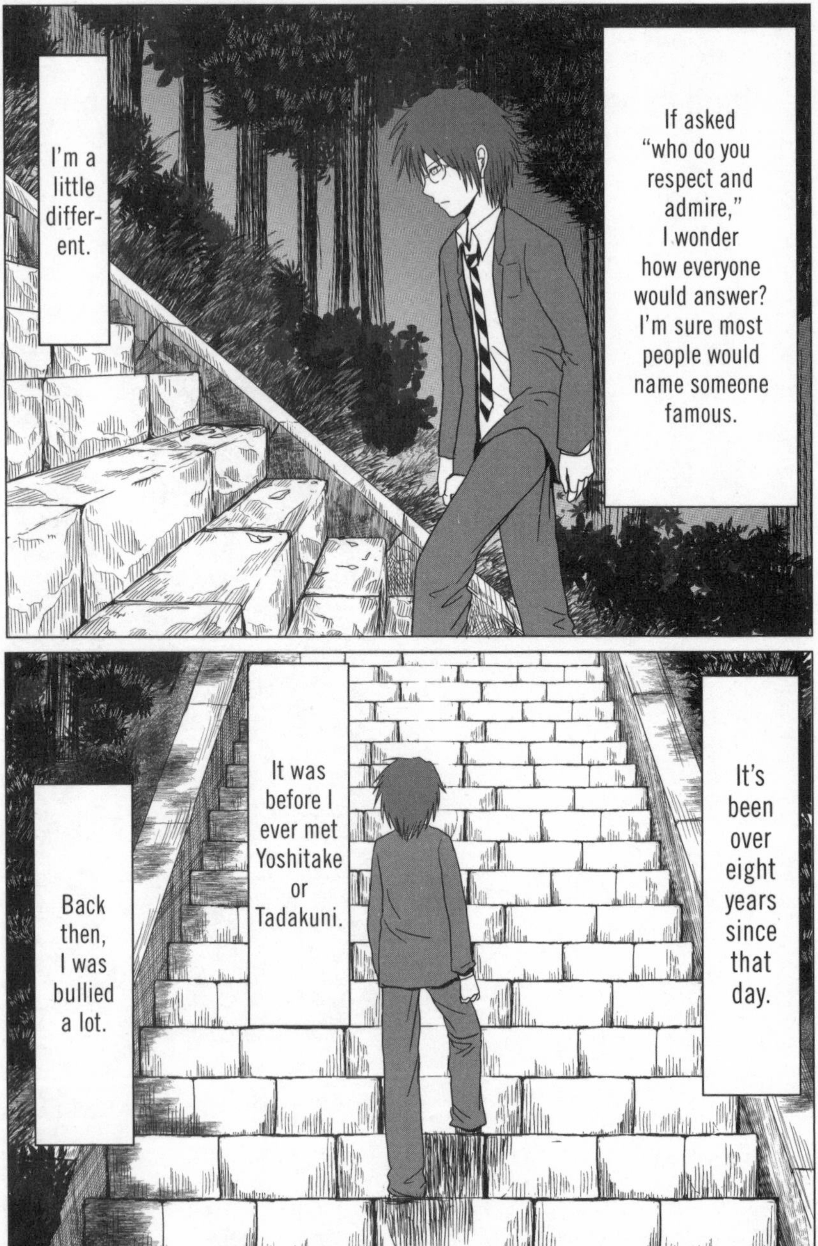
If asked "who do you respect and admire," I wonder how everyone would answer? I'm sure most people would name someone famous.
I'm a little differ-ent.
It's been over eight years since that day.
It was before I ever met Yoshitake or Tadakuni.
Back then, I was bullied a lot.

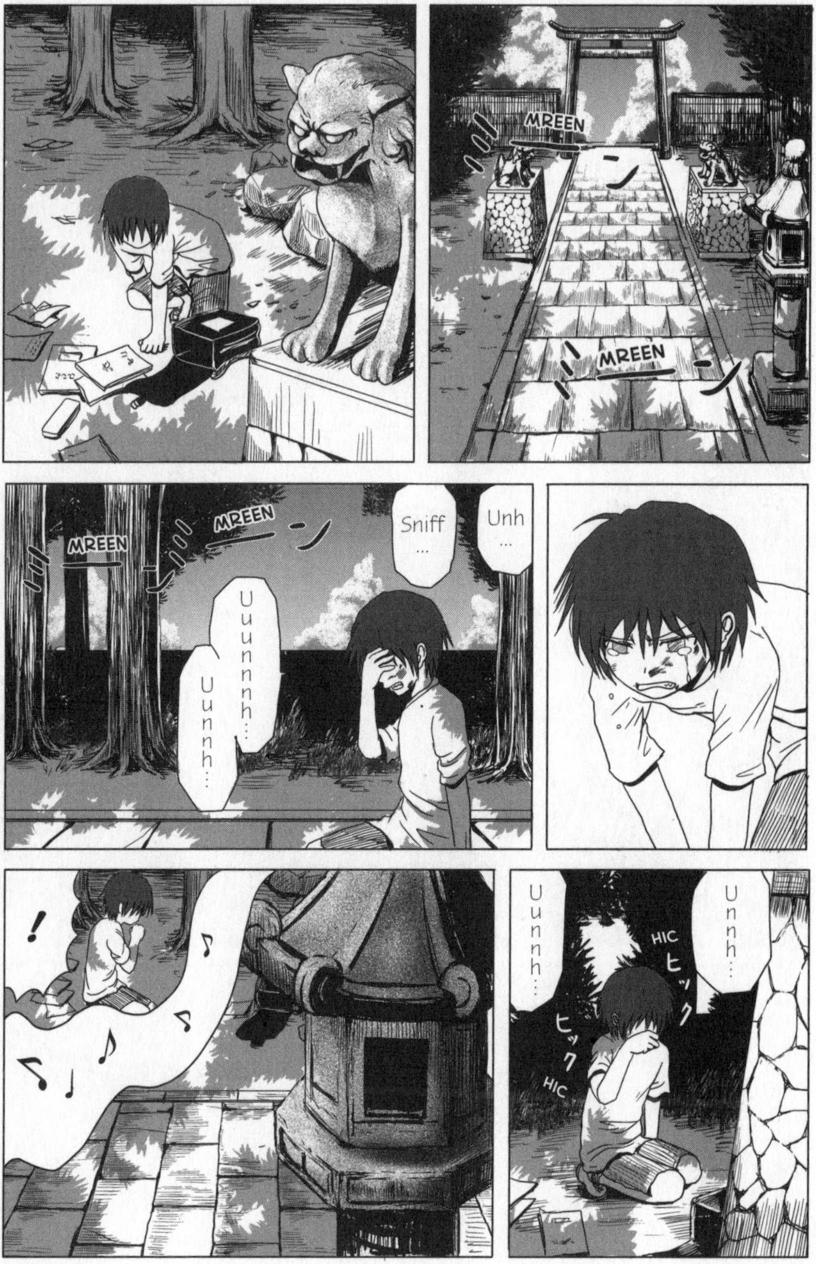
MREEN
MREEN
Unh ...
Sniff ...
Uuunnnh...
Uunnh...
MREEN
MREEN
Unnh...
HIC ヒック
ヒック HIC
Uunnh...
!

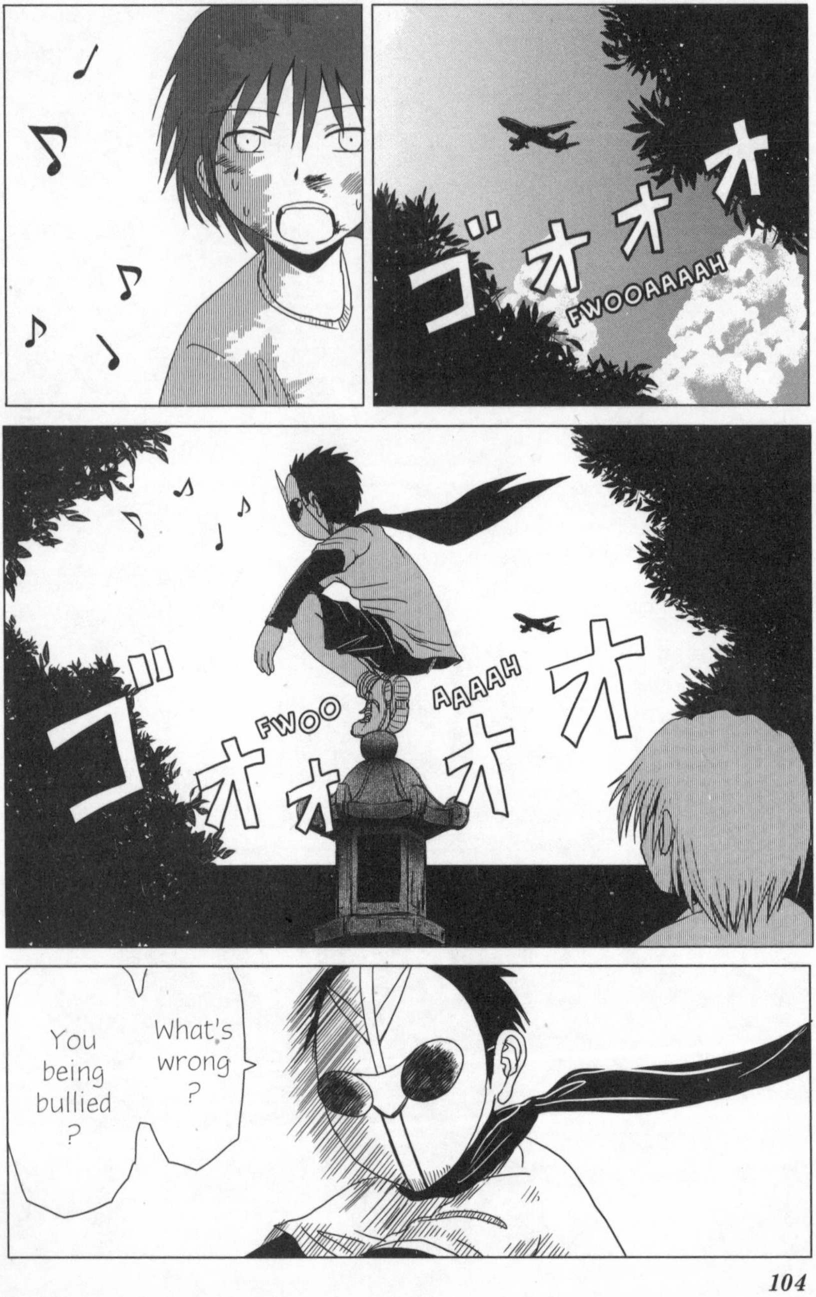
ゴオオオ
FWOOAAAAH
ゴオオオ
FWOO AAAAH
What's wrong?
You being bullied?

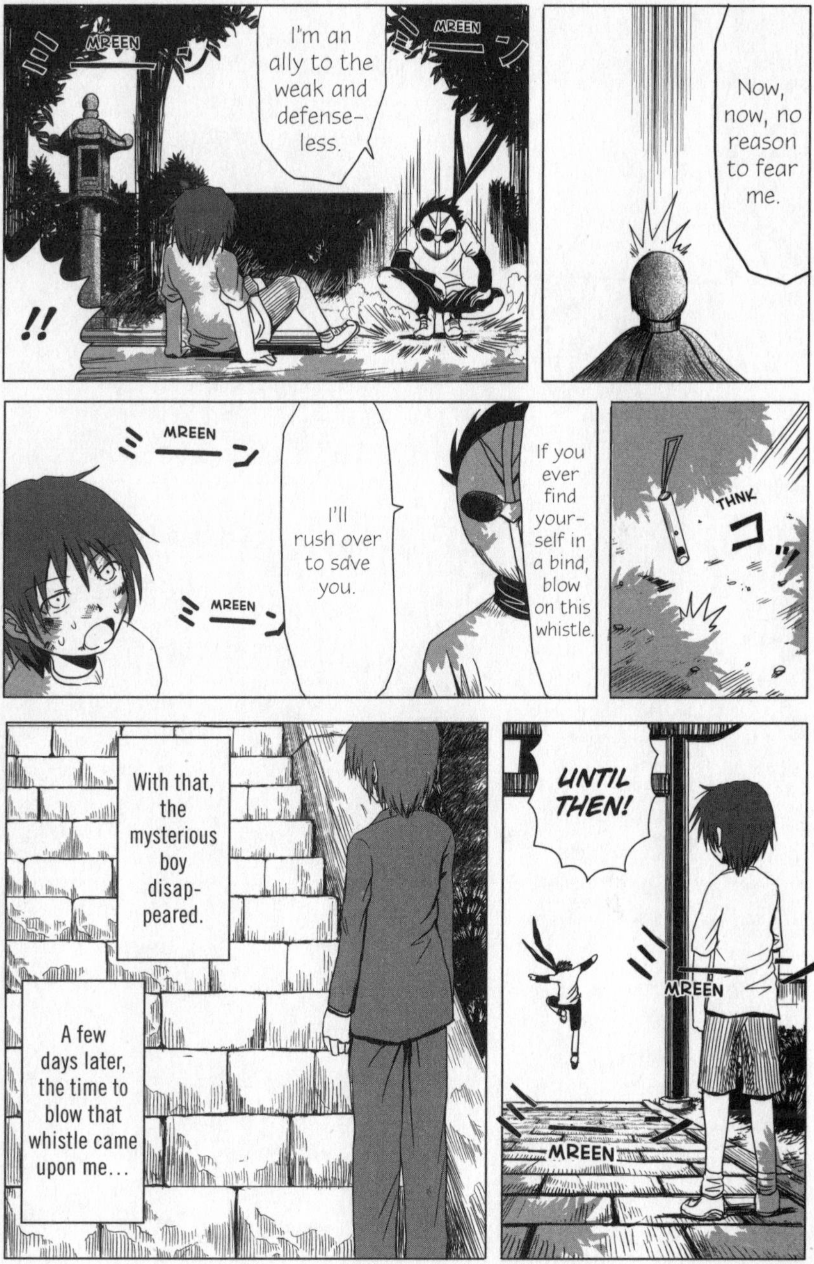
Now, now, no reason to fear me.
MREEN
I'm an ally to the weak and defenseless.
MREEN
!!
THNK
If you ever find yourself in a bind, blow on this whistle.
MREEN
I'll rush over to save you.
MREEN
UNTIL THEN!
MREEN
MREEN
With that, the mysterious boy disappeared.
A few days later, the time to blow that whistle came upon me…

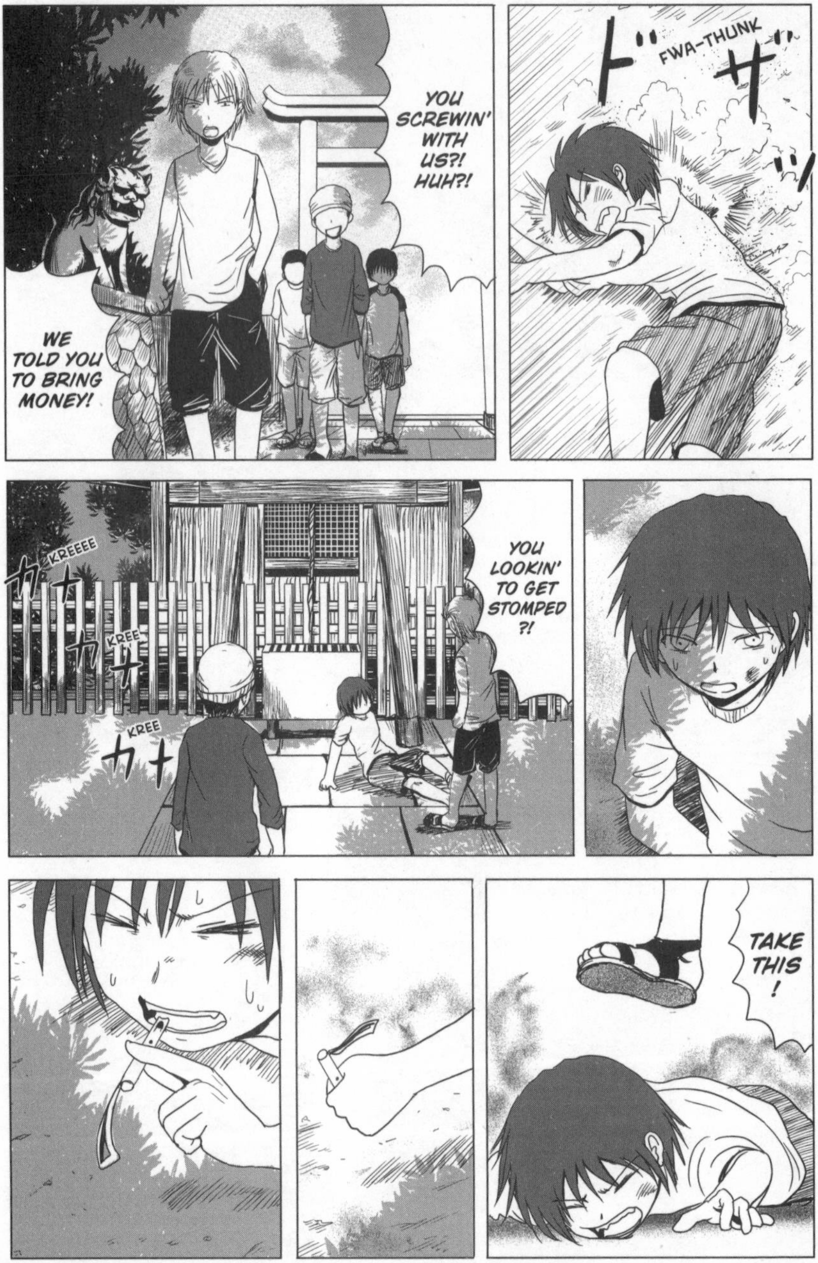

ドザッ
FWA-THUNK
YOU SCREWIN' WITH US?! HUH?!
WE TOLD YOU TO BRING MONEY!
YOU LOOKIN' TO GET STOMPED ?!
カナ
KREEEE
カナ
KREE
カナ
KREE
TAKE THIS !

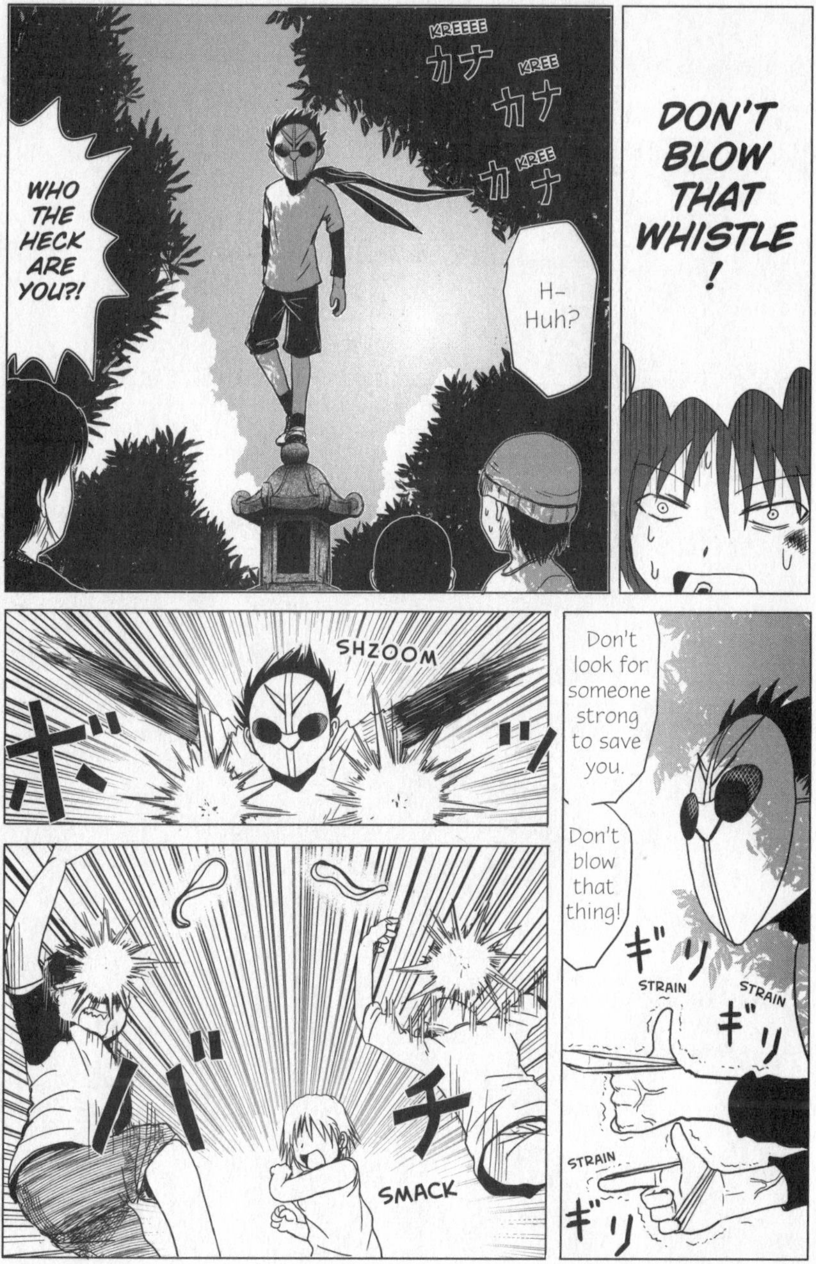
DON'T BLOW THAT WHISTLE!
KREEEE
カナ
KREE
カナ
KREE
カナ
WHO THE HECK ARE YOU?!
H- Huh?
Don't look for someone strong to save you.
Don't blow that thing!
ギリ
STRAIN
STRAIN
ギリ
STRAIN
ギリ
SHZOOM
バチ
SMACK

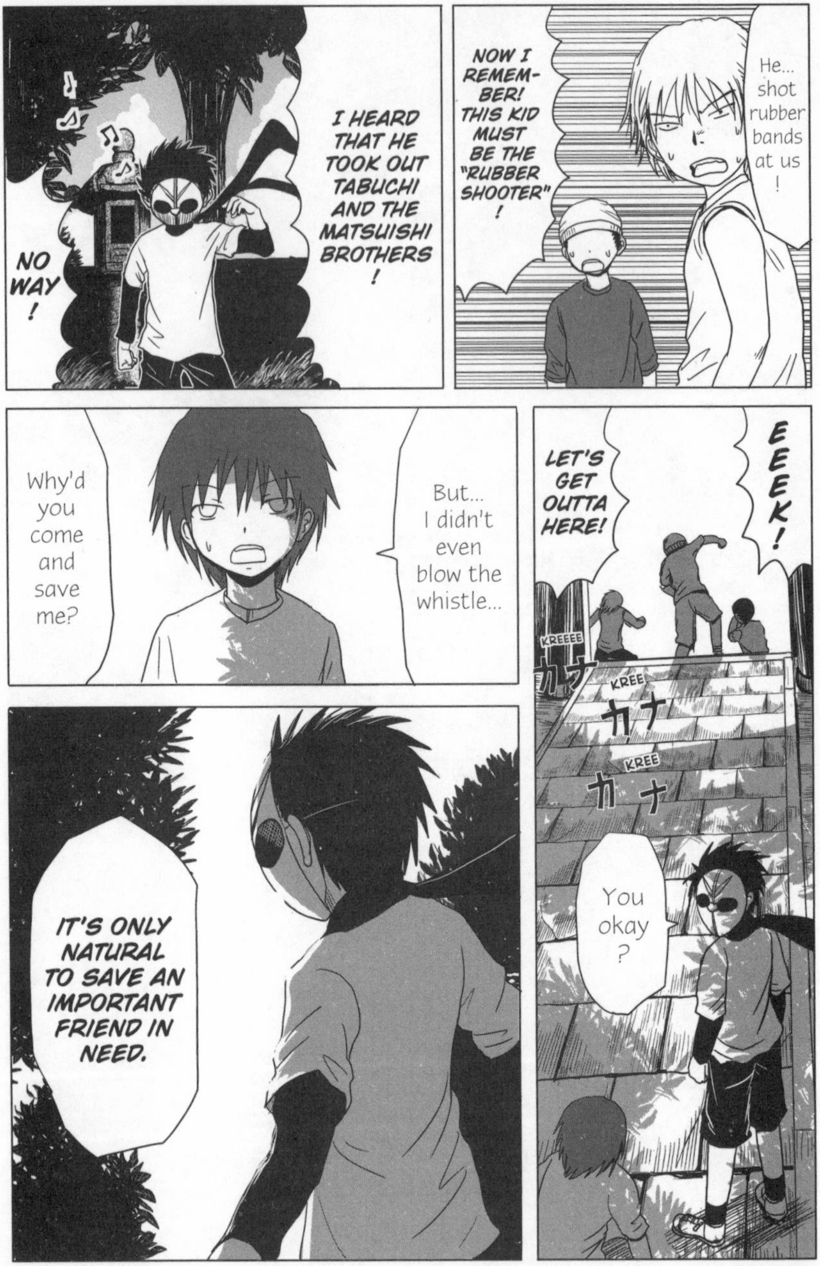
He... shot rubber bands at us!
NOW I REMEMBER! THIS KID MUST BE THE "RUBBER SHOOTER"!
I HEARD THAT HE TOOK OUT TABUCHI AND THE MATSUISHI BROTHERS!
NO WAY!
EEEK!
LET'S GET OUTTA HERE!
KREEE
KREE
KREE
You okay?
But... I didn't even blow the whistle...
Why'd you come and save me?
IT'S ONLY NATURAL TO SAVE AN IMPORTANT FRIEND IN NEED.

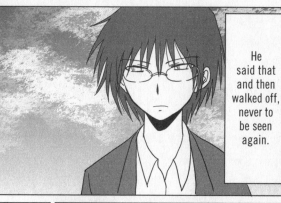

He said that and then walked off, never to be seen again.
I took his words from that day to heart, and I've tried my best to live up to his principles ever since.
Even to this day, I find myself journeying to this shrine whenever I'm feeling discouraged.
Th-That tune!
It's Pachelbel's Canon—it's what he always whistled! Is he up there?!
IS THIS HAPPENING?!
I DON'T BELIEVE IT!
DASH
WILL WE FINALLY MEET AGAIN?!

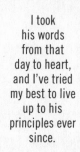

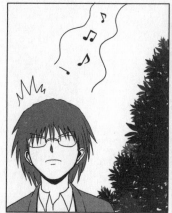

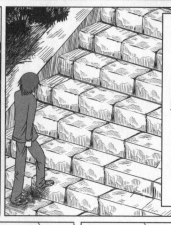

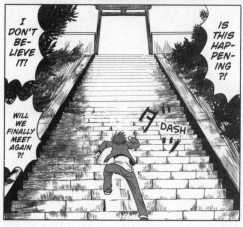

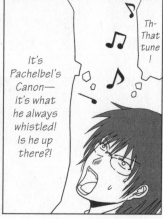

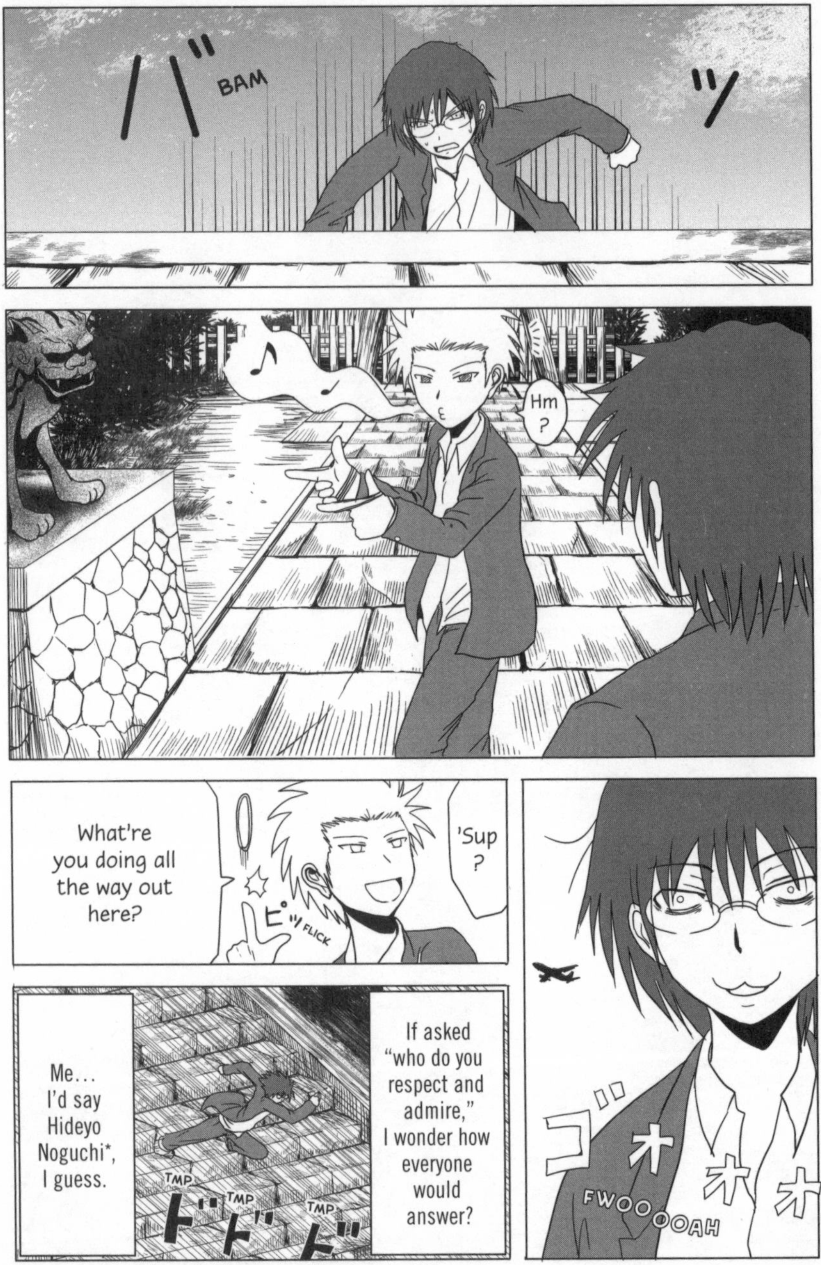
バッ
BAM
Hm?
ゴォオオ
FWOOOOAH
'Sup?
What're you doing all the way out here?
ピッ
FLICK
If asked "who do you respect and admire," I wonder how everyone would answer?
Me… I'd say Hideyo Noguchi*, I guess.
TMP TMP TMP
ドドド

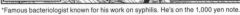

*Famous bacteriologist known for his work on syphilis. He's on the 1,000 yen note.

chapter 30:
high school boys and literature girl. pt. 3

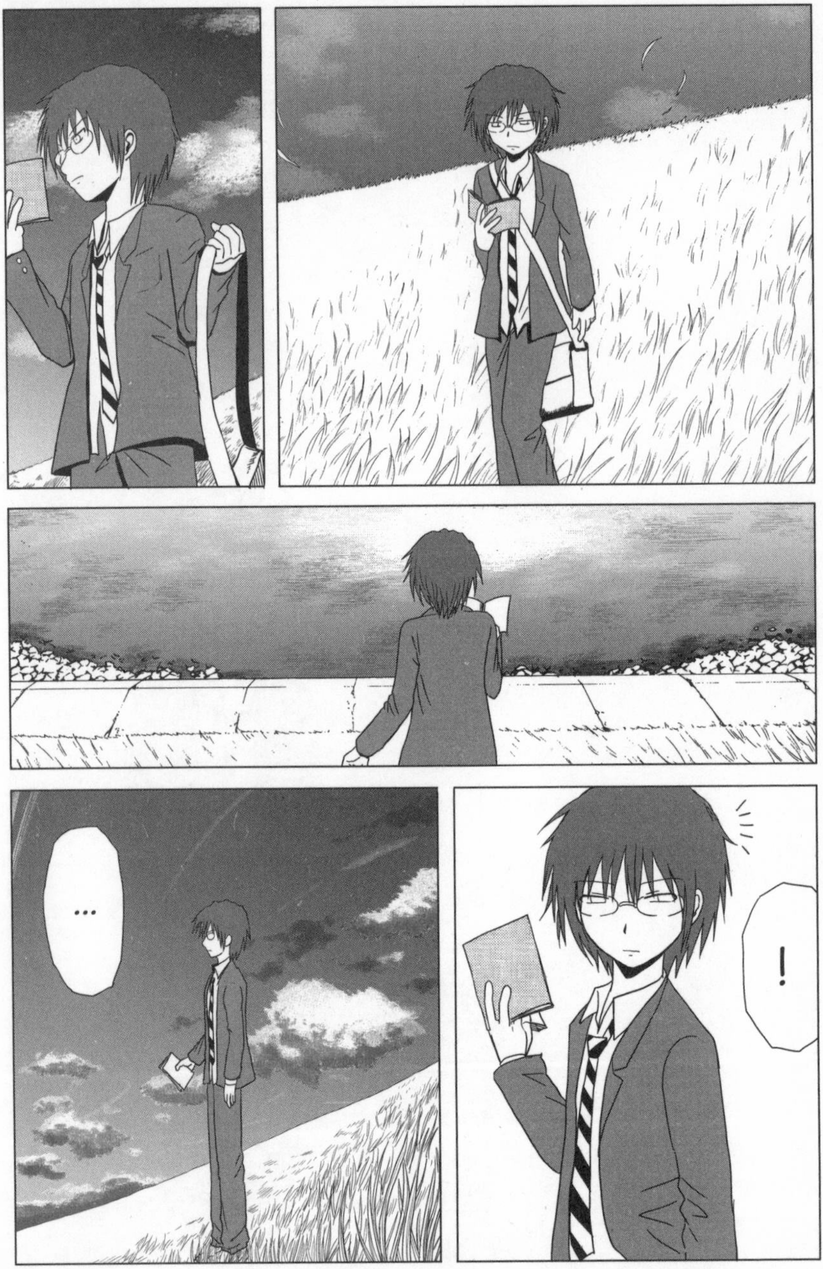
!
...

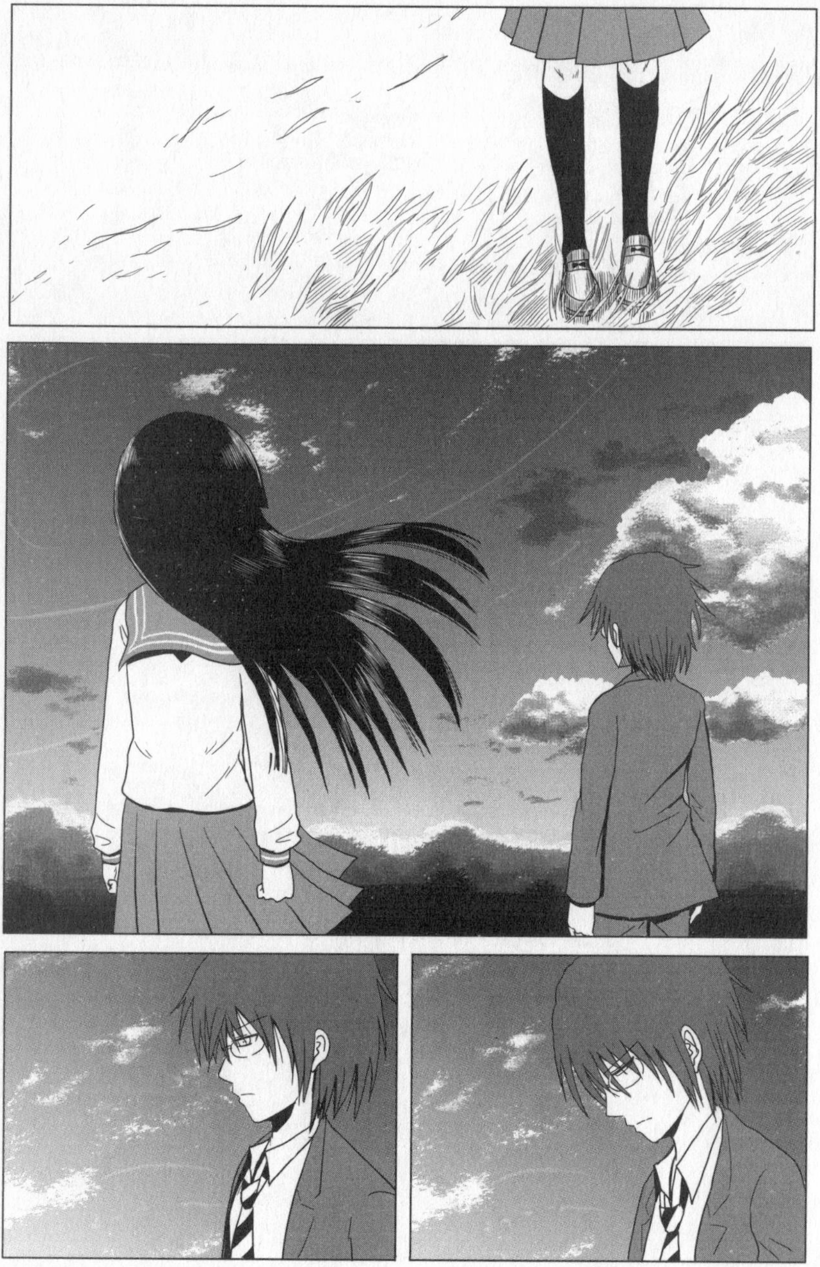

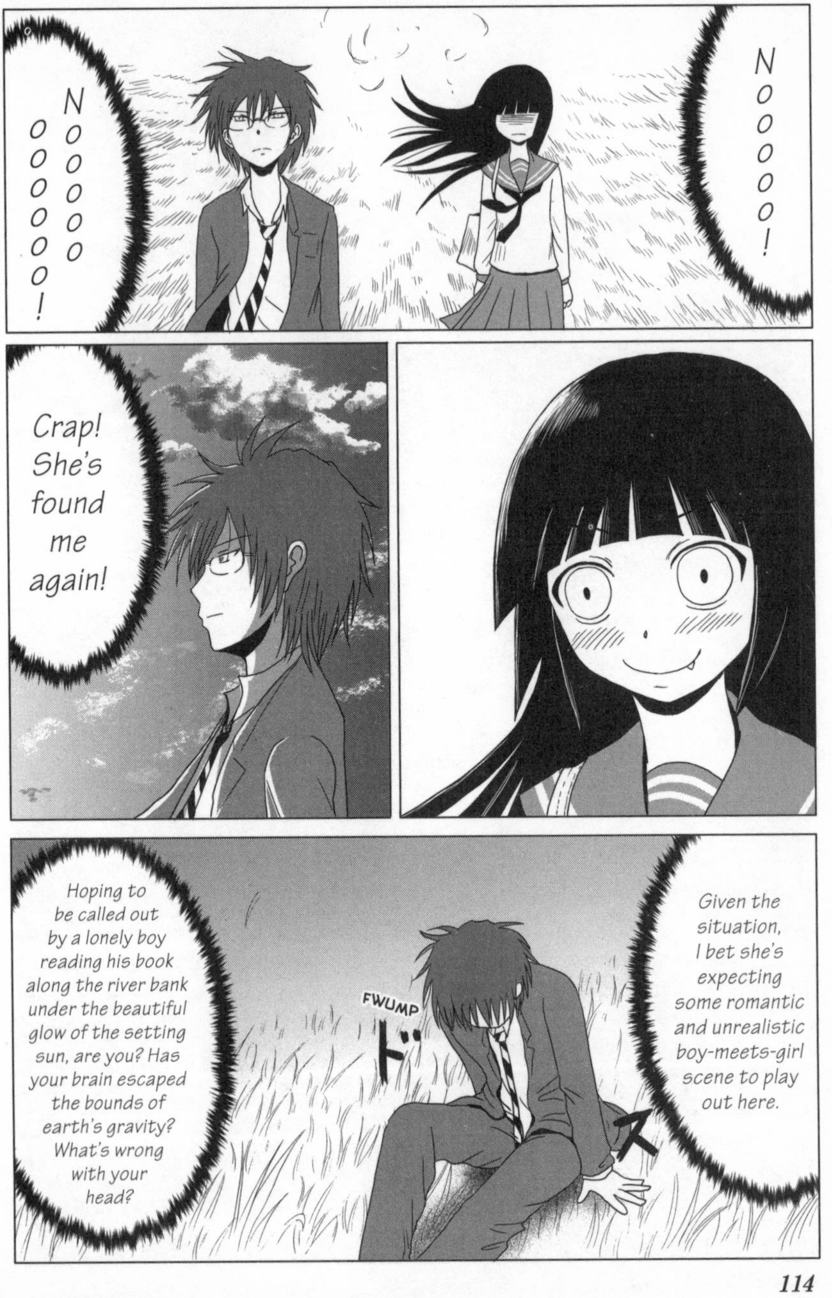
Nooooo!
Nooooooooooo!
Crap! She's found me again!
Given the situation, I bet she's expecting some romantic and unrealistic boy-meets-girl scene to play out here.
FWUMP
ド
Hoping to be called out by a lonely boy reading his book along the river bank under the beautiful glow of the setting sun, are you? Has your brain escaped the bounds of earth's gravity? What's wrong with your head?

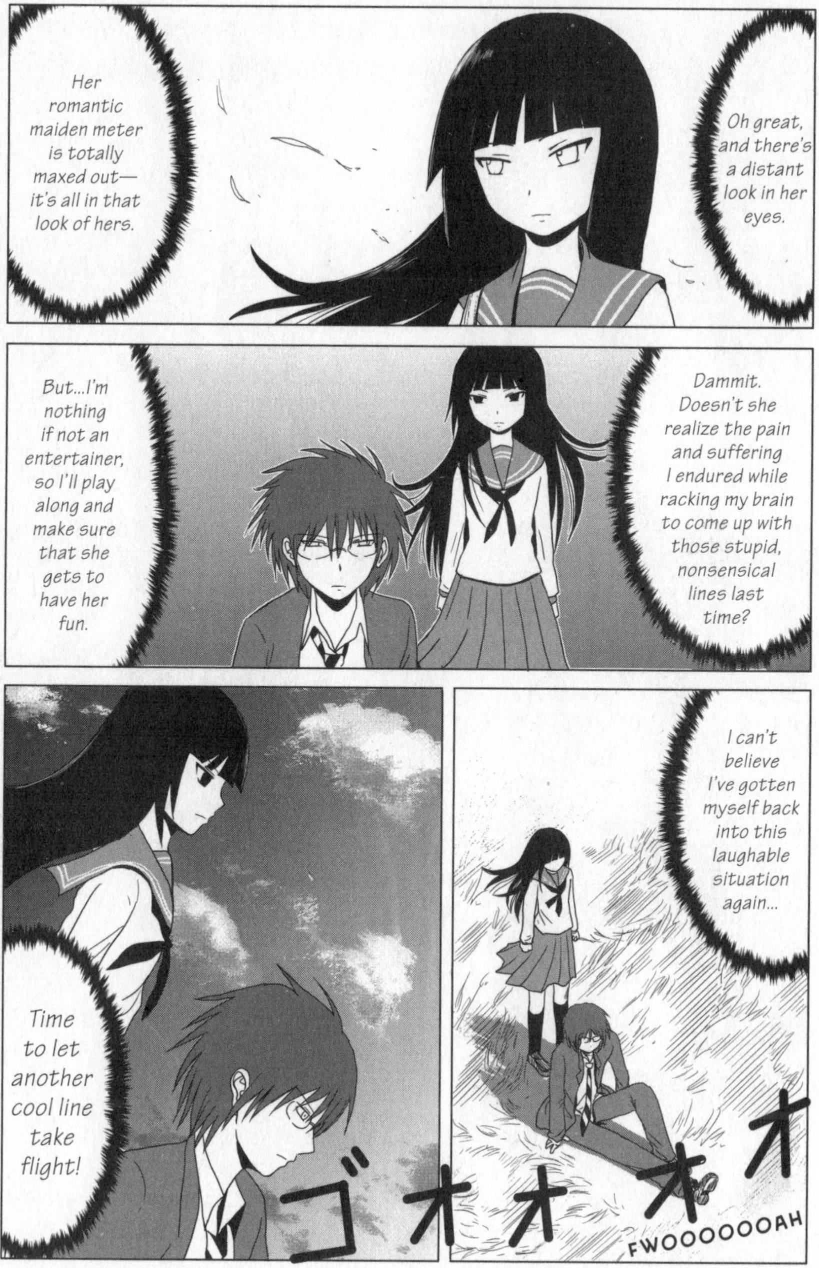

Oh great, and there's a distant look in her eyes.
Her romantic maiden meter is totally maxed out—it's all in that look of hers.
Dammit. Doesn't she realize the pain and suffering I endured while racking my brain to come up with those stupid, nonsensical lines last time?
But...I'm nothing if not an entertainer, so I'll play along and make sure that she gets to have her fun.
I can't believe I've gotten myself back into this laughable situation again...
ゴオオオオ
FWOOOOOOAH
Time to let another cool line take flight!

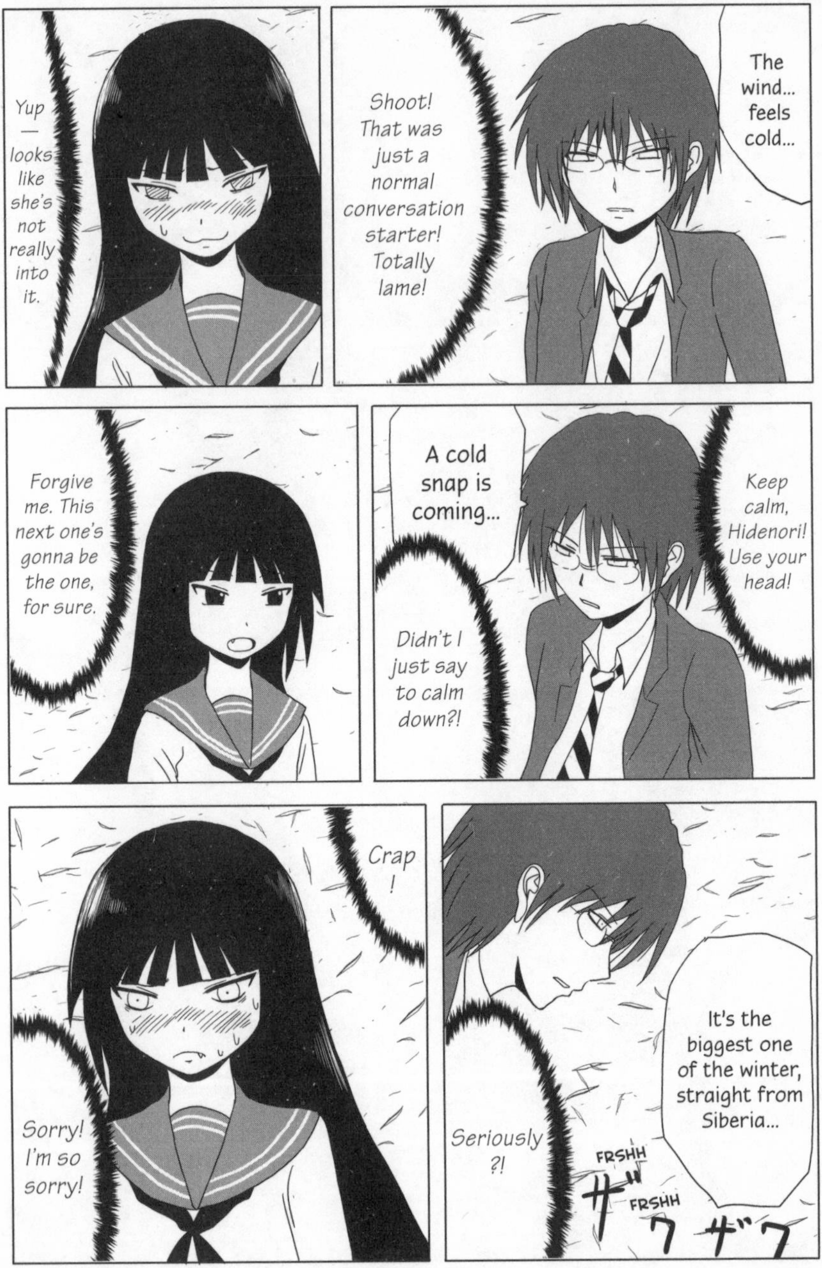
The wind... feels cold...
Shoot! That was just a normal conversation starter! Totally lame!
Yup—looks like she's not really into it.
A cold snap is coming...
Keep calm, Hidenori! Use your head!
Didn't I just say to calm down?!
Forgive me. This next one's gonna be the one, for sure.
It's the biggest one of the winter, straight from Siberia...
Seriously?!
FRSHH
FRSHH
ザワザワ
Crap!
Sorry! I'm so sorry!

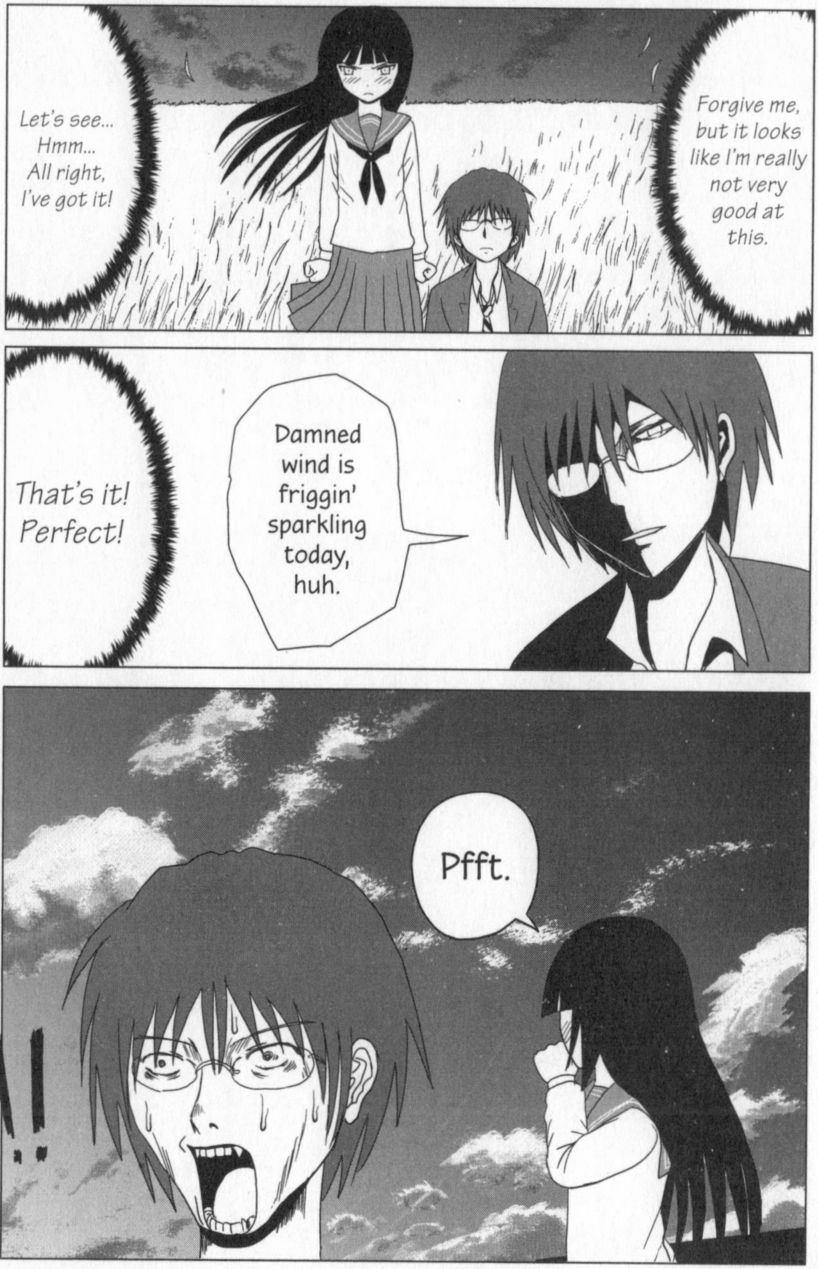
Forgive me, but it looks like I'm really not very good at this.
Let's see... Hmm... All right, I've got it!
Damned wind is friggin' sparkling today, huh.
That's it! Perfect!
Pfft.
!!

the

daily

lives

of

2 high school boys

chapter 31:
high school boys and the holy night

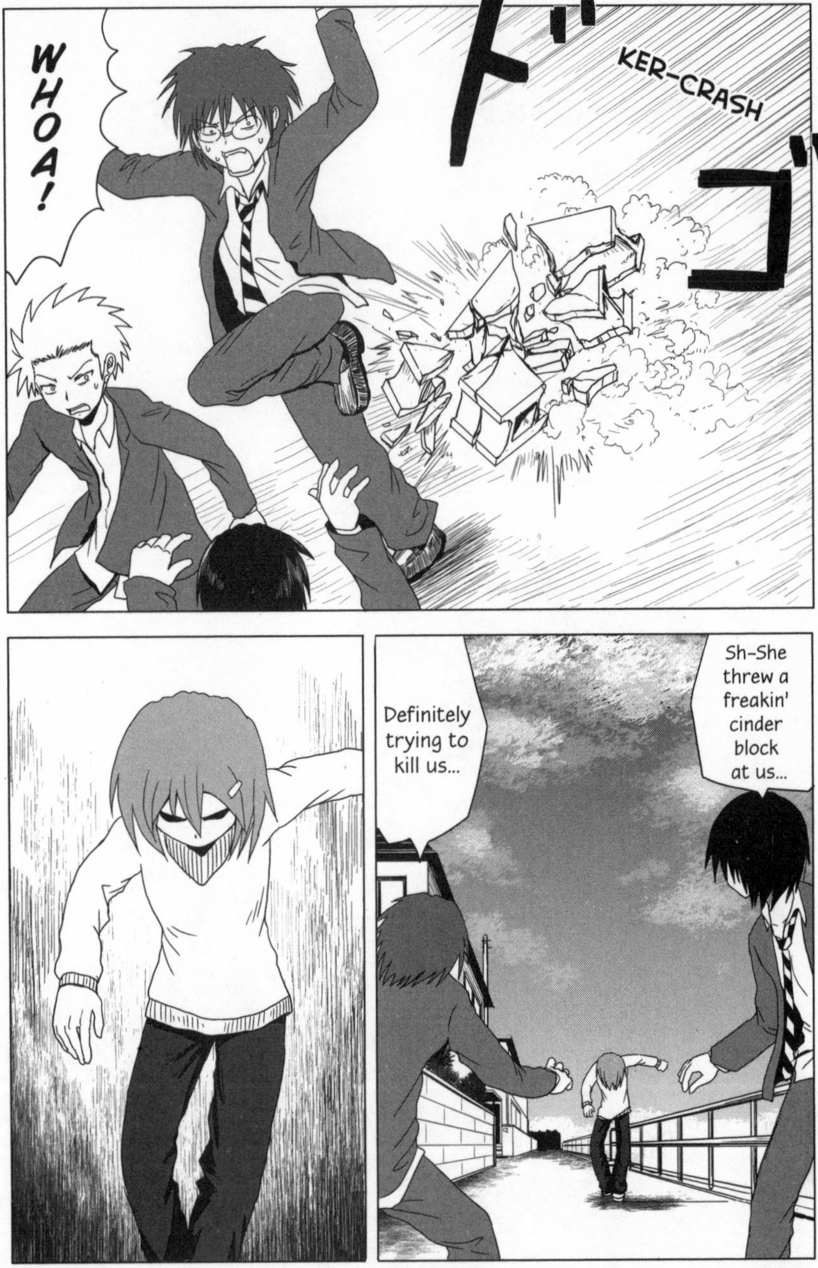
ドゴ
KER-CRASH
WHOA!
Sh-She threw a freakin' cinder block at us...
Definitely trying to kill us...

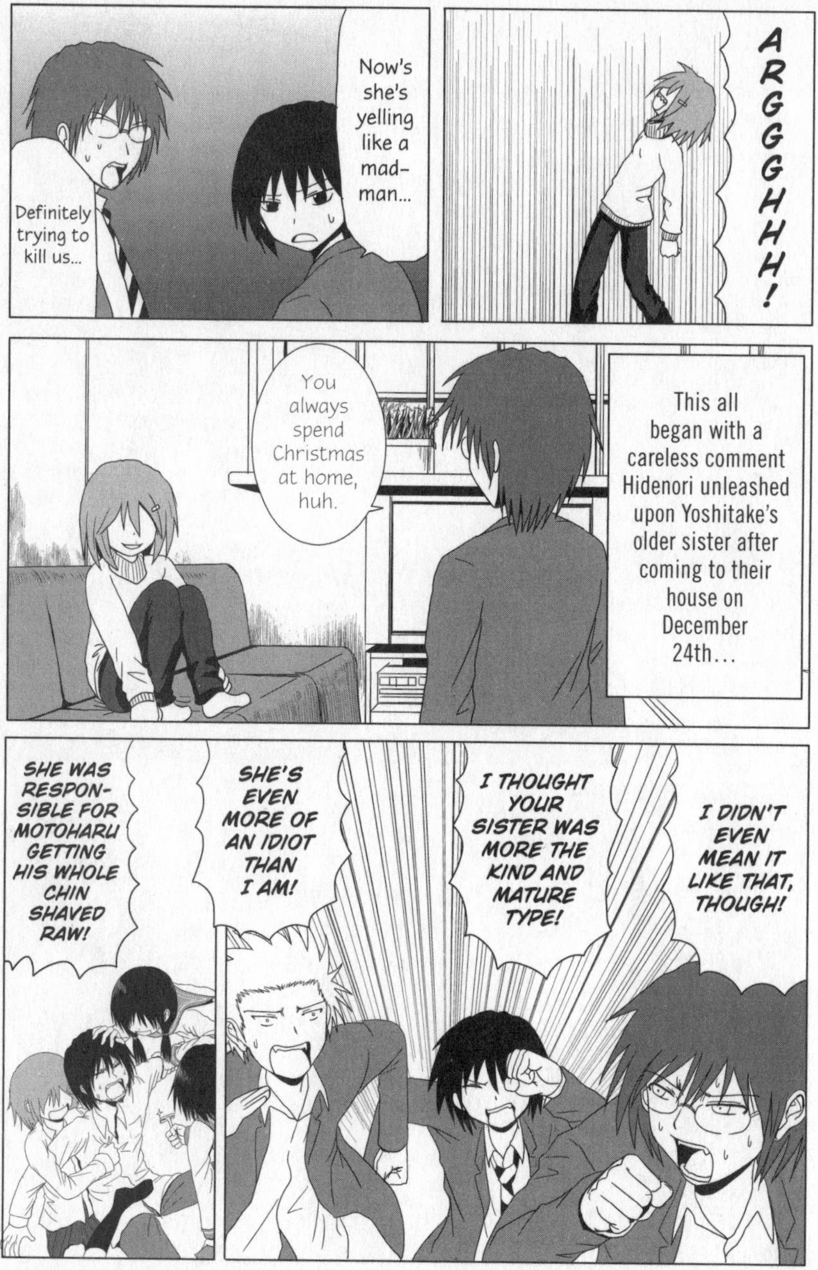
ARGGGHHH!
Now's she's yelling like a mad-man...
Definitely trying to kill us...
This all began with a careless comment Hidenori unleashed upon Yoshitake's older sister after coming to their house on December 24th…
You always spend Christmas at home, huh.
I DIDN'T EVEN MEAN IT LIKE THAT, THOUGH!
I THOUGHT YOUR SISTER WAS MORE THE KIND AND MATURE TYPE!
SHE'S EVEN MORE OF AN IDIOT THAN I AM!
SHE WAS RESPON-SIBLE FOR MOTOHARU GETTING HIS WHOLE CHIN SHAVED RAW!

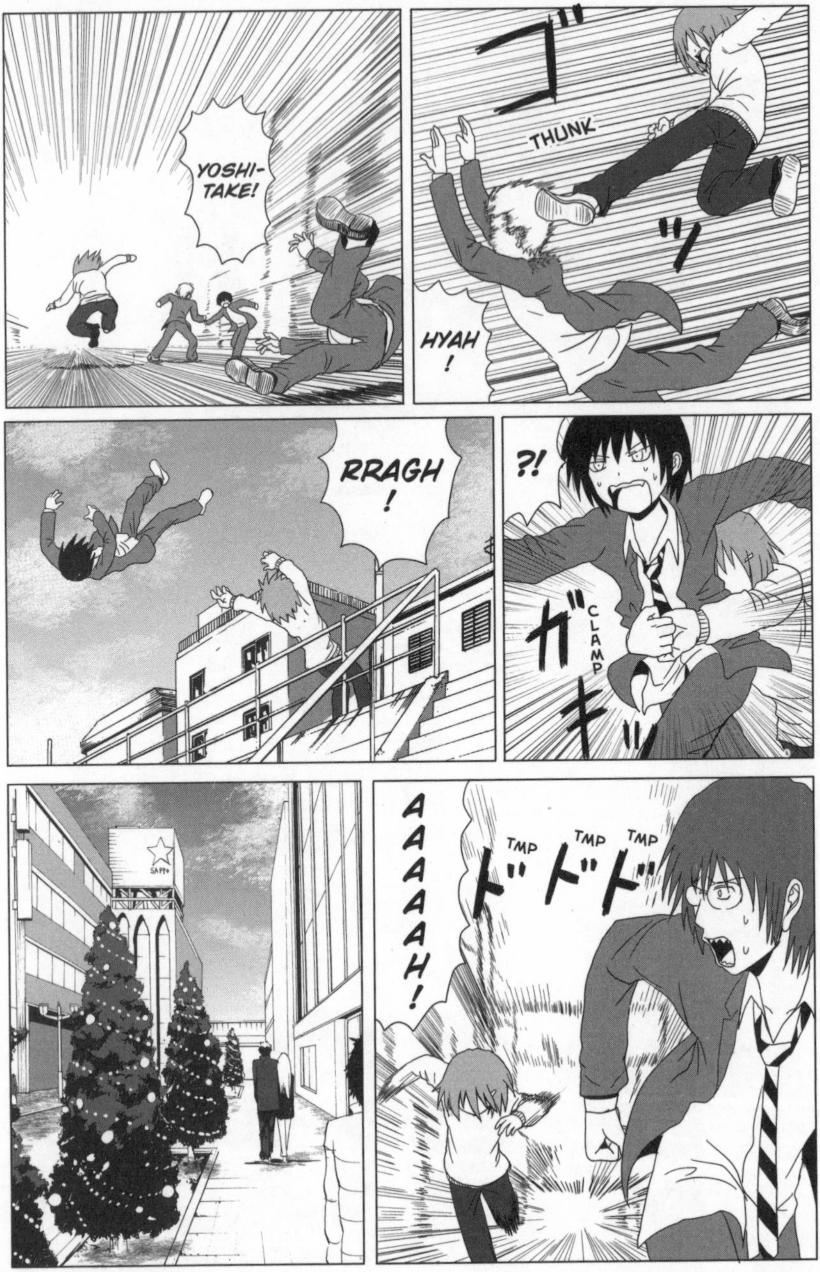
ゴッ
THUNK
HYAH!
YOSHI-TAKE!
?!
ガキッ
CLAMP
RRAGH!
AAAAAAH!
ドドド
TMP TMP TMP

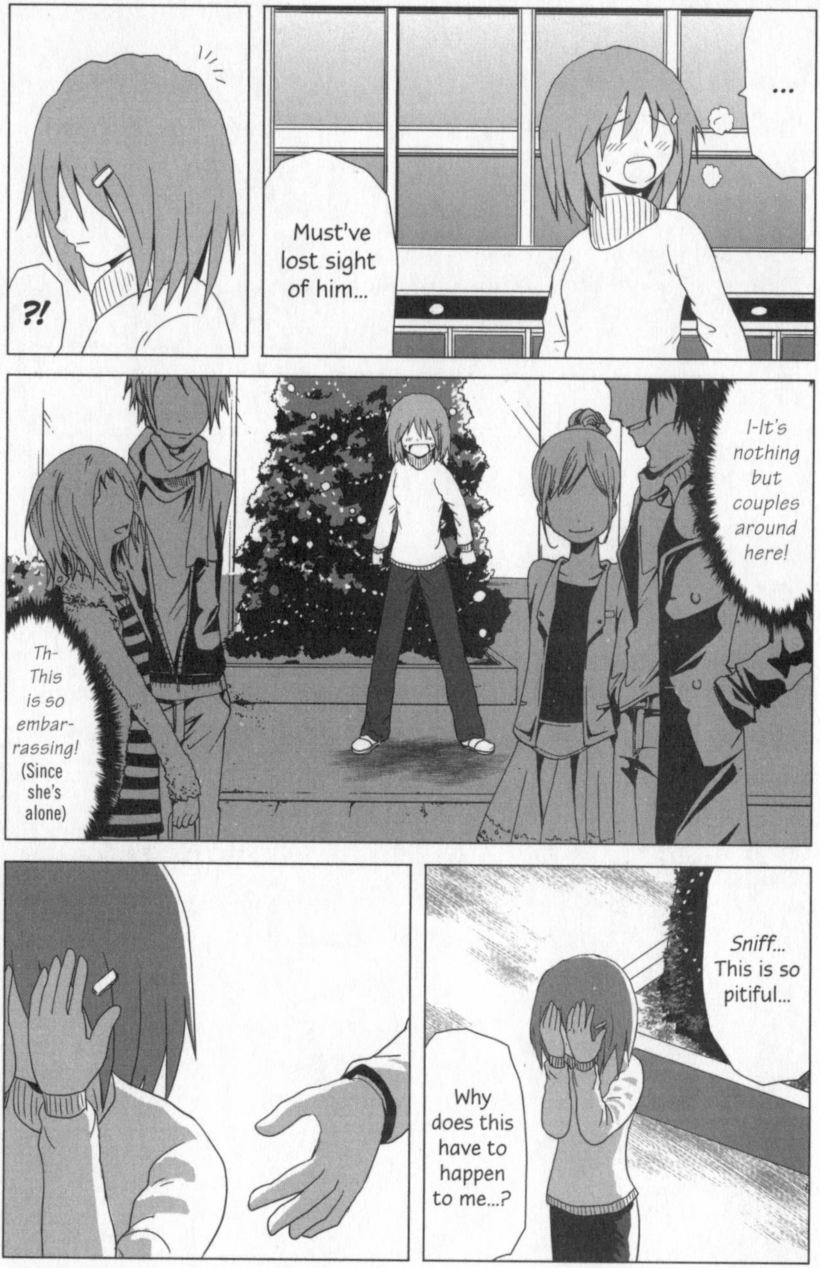
...
Must've lost sight of him...
?!
I-It's nothing but couples around here!
Th- This is so embarrassing!
(Since she's alone)
Sniff... This is so pitiful...
Why does this have to happen to me...?

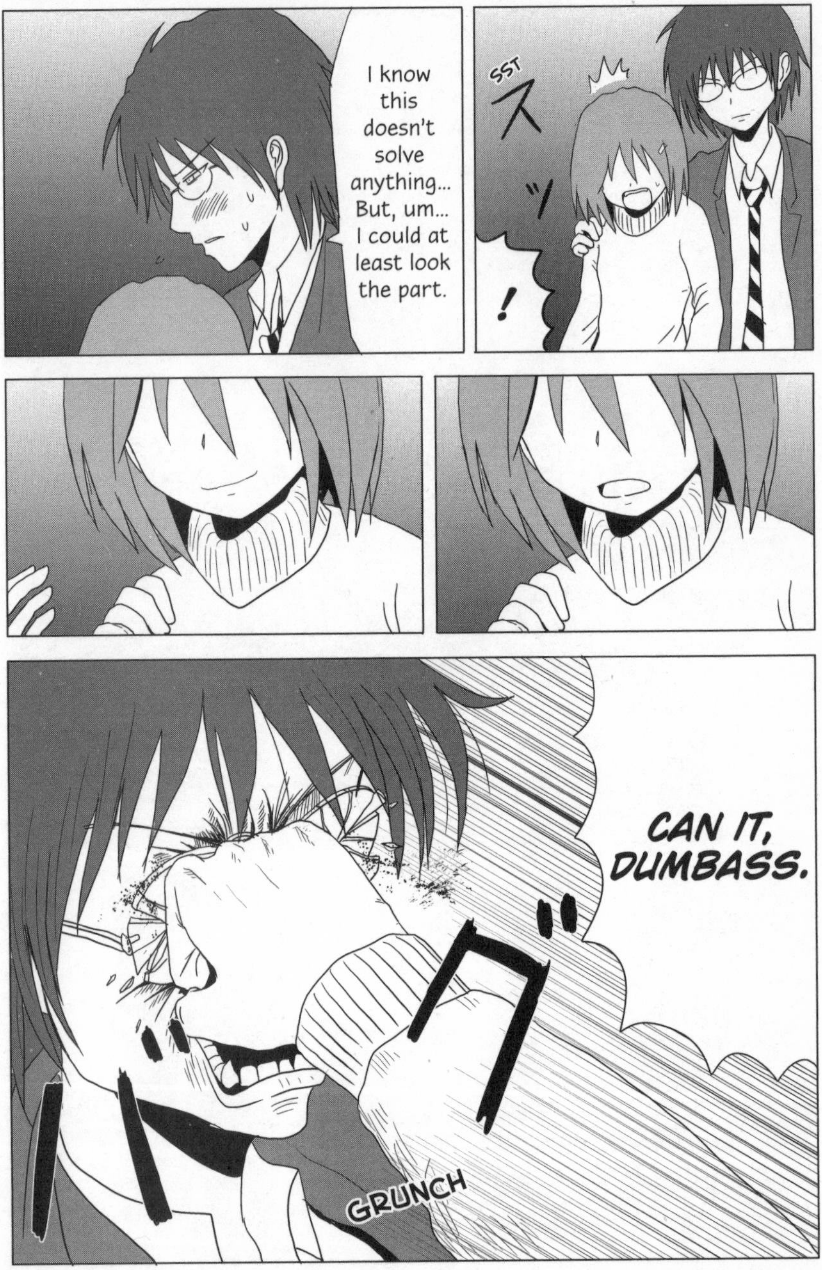
SST
スッ
!
I know this doesn't solve anything... But, um... I could at least look the part.
CAN IT, DUMBASS.
GRUNCH

chapter 32:
high school boys and the new semester

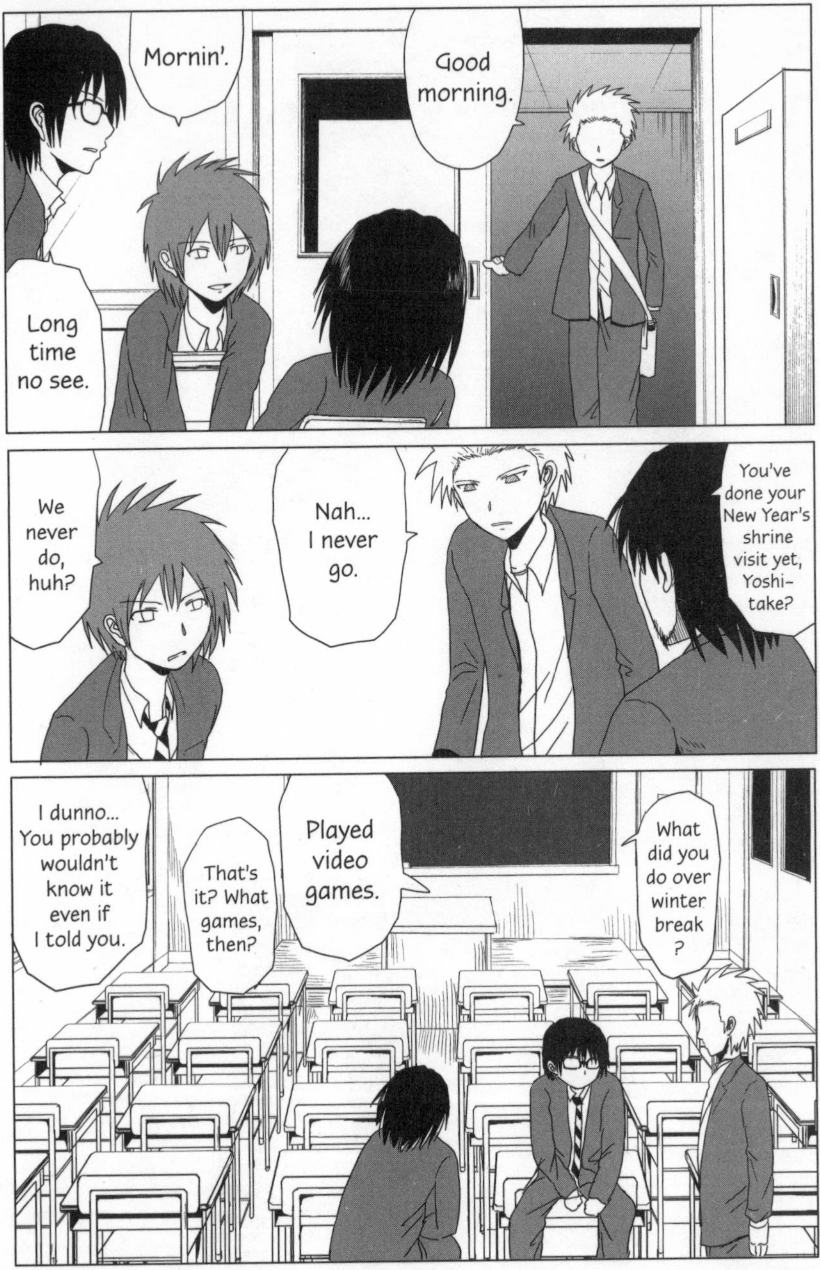
Good morning.
Mornin'.
Long time no see.
You've done your New Year's shrine visit yet, Yoshi-take?
Nah... I never go.
We never do, huh?
What did you do over winter break?
Played video games.
That's it? What games, then?
I dunno... You probably wouldn't know it even if I told you.

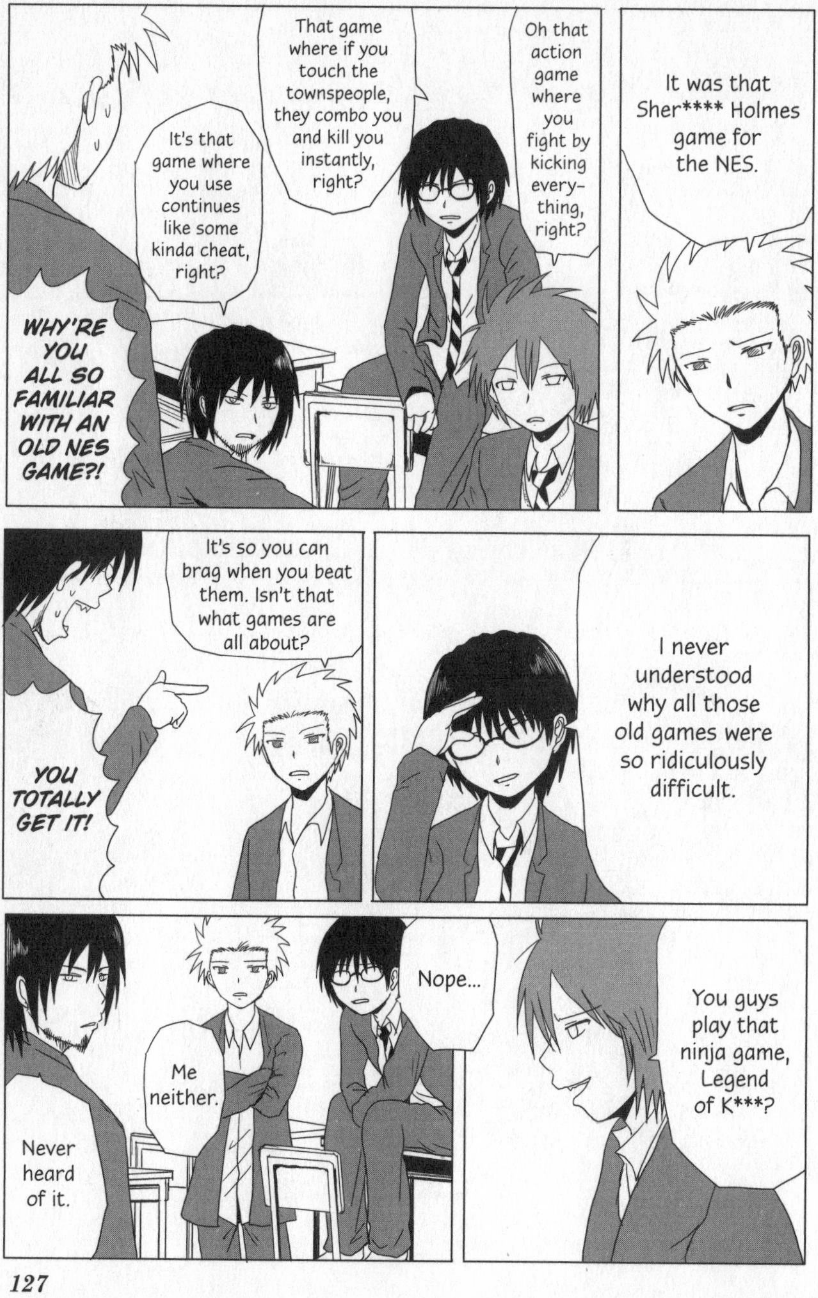
It was that Sher**** Holmes game for the NES.
Oh that action game where you fight by kicking every-thing, right?
That game where if you touch the townspeople, they combo you and kill you instantly, right?
It's that game where you use continues like some kinda cheat, right?
WHY'RE YOU ALL SO FAMILIAR WITH AN OLD NES GAME?!
I never understood why all those old games were so ridiculously difficult.
It's so you can brag when you beat them. Isn't that what games are all about?
YOU TOTALLY GET IT!
You guys play that ninja game, Legend of K***?
Nope...
Me neither.
Never heard of it.

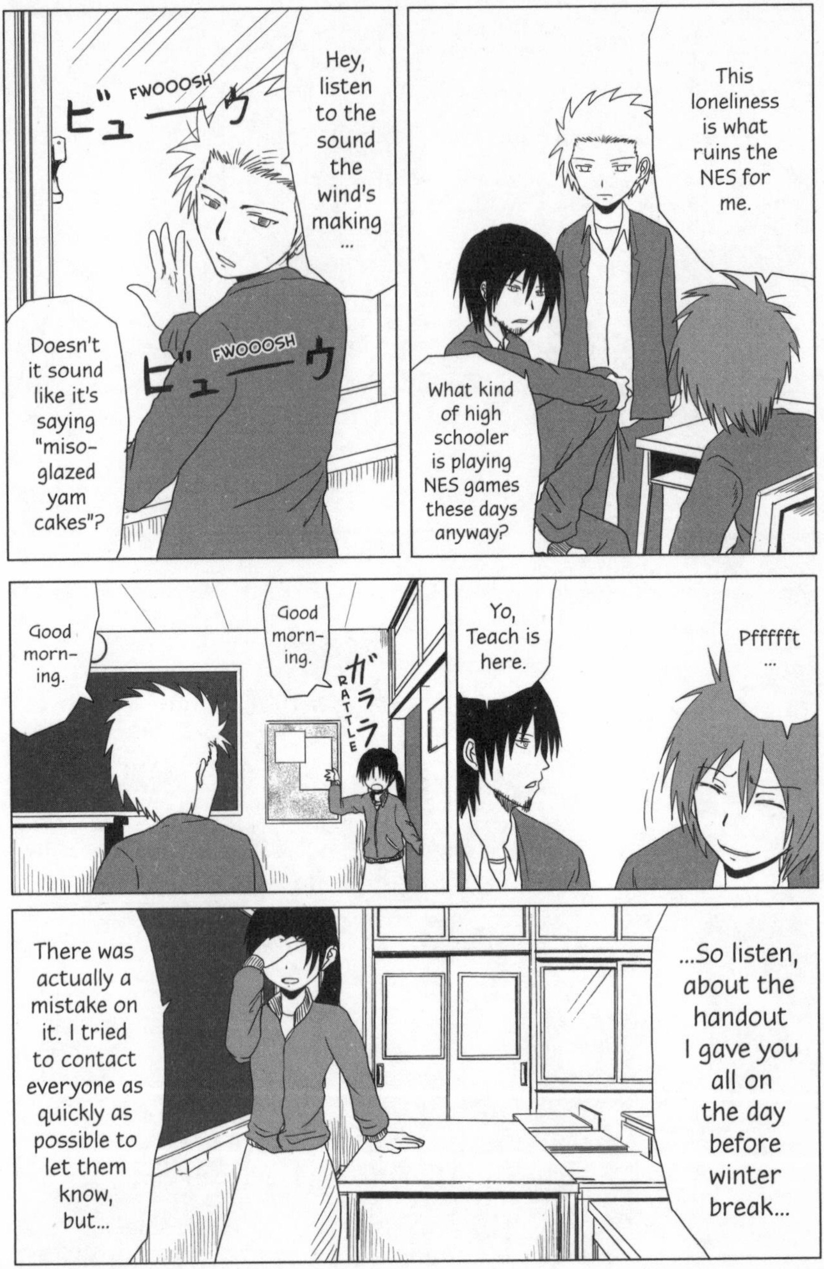
This loneliness is what ruins the NES for me.
What kind of high schooler is playing NES games these days anyway?
Hey, listen to the sound the wind's making ...
ビューウ
FWOOOSH
Doesn't it sound like it's saying "miso-glazed yam cakes"?
ビューウ
FWOOOSH
Pffffft ...
Yo, Teach is here.
Good morn-ing.
ガララ
RATTLE
Good morn-ing.
...So listen, about the handout I gave you all on the day before winter break...
There was actually a mistake on it. I tried to contact everyone as quickly as possible to let them know, but...

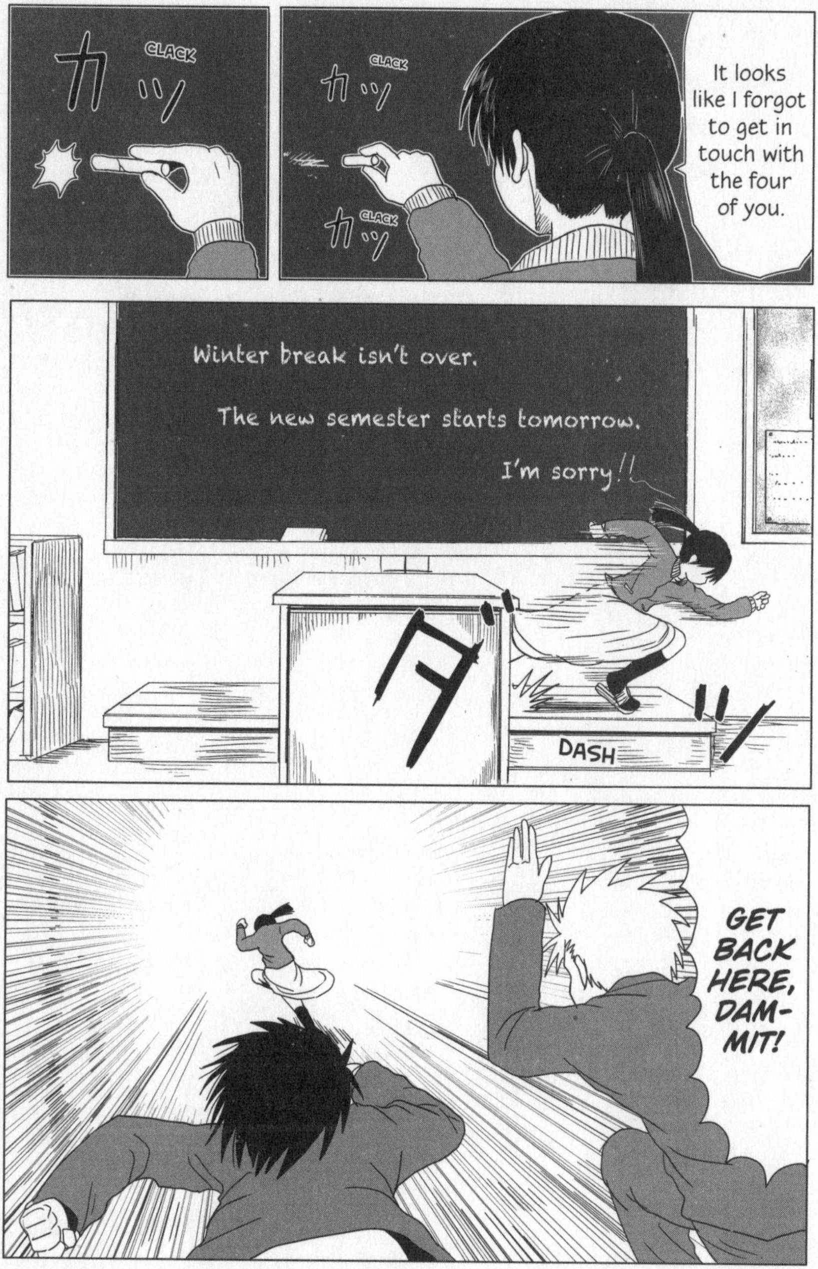
It looks like I forgot to get in touch with the four of you.
カッ
CLACK
カッ
CLACK
カッ
CLACK
Winter break isn't over.
The new semester starts tomorrow.
I'm sorry!!
ダッ
DASH
GET BACK HERE, DAM-MIT!

the

daily

lives

of

2 high school boys

special one-shot: *high school girls are bizarre*

Main Characters:

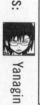

Yanagin

Habara

Ikushima

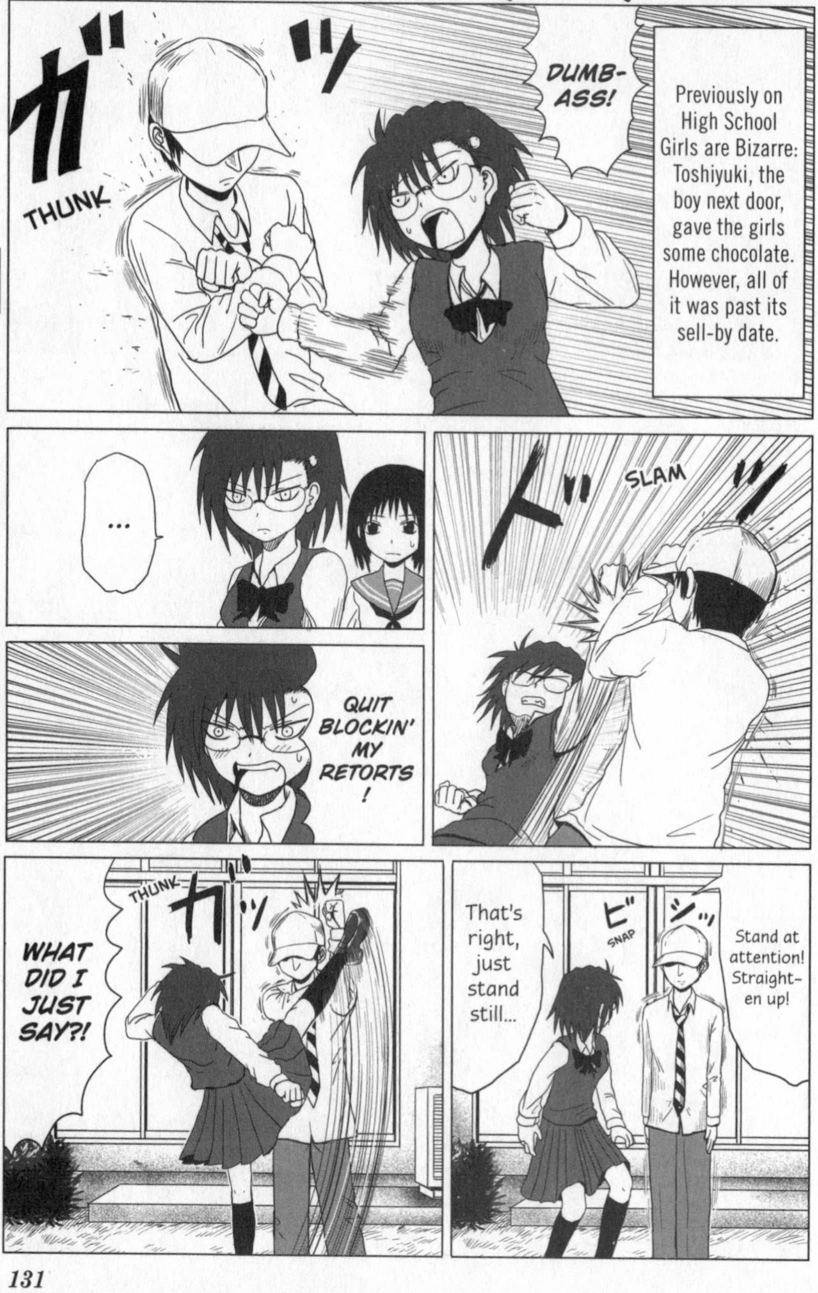
Previously on High School Girls are Bizarre: Toshiyuki, the boy next door, gave the girls some chocolate. However, all of it was past its sell-by date.
DUMB-ASS!
ガッ
THUNK
ドッ
SLAM
...
QUIT BLOCKIN' MY RETORTS!
Stand at attention! Straighten up!
ビシッ
SNAP
That's right, just stand still...
ガッ
THUNK
WHAT DID I JUST SAY?!

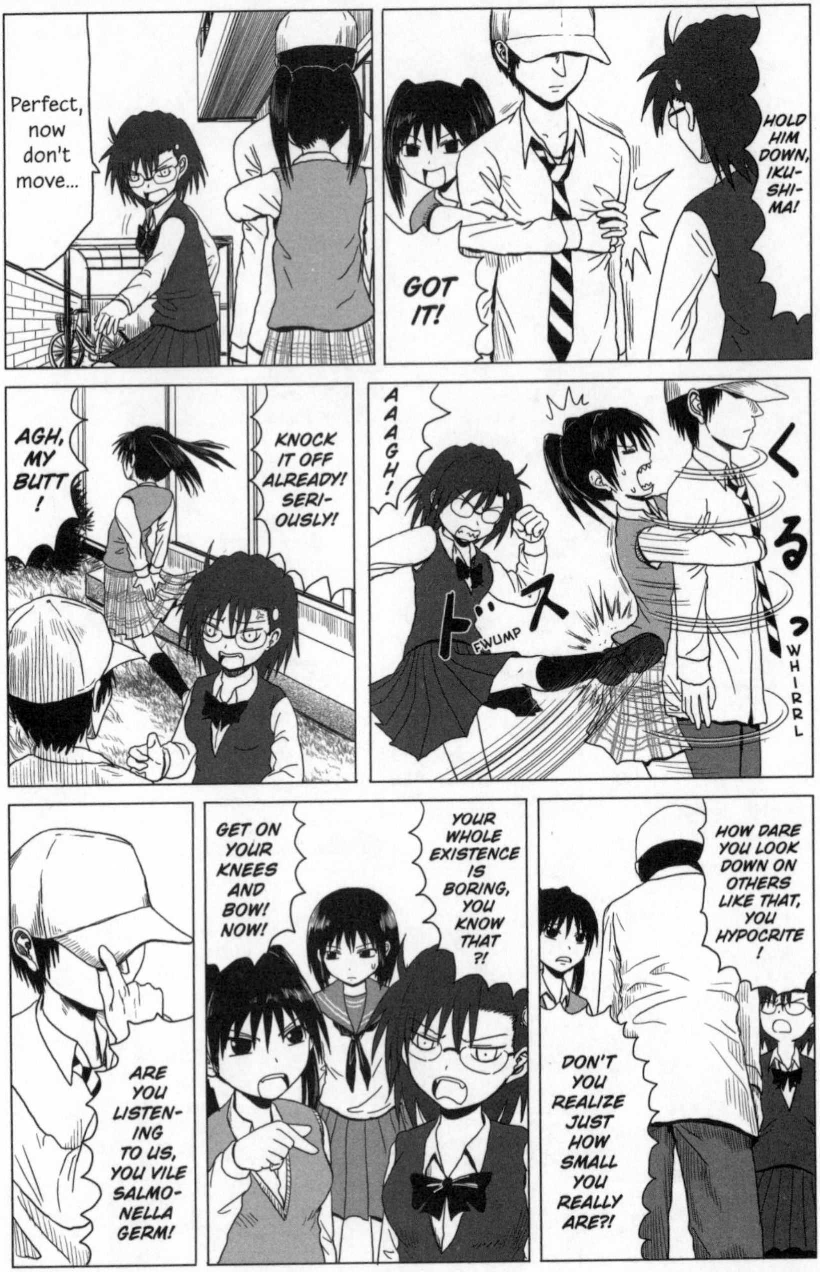

HOLD HIM DOWN, IKUSHIMA!
GOT IT!
Perfect, now don't move...
AAAGH!
くるっ
WHIRRL
ト・・ス
FWUMP
KNOCK IT OFF ALREADY! SERIOUSLY!
AGH, MY BUTT!
HOW DARE YOU LOOK DOWN ON OTHERS LIKE THAT, YOU HYPOCRITE!
DON'T YOU REALIZE JUST HOW SMALL YOU REALLY ARE?!
YOUR WHOLE EXISTENCE IS BORING, YOU KNOW THAT?!
GET ON YOUR KNEES AND BOW! NOW!
ARE YOU LISTENING TO US, YOU VILE SALMONELLA GERM!

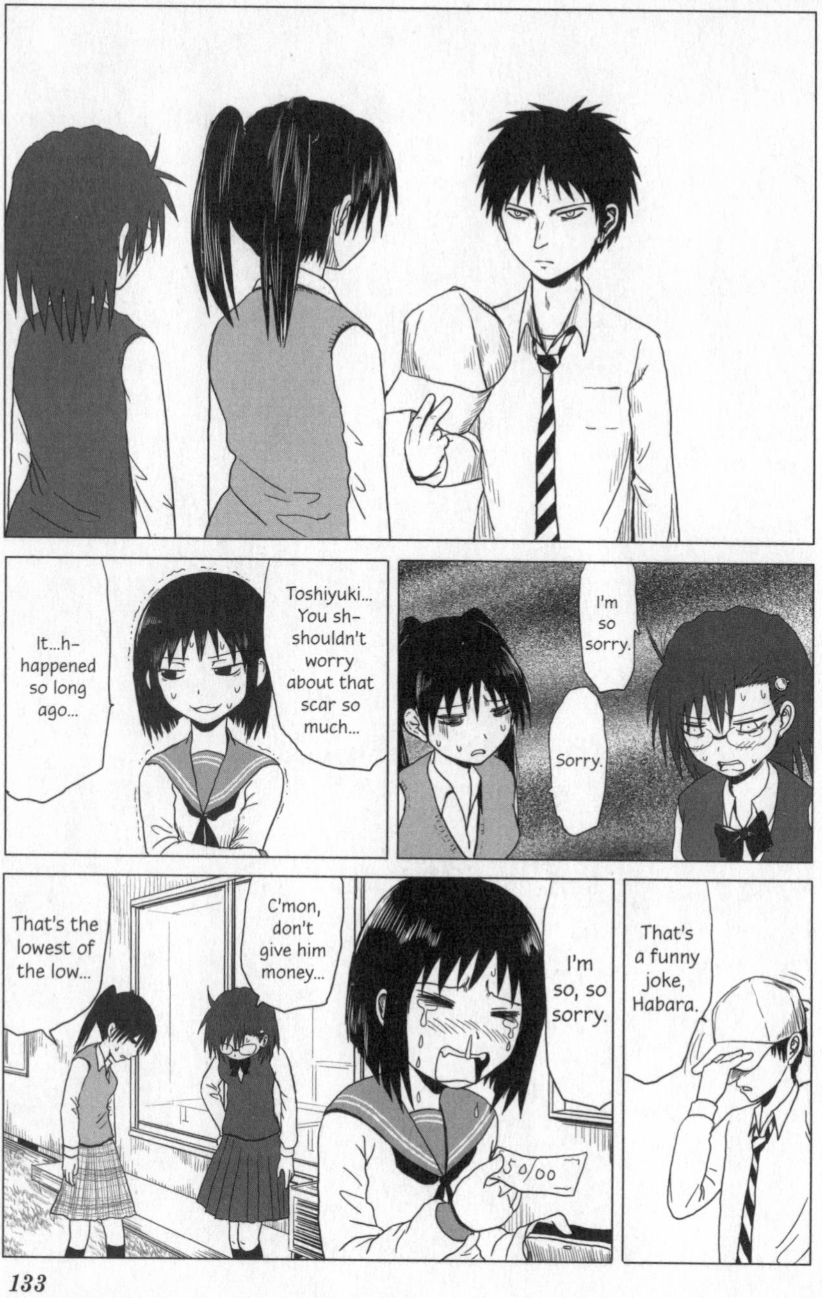
I'm so sorry.
Sorry.
Toshiyuki... You sh-shouldn't worry about that scar so much...
It...h-happened so long ago...
That's a funny joke, Habara.
I'm so, so sorry.
C'mon, don't give him money...
That's the lowest of the low...

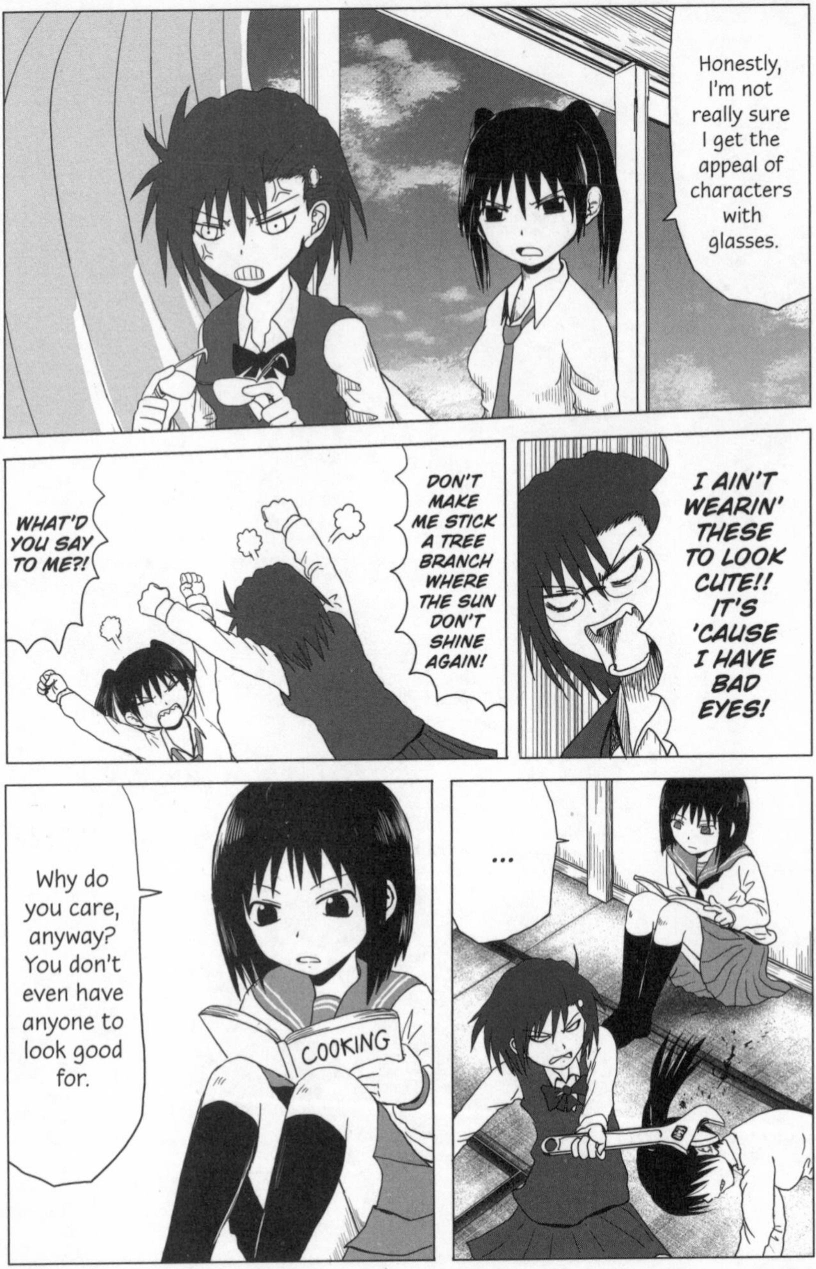
Honestly, I'm not really sure I get the appeal of characters with glasses.
I AIN'T WEARIN' THESE TO LOOK CUTE!! IT'S 'CAUSE I HAVE BAD EYES!
DON'T MAKE ME STICK A TREE BRANCH WHERE THE SUN DON'T SHINE AGAIN!
WHAT'D YOU SAY TO ME?!
...
Why do you care, anyway? You don't even have anyone to look good for.
COOKING

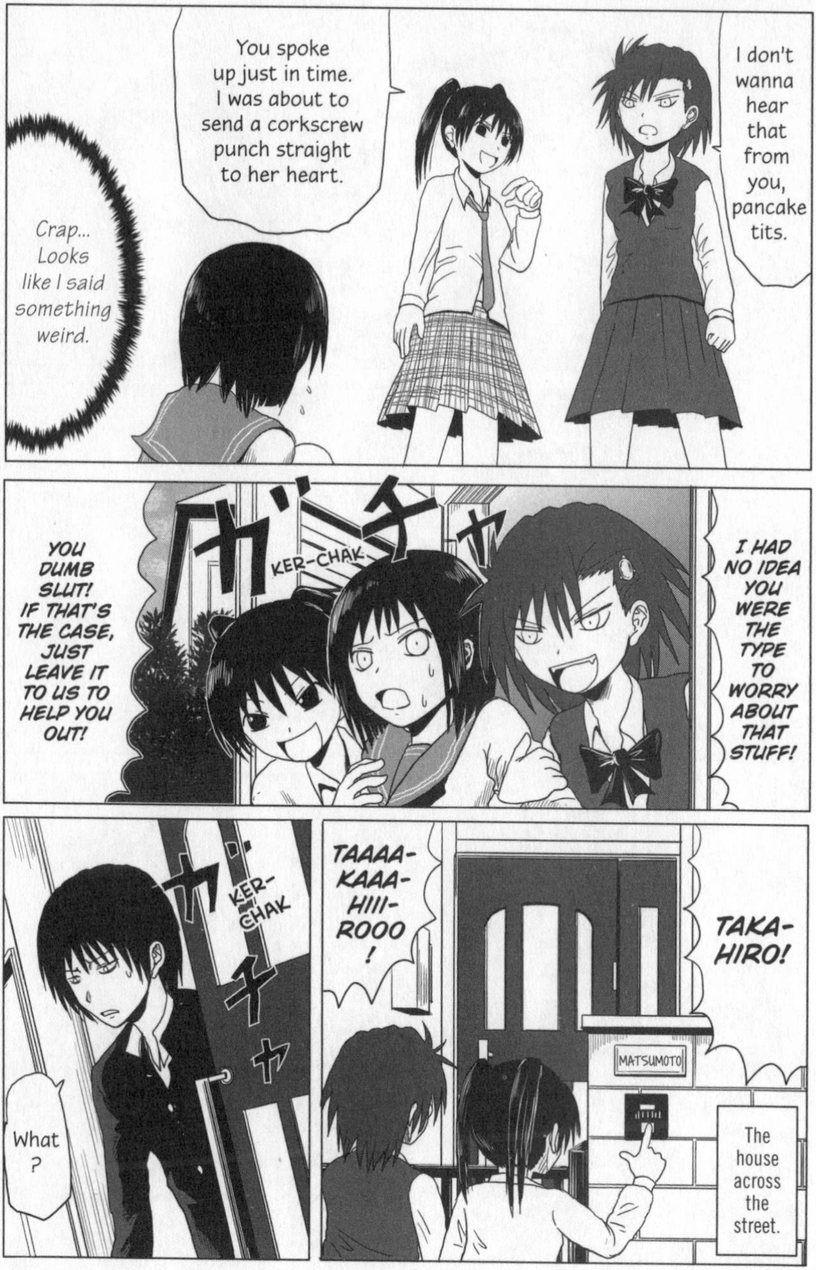
You spoke up just in time. I was about to send a corkscrew punch straight to her heart.
I don't wanna hear that from you, pancake tits.
Crap... Looks like I said something weird.
I HAD NO IDEA YOU WERE THE TYPE TO WORRY ABOUT THAT STUFF!
KER-CHAK
YOU DUMB SLUT! IF THAT'S THE CASE, JUST LEAVE IT TO US TO HELP YOU OUT!
TAKA-HIRO!
TAAAA-KAAA-HIIII-ROOO!
MATSUMOTO
The house across the street.
KER-CHAK
What?

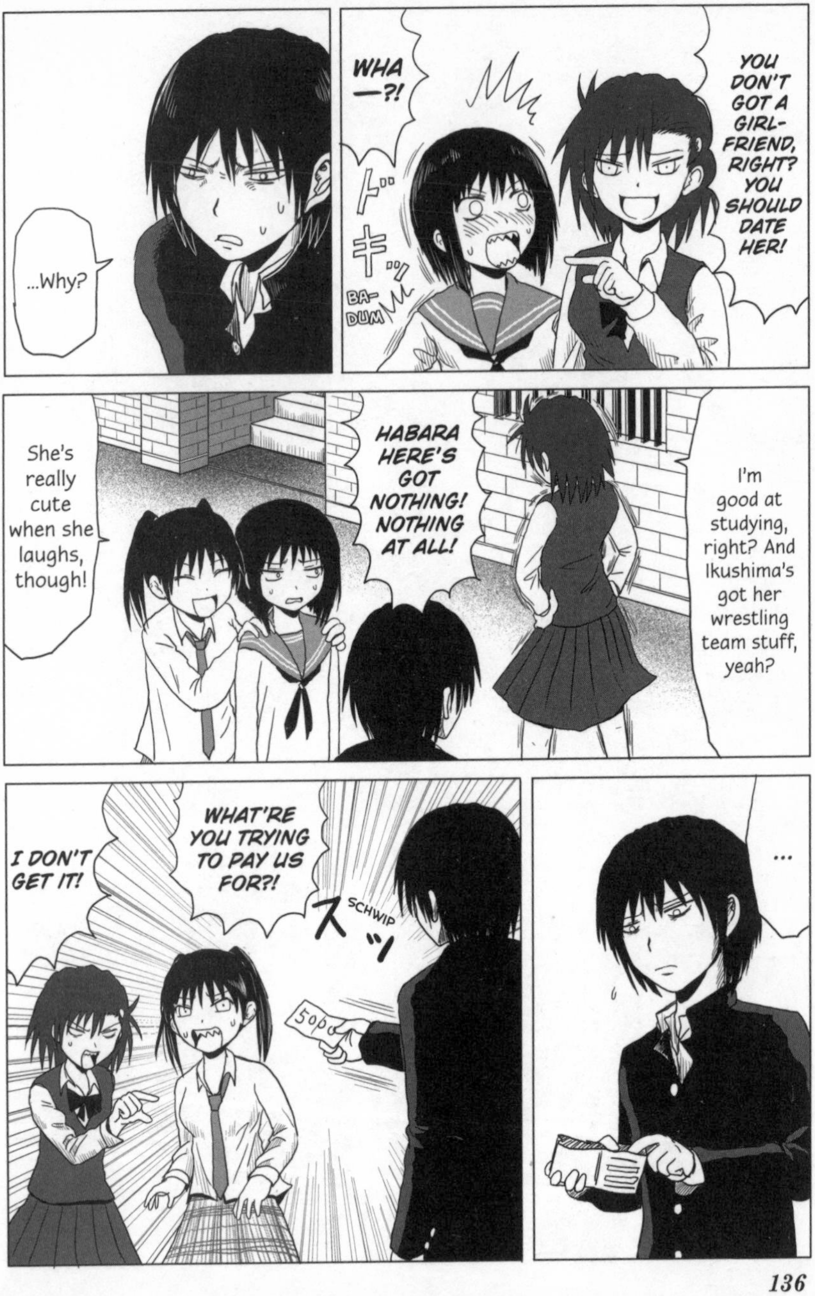
YOU DON'T GOT A GIRL-FRIEND, RIGHT? YOU SHOULD DATE HER!
WHA—?!
ドキッ
BA-DUM
...Why?
I'm good at studying, right? And Ikushima's got her wrestling team stuff, yeah?
HABARA HERE'S GOT NOTHING! NOTHING AT ALL!
She's really cute when she laughs, though!
...
WHAT'RE YOU TRYING TO PAY US FOR?!
I DON'T GET IT!
スッ
SCHWIP

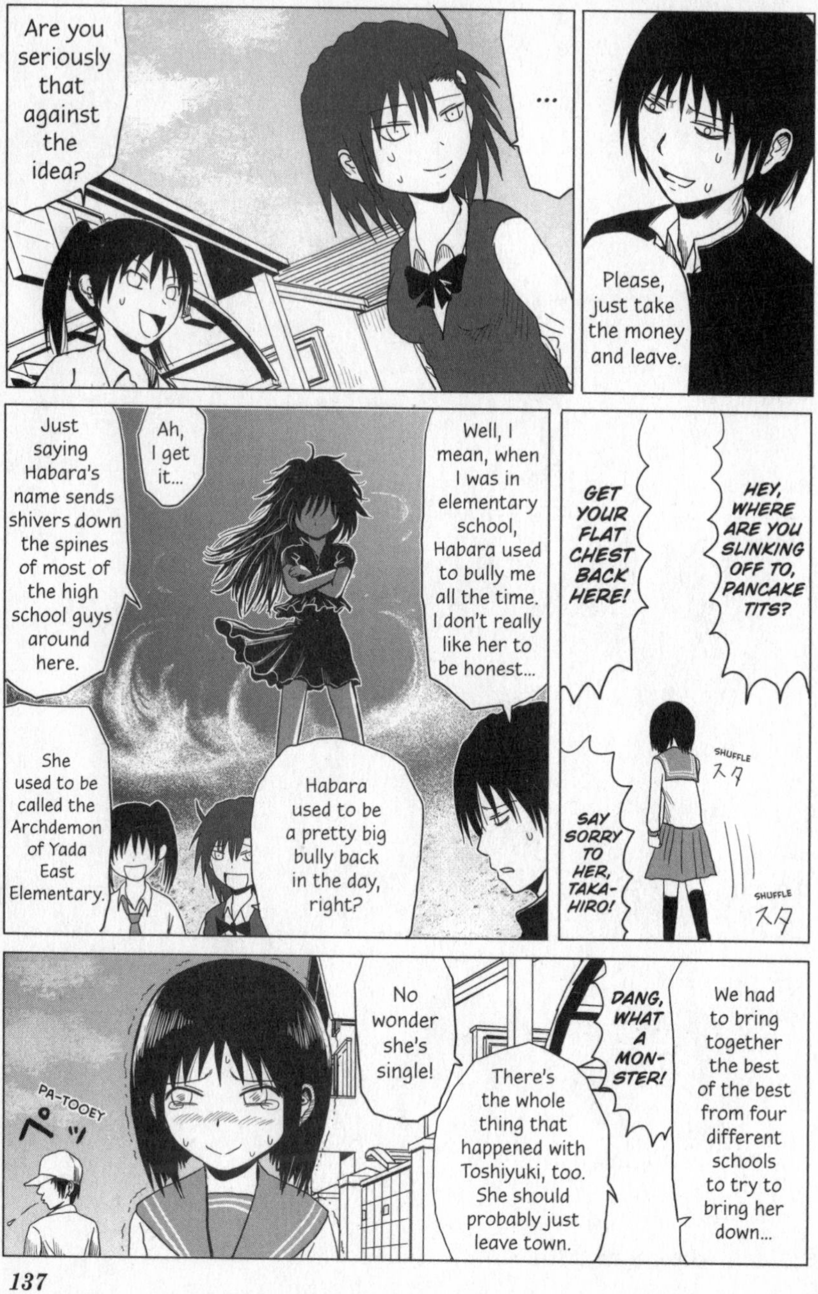
...
Please, just take the money and leave.
Are you seriously that against the idea?
HEY, WHERE ARE YOU SLINKING OFF TO, PANCAKE TITS?
GET YOUR FLAT CHEST BACK HERE!
SHUFFLE スタ
SAY SORRY TO HER, TAKA-HIRO!
SHUFFLE スタ
Well, I mean, when I was in elementary school, Habara used to bully me all the time. I don't really like her to be honest...
Ah, I get it...
Just saying Habara's name sends shivers down the spines of most of the high school guys around here.
Habara used to be a pretty big bully back in the day, right?
She used to be called the Archdemon of Yada East Elementary.
We had to bring together the best of the best from four different schools to try to bring her down...
DANG, WHAT A MONSTER!
No wonder she's single!
There's the whole thing that happened with Toshiyuki, too. She should probably just leave town.
PA-TOOEY ペッ

chapter 6: high school girl power

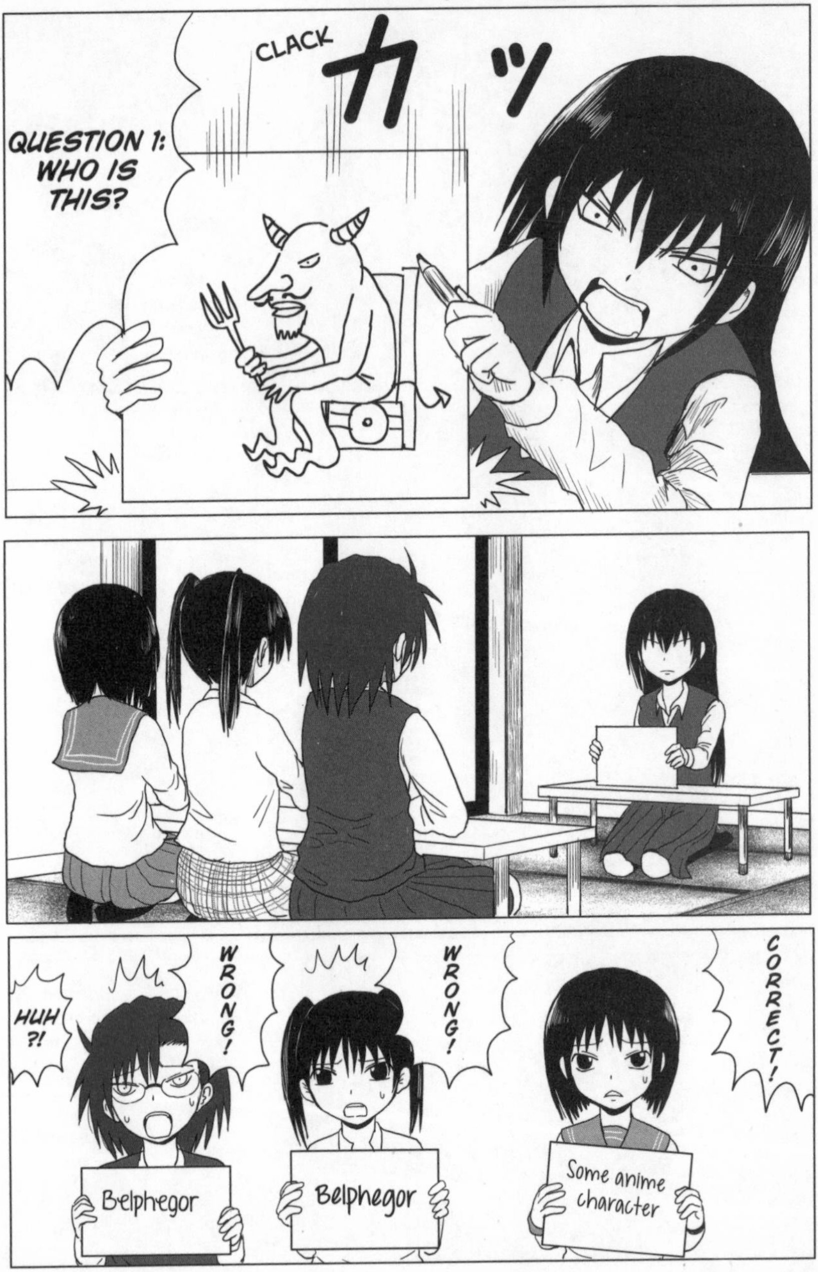
カッ
CLACK
QUESTION 1: WHO IS THIS?
CORRECT!
Some anime character
WRONG!
Belphegor
WRONG!
HUH?!
Belphegor

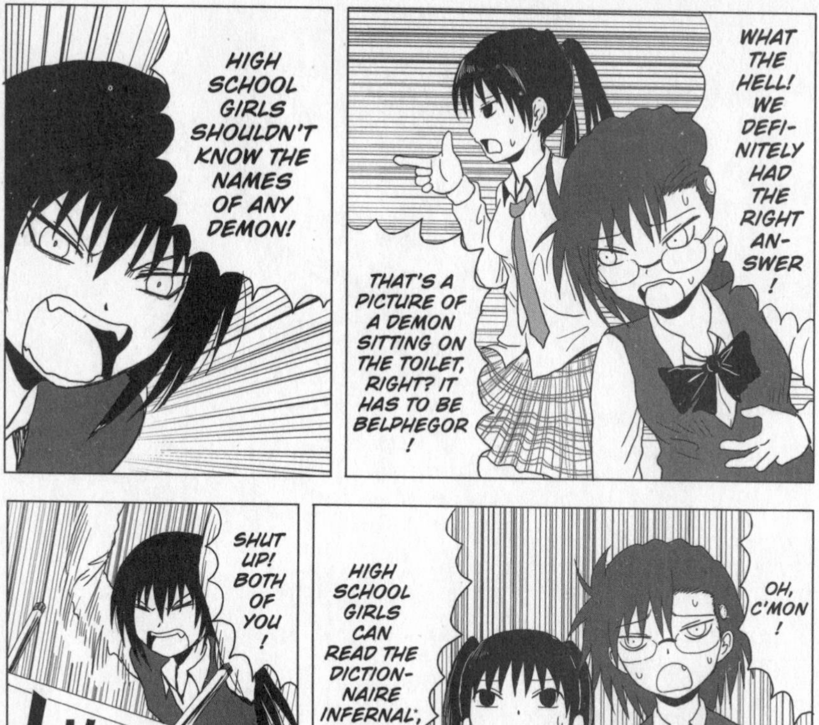
WHAT THE HELL! WE DEFINITELY HAD THE RIGHT ANSWER!
THAT'S A PICTURE OF A DEMON SITTING ON THE TOILET, RIGHT? IT HAS TO BE BELPHEGOR!
HIGH SCHOOL GIRLS SHOULDN'T KNOW THE NAMES OF ANY DEMON!
OH, C'MON!
HIGH SCHOOL GIRLS CAN READ THE DICTIONNAIRE INFERNAL*, WHAT'S THE BIG DEAL?!
SHUT UP! BOTH OF YOU!
ドガァ
FLIP

*A book written by Jaques Collin de Plancy that catalogues demons in great detail.

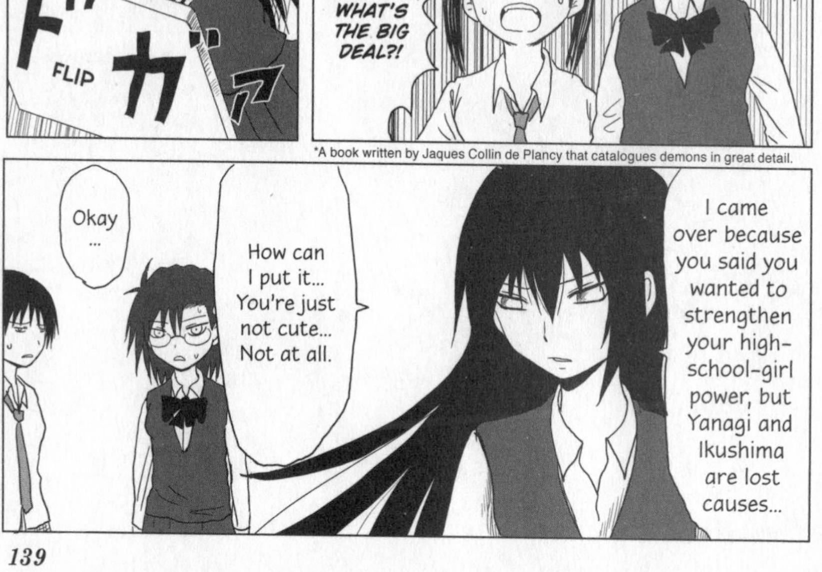
I came over because you said you wanted to strengthen your high-school-girl power, but Yanagi and Ikushima are lost causes...
How can I put it... You're just not cute... Not at all.
Okay ...

YOU GET WHAT I'M TRYING TO SAY?! ALL RIGHT, NEXT QUESTION! WHO IS THIS?!

I feel like I'm going crazy here!

ピ゜ロ゜ーーン
BING BONG

IKUSHIMA!

PERFECT! KEEP ACTING LIKE YOU'RE STUPID! NEXT QUESTION! WHO IS THIS PERSON?!

This is a tough one...

Crap!

OdaNobu

I DON'T KNOW!

Umm ... Uh ...

CORRECT!

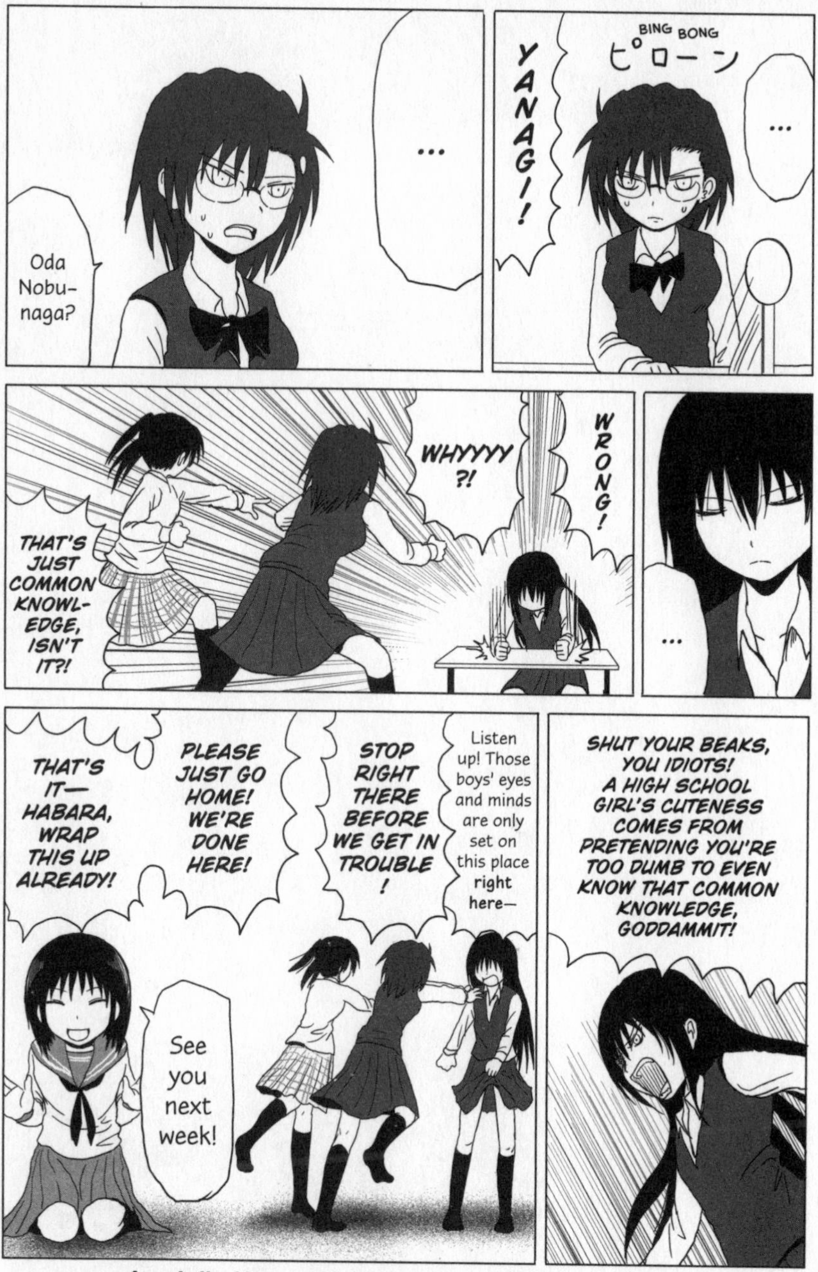

BING BONG
ピローン
...
YANAGI!!
...
Oda Nobunaga?
...
WRONG!
WHYYYY?!
THAT'S JUST COMMON KNOWLEDGE, ISN'T IT?!
SHUT YOUR BEAKS, YOU IDIOTS! A HIGH SCHOOL GIRL'S CUTENESS COMES FROM PRETENDING YOU'RE TOO DUMB TO EVEN KNOW THAT COMMON KNOWLEDGE, GODDAMMIT!
Listen up! Those boys' eyes and minds are only set on this place right here—
STOP RIGHT THERE BEFORE WE GET IN TROUBLE!
PLEASE JUST GO HOME! WE'RE DONE HERE!
THAT'S IT— HABARA, WRAP THIS UP ALREADY!
See you next week!

the daily lives of high school boys vol. 2 - end

the

daily

lives

of

high school boys 2

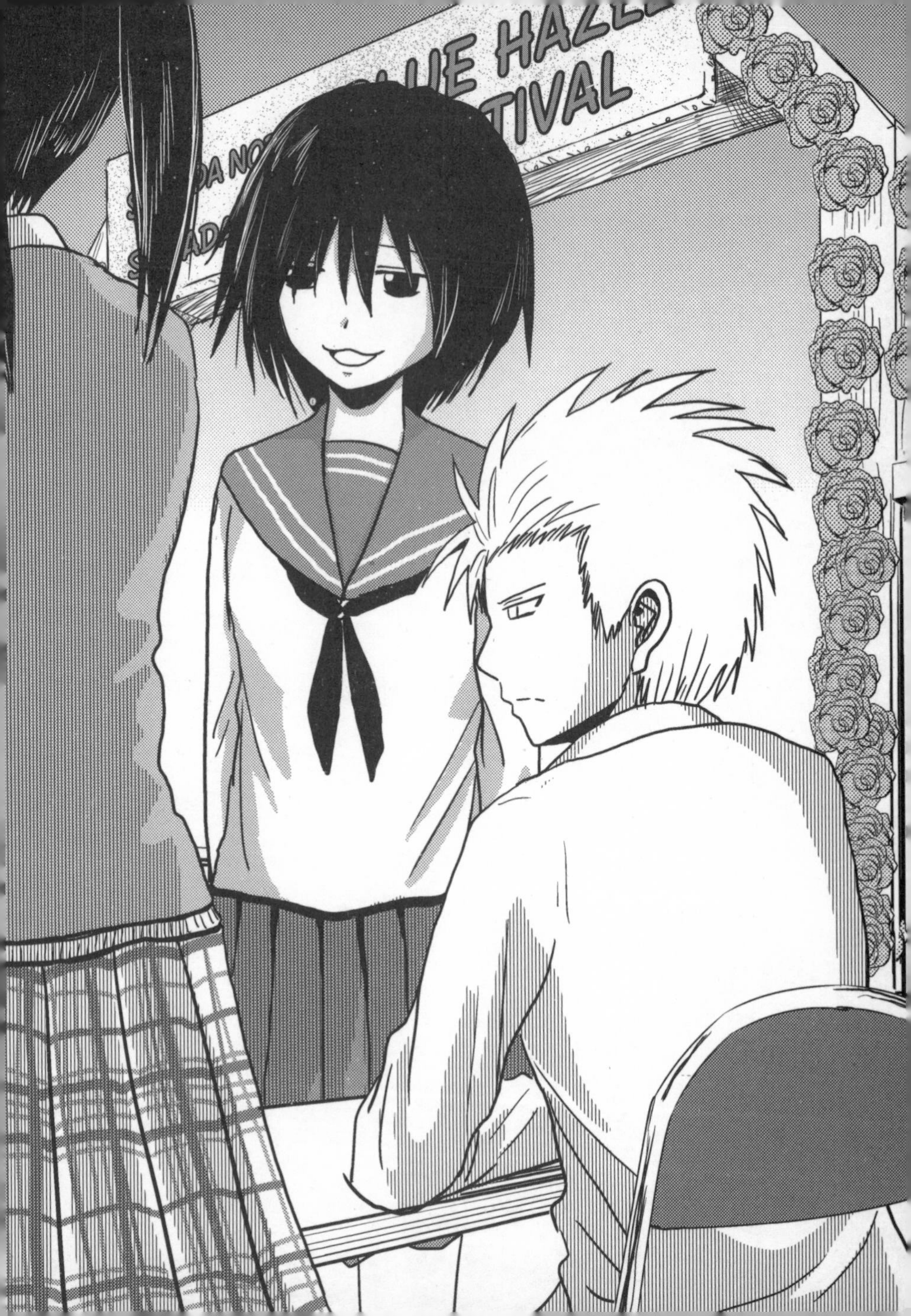

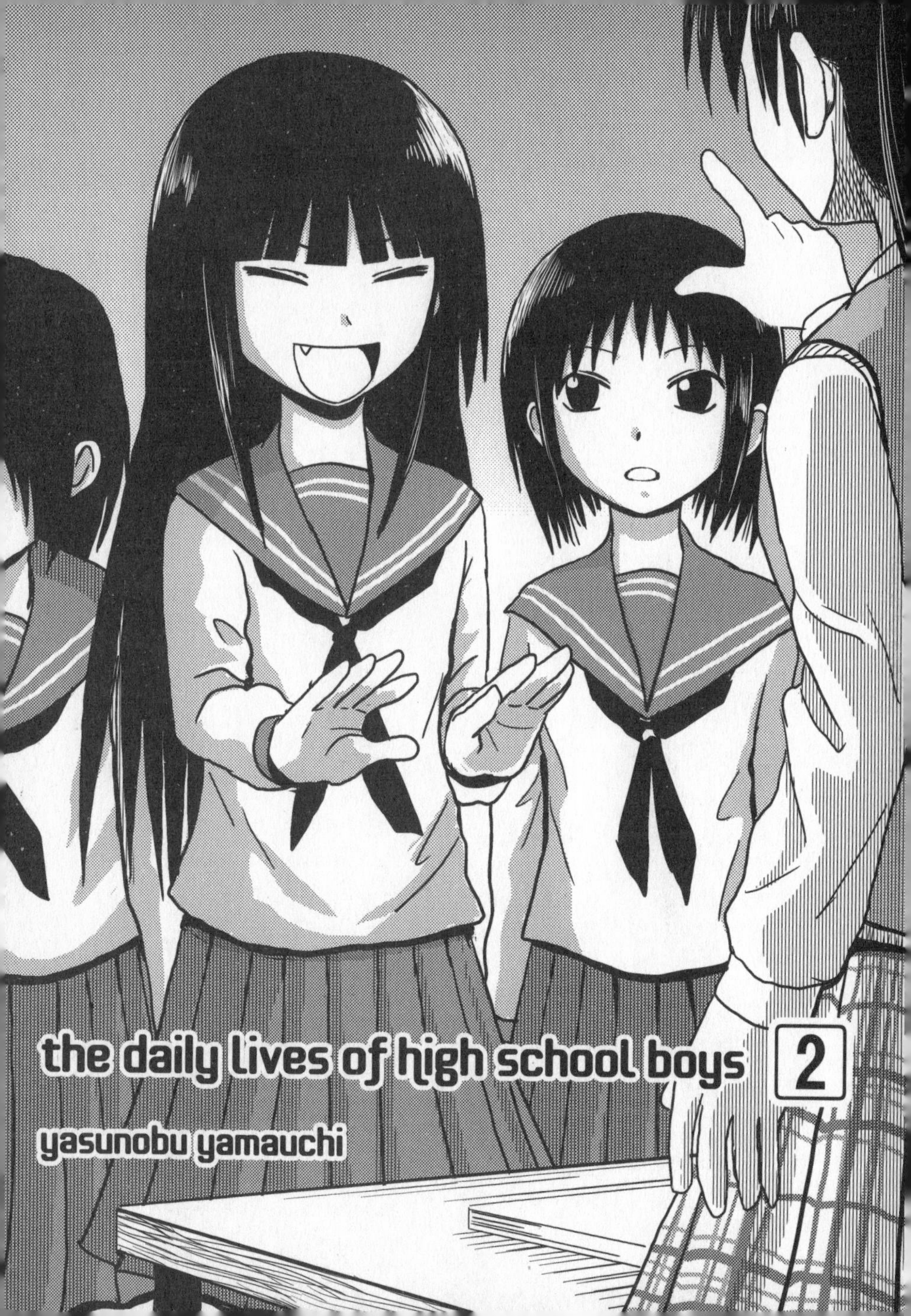
the daily lives of high school boys 2
yasunobu yamauchi

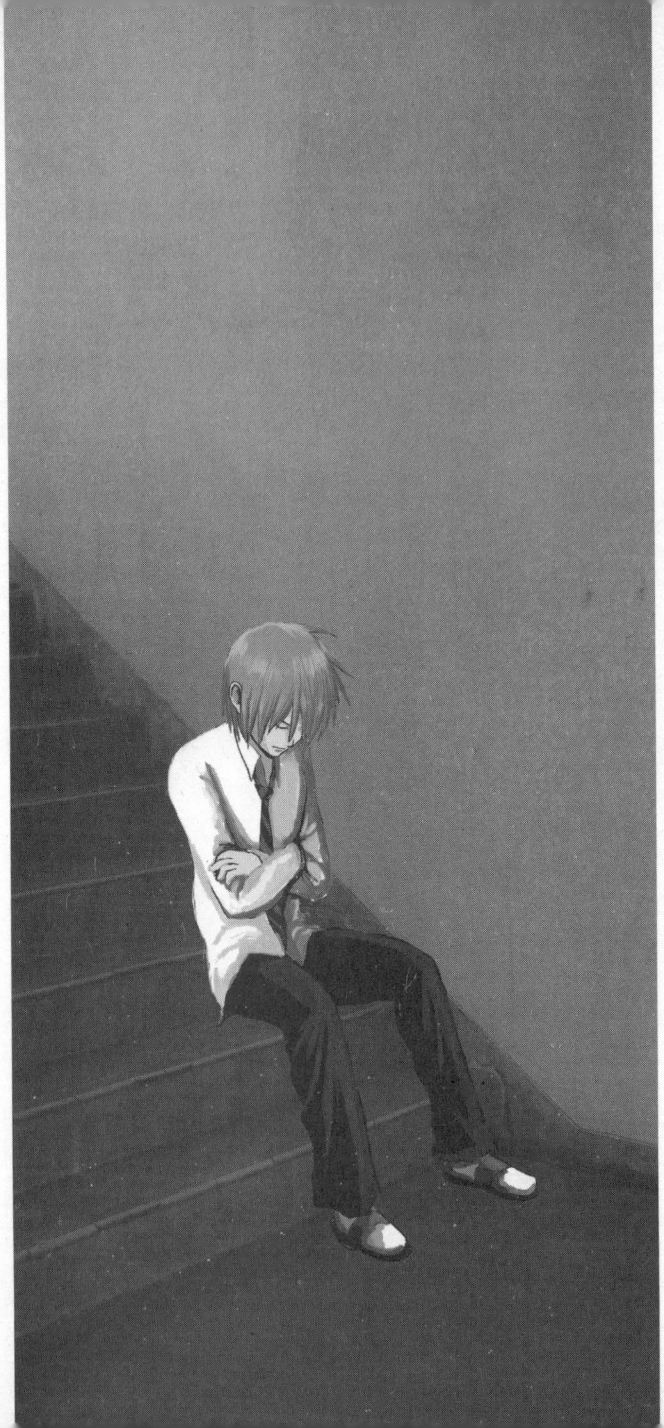

yasunobu yamauchi

It doesn't always happen, but as you can see in the photo above, sometimes my editor and I will butt heads over material to use in the series.

Creating something that we can both be happy with from the beginning is a good thing, of course.

However, clashing with one another and hammering out something we can both be satisfied with can also produce a good manga.

What's being used to draw the manga you casually read might not be ink, but the blood, sweat, and tears of the author, editor, and many other people that are involved in the process.

...Oh, forgive me, it seems that I used the wrong photo here.

the

daily

lives

of

2 high school boys

DAILY LIVES OF
HIGH SCHOOL BOYS

WATCH ON ⊙ crunchyroll®

From the creator of *nichijou*, this surreal-slapstick series revolves around a penniless college student, Midori Nagumo, who lives in an ordinary city filled with not-quite-ordinary people. And as this reckless girl runs about, she sets the city in motion.

Midori is in a bit of a bind. She is in debt, and her landlady is trying to shake her down for unpaid rent. Her best friend refuses to loan her cash since she's wised up to her tricks.

Maybe some bullying would help. Or a bit of petty theft? Neither is sustainable. Maybe getting a job would settle things… But working means less time for fun adventures in the big city…

Volumes 1-9
Available Now!

CITY

Keiichi Arawi

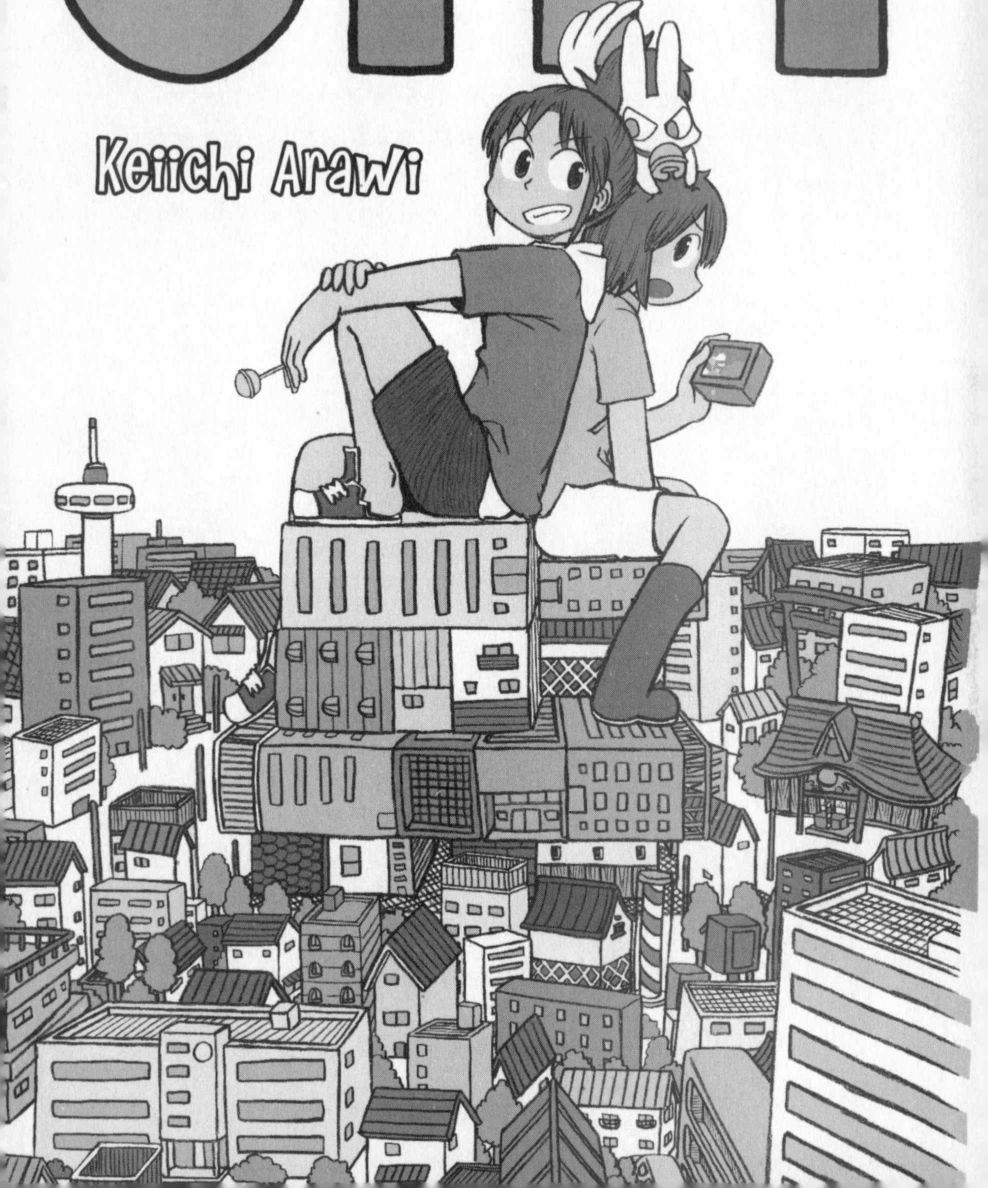

define "ordinary"

in this just-surreal-enough take on the "school genre" of manga, a group of friends (which includes a robot built by a child professor) grapples with all sorts of unexpected situations in their daily lives as high schoolers.

the gags, jokes, puns and random haiku keep this series off-kilter even as the characters grow and change. check out this new take on a storied genre and meet the new ordinary.

all volumes available now!

nichijou

my ordinary life

keiichi arawi

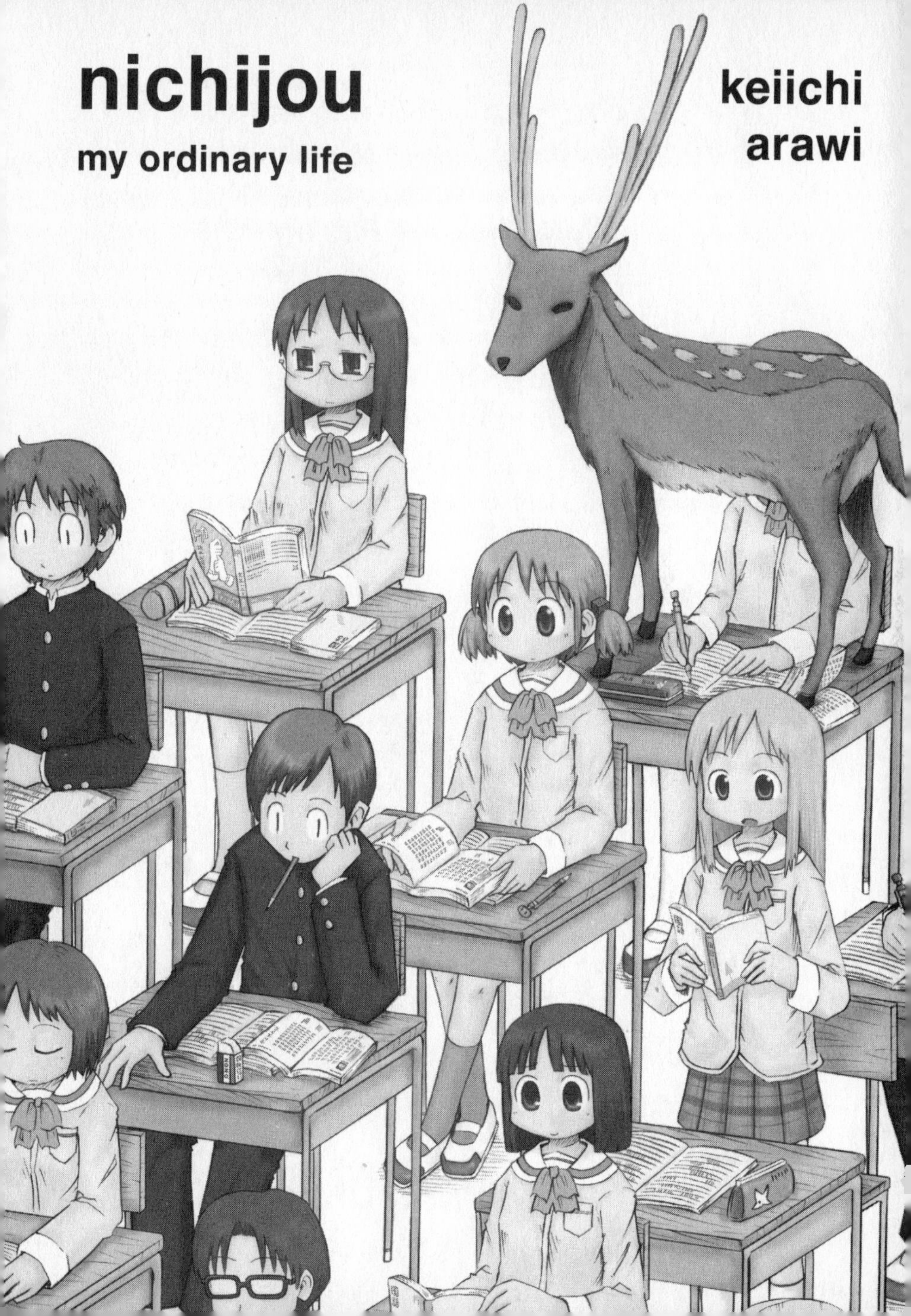

The follow-up to the hit manga series ***nichijou***, ***Helvetica Standard*** is a full-color anthology of Keiichi Arawi's comic art and design work. Funny and heartwarming, ***Helvetica Standard*** is a humorous look at modern day Japanese design in comic form.

Helvetica Standard is a deep dive into the artistic and creative world of Keiichi Arawi. Part comic, part diary, part art and design book, ***Helvetica Standard*** is a deconstruction of the world of ***nichijou***.

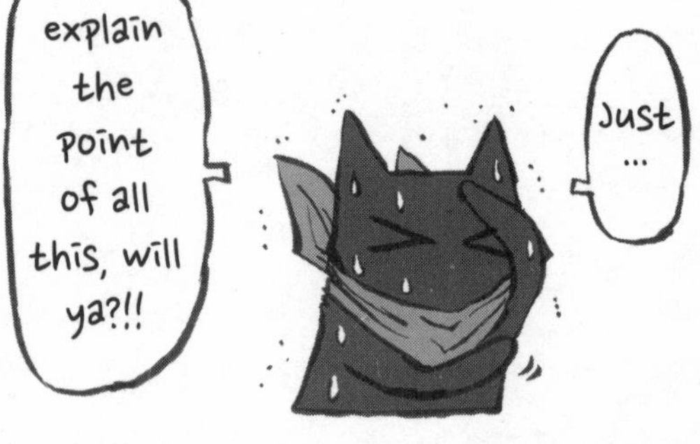
Just ...
explain the point of all this, will ya?!!

Helvetica Standard
Bold

Helvetica Standard
Italic

Both Parts Available Now!

Keiichi
Arawi

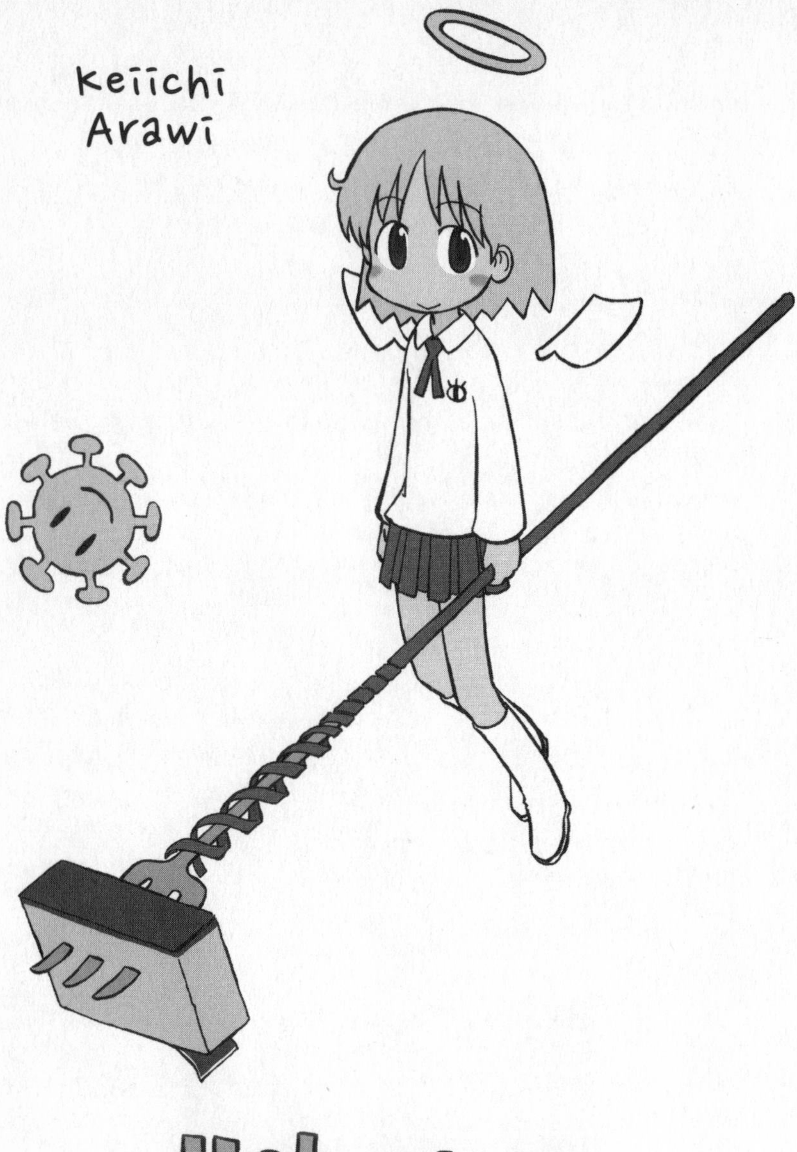

Helvetica
Standard

The Delinquent Housewife!
by Nemu Yoko

Tohru Komukai and his bride-to-be, Komugi, move in with his family just until they find a place of their own. Or, that was the plan, until Tohru suddenly leaves for a long-term business trip overseas, leaving Komugi to fend for herself on her in-laws' turf. While Komugi is pretty, considerate and appears to be an ideal housewife, the truth is she doesn't know how to do a lick of housework, and can't cook at all. Also, she has a secret past as a member of an all-girls *bosozoku* biker gang! The only member of the family to learn these secrets is Dai, Tohru's younger brother, and he helps Komugi keep up appearances until she can learn how to hold her own as a domestic goddess...

ALL VOLUMES AVAILABLE NOW!

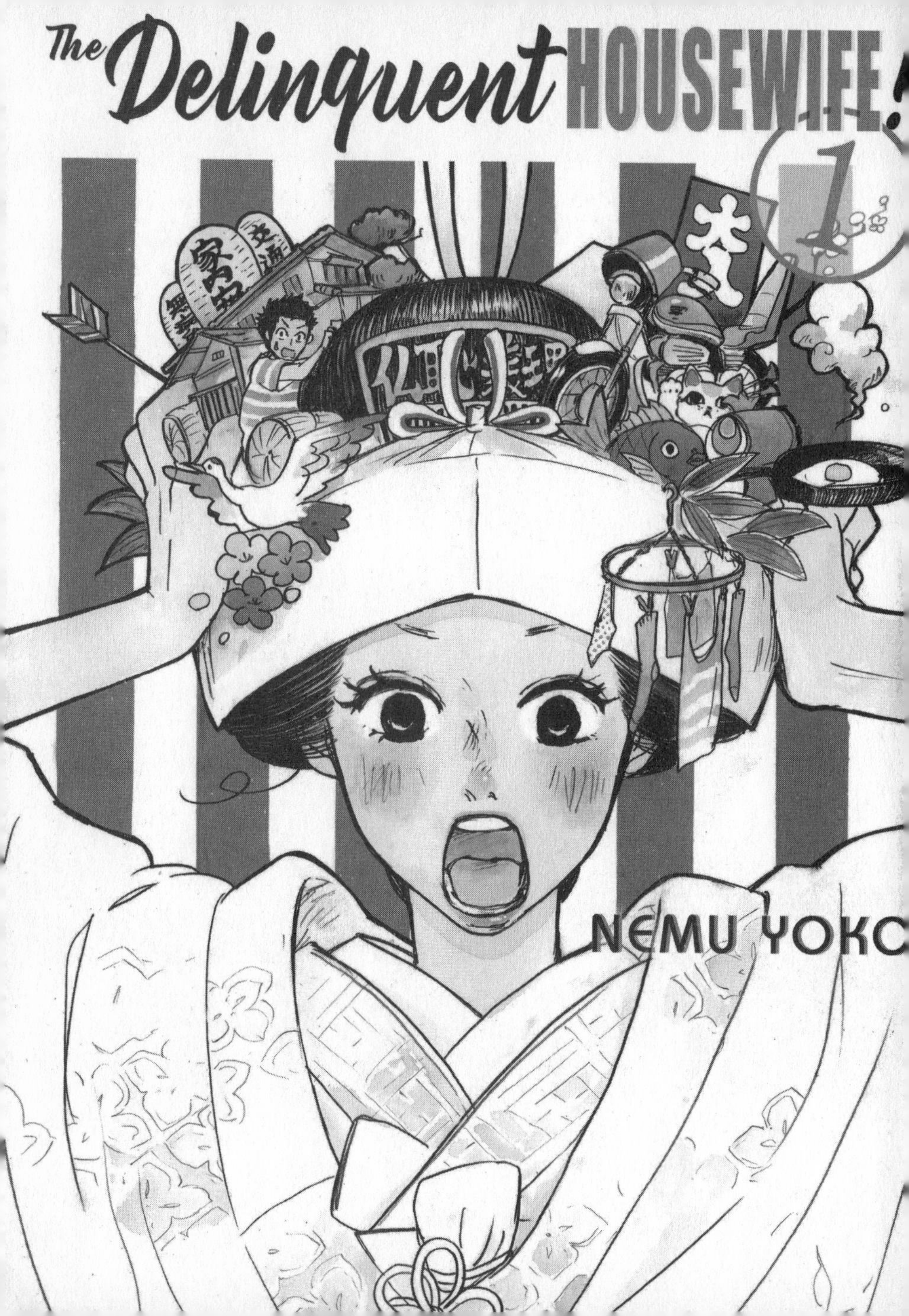
The Delinquent HOUSEWIFE!
1
NEMU YOKO

The Master of Killing Time

Toshinari Seki takes goofing off to new heights. Every day, on or around his school desk, he masterfully creates his own little worlds of wonder, often hidden to most of his classmates. Unfortunately for Rumi Yokoi, his neighbor at the back of the room, his many games, dioramas, and projects are often way too interesting to ignore; even when they are hurting her grades.

Volumes 1-10 available now!

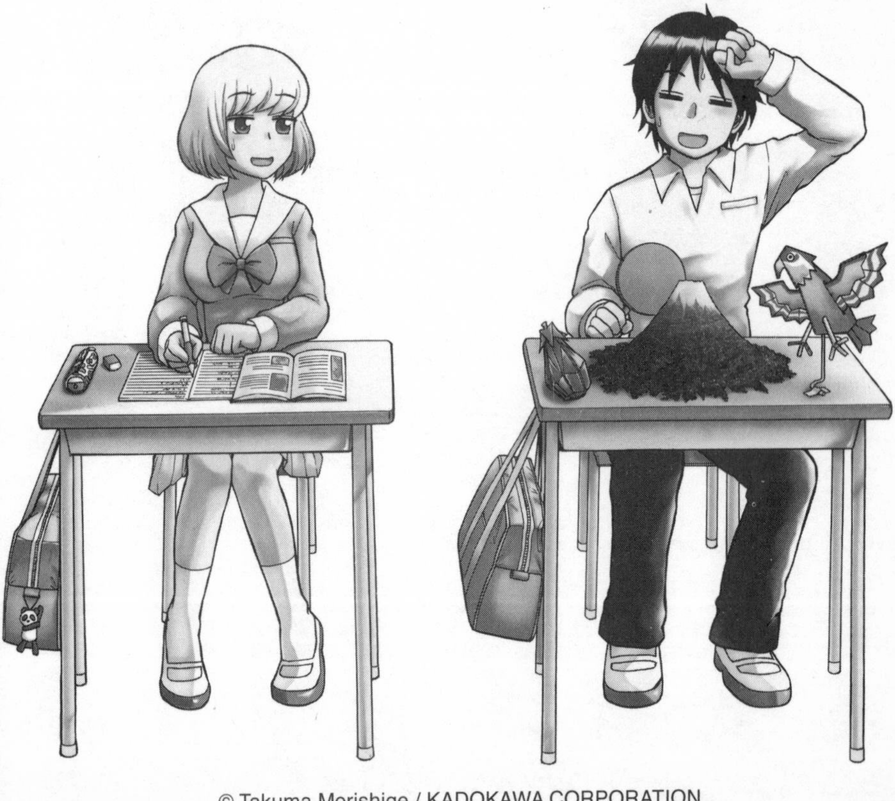

My Neighbor Seki

Tonari no Seki-kun

Takuma Morishige

THE DAILY LIVES OF
HIGH SCHOOL BOYS 2

Yasunobu Yamauchi

A Vertical Comics Edition

Editor: Ajani Oloye
Translation: David Musto
Production: Grace Lu
          Anthony Quintessenza

© 2010 Yasunobu Yamauchi / SQUARE ENIX CO., LTD.
First Published in Japan in 2010 by SQUARE ENIX CO., LTD.
English translation rights arranged with SQUARE ENIX CO., LTD.
and Kodansha USA Publishing, LLC through Tuttle-Mori Agency, Inc.
Translation © 2020 by SQUARE ENIX CO., LTD.

Translation provided by Vertical Comics, 2020
Published by Vertical Comics, an imprint of Kodansha USA Publishing, LLC,
New York

Originally published in Japanese as *Danshi Kokosei no Nichijo 2*
by SQUARE ENIX Co., Ltd., 2010
Danshi Kokosei no Nichijo first serialized in *Gangan Online*, SQUARE ENIX Co.,
Ltd., 2009-2012

This is a work of fiction.

ISBN: 978-1-949980-43-1

Manufactured in the United States of America

First Edition

Kodansha USA Publishing, LLC
451 Park Avenue South
7th Floor
New York, NY 10016
www.readvertical.com

Vertical books are distributed through Penguin-Random House Publisher Services.